PRAISE FOR BOB DYLAN

"I saw Bob Dylan in concert shortly after his conversion experience and was amazed by the raw courage it took to sing those new songs to increasing anger from his old fans and refuse to sing his earlier hits. Eventually he came to understand that he could pick and choose and integrate many of his old songs with the new and march forward as a man of faith. That's the Dylan we meet in *Bob Dylan: A Spiritual Life.*"

—PAT BOONE

"Scott Marshall, in his book *Bob Dylan: A Spiritual Life*, reflects on the spiritual expressions of one of our country's greatest artists, and there is no shortage of material from which to learn."

—PRESIDENT JIMMY CARTER

"Bob Dylan will not be labeled. For five decades now, he has avoided the trappings of every group that has wanted to claim him as their own. Call Dylan whatever you want, but the name won't stick. What does stick is his music, in part because his songs contain a deep, abiding spirituality that moves listeners like me more than the songs of any other artist."

—SCOTT DERRICKSON, DIRECTOR OF *DOCTOR STRANGE*

"Bob has always been rock and roll's poet laureate. A lyricist confesses a lot—we're sort of our own psychotherapists—and "Gotta Serve Somebody" is as close to a modern-day hymn as anything I can think of. Bob's spirit is captured effectively in *Bob Dylan: A Spiritual Life*. If you can't trust Bob Dylan, who can you trust?"

—ALICE COOPER

"Bob Dylan has been an inspiration to me throughout my career and I've been deeply affected by his spiritual journey. Rock and roll is at its best when it asks the important questions, as Bob has always done in his work, and there is no more important question than the question of God. *Bob Dylan: A Spiritual Life* provides the final answer to those who doubt or minimize Bob's spiritual commitment. His faith remains solid. He is the prophet of our generation and we ignore his warnings about a slow train coming at our own peril."

—GARY CHERONE, LEAD SINGER, EXTREME, VAN HALEN

"A pointillist rendering of a man's spiritual evolution . . . cross-referencing over five decades of interviews and friendships, distilled from hundreds of artistic, religious and personal sources, *Bob Dylan: A Spiritual Life* succeeds mightily in documenting Bobby Dylan Zimmerman's continuing (and often misunderstood) personal reconciliation of two faiths."

—NOEL PAUL STOOKEY OF PETER, PAUL AND MARY

"I always have a hard time writing anything down about Bob Dylan. Feels like he might want it that way. I saw Bob Dyln on my thirteenth birthday. Flew home for it. Felt like he ushered me into adulthood properly. I grew up with his songs—and somehow his songs have grown up with me as well. His words come in and out of my life like apparitions, appearing in mercurial forms ranging from the hipster iconoclast to the suburban prophet. Dylan's songs have guided me from young aimless angst to a hope that is busy being born. Whatever he was singing about, I always felt like Dylan made me a believer."

—JON FOREMAN, SWITCHFOOT

"Scott Marshall has performed the important task of bringing light to the mystery of how the man who warned us not to follow leaders lectured us fifteen years later that we had to serve somebody, since he talked to just about everybody who had insight into Dylan's thinking at the time of his famous Slow Train Coming run at San Francisco's Warfield Theatre. Painstaking footnotes manifest the level of dedication to research."

—JACK MCDONOUGH, FORMER BILLBOARD CORRESPONDENT AND AUTHOR OF *SAN FRANCISCO ROCK: THE ILLUSTRATED HISTORY, 1965–1985*

"Mr. Marshall skillfully weaves his tale with relevant quotes as Dylan travels from seeing the Bible as 'just literature' to believing 'in the Bible, literally.'"

—ANDREW MUIR, AUTHOR OF *ONE MORE NIGHT: BOB DYLAN'S NEVER ENDING TOUR* AND *SHAKESPEARE IN CAMBRIDGE: A CELEBRATION OF THE SHAKESPEARE FESTIVAL*

"With *Bob Dylan: A Spiritual Life*, Scott Marshall takes Dylan's idiosyncratic faith walk seriously enough to bear with the obfuscation, jokes, and sleight-of-hand that have always been a non-negotiable part of the journey. By doing so, Marshall patiently (and respectfully) connects the dots left behind by the artist himself over a half-century recording career. The result is the richest, most complete understanding of Dylan the Radical Monotheist to date."

—TONY NORMAN, *PITTSBURGH POST-GAZETTE*

"*Wow, oh my*, and *thank-you* are the words that kept coming to mind as I read Scott Marshall's masterly written *Bob Dylan: A Spiritual Life. Wow* for the extent of research, which is top-notch; *Oh my* for the scores of facts and anecdotes I'd never run across before (and I've been reading Dylan bios for decades!); and *thank-you* for what is probably the best-argued book on the enduring biblical pulse at the heart of Dylan's music. As the author himself says, 'Why bet against Dylan having a place at that heavenly welcome table?' Wow, oh my, and thank-you, Scott Marshall!"

—ROBERT HUDSON, EDITOR, ZONDERVAN; AUTHOR, *THE CHRISTIAN WRITER'S MANUAL OF STYLE* AND *KISS THE EARTH WHEN YOU PRAY*

"Scott Marshall comes as close as anyone ever will to documenting the complete and complex record of Bob Dylan's continuing spiritual journey."

—JEFFREY GASKILL, PRODUCER, *GOTTA SERVE SOMEBODY: THE GOSPEL SONGS OF BOB DYLAN*

"The concept of examining Bob Dylan and spirituality is an intriguing one. As a devoted student of Dylan, I can't wait ot see where this story leads. All things considered, it seems central to a real understanding of the maestro."

—MICHAEL LEVINE, HOLLYWOOD PUBLICIST AND AUTHOR OF *GUERILLA PR*

"A number of Bob Dylan's songs—*Blowin' In the Wind, I Shall Be Released,Knockin' On Heaven's Door*, among others—have always struck me as modern hymns. Discerning a consistent theme of monotheism in Dylan's vast and divergent canon of works reflects the extraordinary passion that his spiritual biographer, Scott Marshall, brings to his subject. For nearly two decades, Marshall has been studying and writing about Dylan's religious views and spiritual odyssey; the result is this book, the Bible on Dylan's religiosity and a seminal contribution to the literature on this towering cultural—and yes, spiritual—figure of our time."

—JAMES ROSEN, FOX NEWS CHIEF WASHINGTON CORRESPONDENT AND EDITOR OF THE *NEW YORK TIMES* BESTSELLER *A TORCH KEPT LIT: GREAT LIVES OF THE TWENTIETH CENTURY* (BY WILLIAM F. BUCKLEY, JR.)

"Well researched and energetically argued, a challenging new view of a complicated man."

—ERIC ALTERMAN, AWARD-WINNING AUTHOR AND COLUMNIST AT *THE NATION*

"Bob Dylan is a Jew and a Christian and a steadfast contrarian. Scott Marshall provides a balanced, comprehensive account of the Nobel Prize winner's spiritual life—a mysterious journey of biblical proportions."

—DON LATTIN, LONGTIME RELIGION WRITER AT THE *SAN FRANCISCO CHRONICLE* AND THE AUTHOR OF *CHANGING OUR MINDS*

"With lucid prose and a compelling narrative, Scott Marshall demonstrates that Bob Dylan's religious sensibilities have been constant throughout his remarkable career, not episodic. This book contributes significantly to our understanding of the enigmatic Nobel laureate."

—RANDALL BALMER, EMMY AWARD NOMINEE; CHAIR OF RELIGION, DARTMOUTH COLLEGE

BOB DYLAN

A Spiritual Life

SCOTT M. MARSHALL

A POST HILL PRESS BOOK
ISBN: 978-1-63758-096-7
ISBN (eBook): 978-1-63758-097-4

Bob Dylan:
A Spiritual Life

Interior Design by Mark Karis

Post Hill Press
New York • Nashville
posthillpress.com

Published in the United States of America

To my wife: an incredible woman, an invaluable therapist/social worker, an excellent photographer, and absolute best friend.

CONTENTS

FOREWORD

BOB DYLAN WILL NOT BE LABELED. For five decades now, he has avoided the trappings of every group that has wanted to claim him as their own. Call Dylan whatever you want, but the name won't stick. What does stick is his music, in part because his songs contain a deep, abiding spirituality that moves listeners like me more than the songs of any other artist.

In theory, I suppose, I should be bothered by Scott Marshall's book, since it could be argued that *Bob Dylan: A Spiritual Life* is an attempt to label Dylan as a man of faith. But while the book does at times feel like an apologetic for Dylan's enduring Christianity, it also rigorously evidences his continuing Judaism, and as a result, I found myself once again marveling at Dylan's refusal to be pinned down. And Dylan is no mere contrarian. He doesn't cast off labels by simply arguing against them, but, instead, his words and actions force the titles thrust upon him to fall away because of their obvious incompleteness.

That said, Marshall's book is a deeply compelling documentation of Dylan's belief in the biblical God of both the Old and New Testament. For those of us who are religious and love Dylan's music, this topic is of obvious interest. But what matters most about this book to me personally is that it has expanded the way I think about Dylan's musical library. Since reading these pages, I have begun to think of the religious and spiritual dimensions of Dylan's music in a less linear fashion: I no longer think of *Slow Train Coming, Saved,* and *Shot of Love* as his "Christian" records, but instead I fancy the idea that when Dylan recorded them he was being topical, as if Jesus were the present subject on his *Theme Time Radio Hour* show. Perhaps instead of spreading these songs of religious devotion throughout his body of work—as U2 has done—he instead stacked them into three dense albums, and now spreads them out in concert amongst the rest of his songs. U2 has been called the most Christian mainstream band in the world, but isn't there more Christianity in the aforementioned three Dylan records than all of U2's records combined? Perhaps by stacking these songs into three back-to-back albums, Dylan aggressively took on the label of "born-again Christian" only to abandon the limitations of that label by returning to his Jewish roots with the brilliant album *Infidels*.

Maybe Dylan really does live according to the title of my favorite of his albums, *Time Out of Mind.* Perhaps all of his songs were meant to transcend the time-bound events that gave birth to them, and each song has never meant more or less than it does now. Maybe "The Times They Are A-Changin'" isn't just a '60s revolution song and "Gotta Serve Somebody" isn't just a born-again era song. Each of them was that, of course, but after reading this book, I am thinking that Dylan's songs have a kind of unique right to exist far beyond their original context because Dylan has never recanted a single line from a single song. I do know that, in the end, Dylan's personal faith—what he believes or doesn't believe—is ultimately between him and his God. What matters to me, and what should matter to the readers of this book, are his songs.

I agree with Dylan that he is a man with a true calling. I believe that whatever his dogma (or lack of it), he is a man uniquely touched by God, called forth to usher truth and beauty into the lives of those of us who are listening.

—SCOTT DERRICKSON, DIRECTOR OF *DOCTOR STRANGE*

ACKNOWLEDGMENTS

THE MANUSCRIPT WOULD BE SOMEWHERE, incomplete in a disorganized home office and mind if not for my wife. Many thanks, Amy Lynn Roseberry Marshall; take a well-deserved bow. Think I'll stick with you, baby, until the wheels fall off and burn. Mercy guide us.

Roots that run deep: Big tip of the hat to Mark Joseph who suggested the idea for this book in 2004 when it didn't make much sense (to me). Over the years he fought on my behalf in the trenches—pitching the manuscript to a variety of publishers, some mainstream publishers in New York City (nearly landed a deal), and then found an agent who gave it the good college try for a season, to no avail—and for all of that I'm greatly appreciative. In 2016, he secured a deal. Others who've meant much in this long journey include: Daniel Evearitt; Jeff Gaskill; Veronica Keohane; Jonathan Lauer; Doug LeBlanc; Mick & Laurie McCuistion; Anne Nicolson (faithful godmother, fellow Dylan fan); Tony Norman; Warren Smith; Tim Stark. (I await your tome, brother!)

Significant helpers along the way: Dave Kelly; Regina McCrary; and Maria Muldaur—and each of my interviewees; Roe Andersen; Benyamin Cohen (thanks for the $25.00, and the open door; your successor owes me $75.00); Joseph Farah (a Dylan fan, and a believer in the manuscript); Doc Hensley; Joyce Jackson (apology for the omission last time around); Mark Karis; Brian Lamb (much inspiration from BookNotes and BookTV); John Lawing; Drew Lawson; Jessica Reis Matthews (great help at what we thought was the midnight hour); Davin Seay & Mary Neely; Michael Ray "Smitty" Smith; and Geoff Stone.

Dylan authors: Michael Gray; Clinton Heylin (as for Dylan books penned, not a soul comes close); Bob Hudson; Stephan Pickering (one of the first on the scene and still reaching); Christopher Ricks (freethinking atheist hospitable to Gospel Bob; Anthony Scaduto; and Don Williams.

Inspiration via friends, acquaintances, and great sources: Kark Erik Andersen; Derek Barker; Jimmers Baxter, poet; Steve Beard; James Earl Carter, Jr. (for the note, and for taking a look); Sean Curnyn; Jerry Fliger; Marty Grossman; Jessica Handwork and her boys; Darren Harbert; Leon Hartwell, poet; Gail Justin; Alec (sternum) Lauriault; Bob Levinson; Terry Mattingly; Ed Newman; Bill Pagel; Michel Pomarede (*the* Dylan bibliophile); Tom Porter (when the kiddos fly the coop, I await your book on The Boss); Markus Prieur; Jason Robb; Bob Ryan; Heather Samsa; Curt Wanner (extraordinary Ph.D on Falwell, Robertson, and Osteen); Donald T. Williams; and The Two Riders—John Wraith & Mike Wraith.

Former (and current) students: Emmanuel College; Hart County High; North Georgia College & State University (now UNG); North Georgia Technical College; Toccoa Falls College; and Truett-McConnell University.

Family: The Adams family; Cinnie Brown; John, Amy, Grace, and Greta LaFrentz (Amy escorted me to my first Dylan gig in 1990 and treated me to one in Huntsville in 2016); a great man and surgeon (retired), my father, Walter Haskell Marshall Jr., and his better half, my amazing mother, Jean Marshall; the Masseys (including cousin Justin who managed to eventually read my last book while on the toilet); Matt, Grace, Emma, Matthew, and Marshall (Grace, I expect a signed copy of the Yonder Mountain book down the road); The Roseberry clan: Fred Jr., Marilyn, Rob (Motley Crue!) and Marcie, Kristin and her children—Hanna, Nathan, Abby, and Andrew—and her birds; Lydia; Nancy; the Summers; the Tippits; and the Wrights.

In memoriam: Ian Bell (1956–2015); Bert Cartwright (1924–1996); John Gibbens (1959–2015); Dave Governor (1968–2011); Mike Handwork (1970–2014); James Hill (1916–2000); Christopher Hitchens (1949–2011); John Hume (1959–2012); Carol Lauriault (1940–2008); Mike Marqusee (1953–2015); Walter Marshall (1907–1996); Helen Marshall (1906–1997); Bill Mauzy (1967–2015); Earl Maxon (1913–2004) and Dolores Maxon (1916–2008); Eddie Morrison, Jr. (1949–1999); "Poppa" George Mosteller (1926-2013); Randy Nordstedt (1968–1994); Bill Parr (1953–2012); Sy Ribakove (1928–2013); Robert Shelton (1926–1995); and Stephen Webb (1961–2016); Dave Whiting-Smith (1961–2006); Paul Williams (1948–2013).

1

CHIEF COMMANDER BLUES

Listen, God, look closely after him. He's more fragile than most people.

—JOAN BAEZ, IN HER AUTOBIOGRAPHY *DAYBREAK* (1968)

I'm preachin' the Word of God / I'm puttin' out your eyes

—BOB DYLAN, "HIGH WATER (FOR CHARLEY PATTON)," 2001

"WHEN I THINK OF MYSTERY, I don't think of myself," Bob Dylan once charmingly quipped. "I think of the universe, like why does the moon rise when the sun falls? [Why do] caterpillars turn into butterflies?"[1] Dylan has refused to buy into the myth that his art is an unsolvable mystery. Speaking of his songwriting and performing, he said this to a journalist in 2001: "I've had a God-given sense of destiny. This is what I was put on earth to do."[2]

Destiny or fate is something Dylan believes in. In fact, Jack Fate is the character he plays in his most recent film, *Masked and Anonymous*. "Dylan is very accepting of the life he was given to live. He is resigned, he is content, and he is reminiscent," writes author Ronnie Keohane. "In *Masked and Anonymous*, Dylan tells us that though it has been a wild ride—full of treachery and loyalty, hatred and gracious love, callousness and compassion, violence and passion—he and his alter ego, Jack Fate, have rode it well."[3]

As to when the alleged mystery began, Dylan aficionados can recite the basic, immutable facts. In Duluth, Minnesota, on a spring evening in 1941—May 24 at 9:05 p.m. to be precise—Beatrice Zimmerman gave birth to her first child, a baby boy, in St. Mary's Hospital. Abraham Zimmerman, the son of Jewish immigrants from Odessa, Russia, was the proud new father of this same baby boy who would, one day, be pondering the mysteries of the universe, the moon and the sun, and caterpillars turning into butterflies.

"The birth certificate is filed May 28, 1941, coinciding with the circumcision ceremony," writes Dave Engel in his book *Just Like Bob Zimmerman's Blues*. "*Brit milah*, or *bris*, signifies God's covenant with Abraham. The operation is performed by a religiously schooled *mohel* in the presence of relatives and congregation members; a big party follows."[4]

In 1968, biographer Robert Shelton asked Dylan's father if his son studied the biblical language and knew the whole Hebrew ritual. "Bobby could speak; he knew 400 Hebrew words," remembered Abraham Zimmerman. "Literally, he could speak Hebrew like they do in Israel today. Rabbi Reuben Maier took great pride in him [during his bar mitzvah preparation in 1954] and took him to show him off one Friday night. The rabbi would say the sentence in English and Bobby would say it in Hebrew."[5]

It is ironic that the seemingly inconsistent Bob Dylan—who occupies such hallowed space in the countercultural decade of the 1960s—has been so consistent in assuming that God exists. When asked by Neil Spencer of *New Musical Express* about the "compatibility" between his interest in Judaism (his visits to Israel in 1969–1971) and his controversial beliefs of 1979-1981, Dylan simply replied, "There's really no difference between any of it in my mind."[6]

In 2003, Larry Charles—the man who co-conspired with Dylan on the much-maligned *Masked and Anonymous*—spoke about this very topic. "I think when he was 'born again,' he was just expanding his feeling about religion and God," said Charles. "In his mind—this is my interpretation—I don't think he saw such a disconnect between his Judaism and his Christianity. I think he sees it all as streams running from the same source. His definition of religion, his definition of God, is a very broad one and encompasses a lot of traditions, and I don't think they are in conflict with each other."[7]

For Charles to say that he thought Dylan was "expanding" his feeling about God after being "born again" is an intriguing assertion. Dylan believed Jesus was God. Many fans who follow Dylan might wonder how that could amount to an expansion of feeling about God. For some observers, this whole issue is irrelevant and apathy abounds.

"For the past twenty years the only puzzle with each new Dylan album has been whether this serial monotheist is now a Christian or Jew, and most people I know stopped caring long ago,"[8] said Francis Davis of the *Atlantic Monthly* in 1999. But Bob Dylan's spiritual odyssey hasn't been the suddenly monotheistic one of the last two decades as Davis and others might have us believe. It's not as if the songwriter was your run-of-the-mill atheist prior to all hell breaking loose in the wake of *Slow Train Coming* (1979), *Saved* (1980), and *Shot of Love* (1981).

Despite the indelible image of a cynical, persnickety, and perhaps agnostic Dylan of the mid-1960s, there is a mountain of evidence to suggest that he has been preoccupied with God from the very start. "The singular and special power of Dylan's music can be attributed to his fated obsession with the mysteries of Jehovah, setting him apart from the ruinous equivocations of Eastern doctrines,"[9] observed Davin Seay and Mary Neely in their 1986 book, *Stairway to Heaven: The Spiritual Roots of Rock 'N' Roll.*

Whether Judaism or Christianity, or perhaps a well-adjusted mixture, there are pretty much no "gods" in the Bob Dylan narrative (except to point out their futility)—just good old-fashioned monotheism.

Although some Dylan fans look the other way when it comes to the religious or spiritual angle of the Robert Allen Zimmerman story, there are those who have remained interested. Back in 1980, a twenty-nine-year-old Daniel Evearitt moved with his wife, Karen, to Rockland County, New York. Over the course of the decade, he pursued two degrees at nearby Drew University. The Evearitts, a committed Christian couple, were the caretakers at a local Conservative synagogue and lived above the Hebrew school on the property. Their responsibilities included cutting the grass, setting up meetings, custodial duties, and on Fridays and Saturdays (because of the Sabbath), turning on the lights and the heat or air.

Evearitt, having attended his first Dylan concerts at Madison Square Garden in 1974, was well aware of the recent shakeup in Dylan's spiritual journey. He recalled conversations with the rabbi and others in this Jewish community who followed and appreciated Dylan's music. The three albums *Slow Train Coming, Saved,* and *Shot of Love* caused substantial discomfort but they also formed the hope and idea of yet another Dylan phase. "Their view was 'This too shall pass,'" remembered Evearitt.

In 1987, Evearitt and some of his Jewish brethren from Rockland County attended a Dylan and the Grateful Dead concert at Giants Stadium in East Rutherford, New Jersey. Opposing views, theologically speaking, couldn't keep friends from sharing a mutual love—Bob Dylan's music. Fittingly, Dylan opened with "Slow Train" and closed with "Knockin' on Heaven's Door." Over a decade earlier, Evearitt's awareness of Dylan's music was evident when he penned an article in 1976 for *Christianity Today*; he thought then that Dylan's lyrics had something to say to a Christian crowd. The two-time author and retired theology professor remembers buying some bootleg albums in New York's Greenwich Village in 1970 and discovering Dylan's "Long Ago, Far Away."[10]

It's not a stretch to think of Dylan's songs being appreciated by some theology professors. Or any kind of professor, really (Neil Corcoran's 2002 book, *'Do you, Mr. Jones?': Bob Dylan with the Poets and Professors* might serve as exhibit A). Even the sciences aren't immune from the cultural ubiquity that is Dylan. For example, Lisa Randall took the trouble to explain how she arrived at the primary title of her 2011 book, *Knocking on Heaven's Door: How Physics and Scientific Thinking Illuminate the Universe and the Modern World.*

"I first heard the phrase 'knockin' on heaven's door' when listening to the Bob Dylan song at his 1987 concert with the Grateful Dead in Oakland, California," wrote Randall, a professor of physics at Harvard University. "Needless to say, the title of my book is intended differently than the song's lyrics, which I still hear Dylan and Jerry Garcia singing in my head. The phrase differs from its biblical origin as well, though my title does toy with this interpretation. In Matthew, the Bible says, 'Ask, and it shall be given you; seek, and ye shall find; knock, and it shall be opened unto you: for everyone that asketh receiveth; and he that seeketh findeth; and to him that knocketh it shall be opened.'"

Before Randall reflected on how different the philosophy and goals of science are from those of religion, she engaged in a bit of hermeneutics on her previously quoted passage from the Gospel of Matthew:

> According to these words, people can search for knowledge but the ultimate object is to gain access to God. People's curiosity about the world and active inquiries are more stepping-stones to the Divine—the universe itself is secondary. Answers might be forthcoming or a believer might be spurred to more actively seek truth, but without God, knowledge is inaccessible or not worth pursuing. People can't do it on their own—they are not the final arbiters.[11]

Back in 1965, music critic Ralph Gleason was conducting an inquiry of his own: "I played portions of the new Dylan album [*Highway 61 Revisited*] for a young man studying for the priesthood. 'He's a preacher,' he said, 'he ought to be speaking in the cathedrals.' He is. It's only that the cathedrals, too, are different."[12]

A significant transaction has been going on for five decades now between Bob Dylan and his audience. Its manifestations—for better or worse—show no sign of quitting anytime soon. Who can know the religious or spiritual journey of your average Bob Dylan fan? Though the book has not been written on *that*, there are undoubtedly orthodox, conservative, and reformed Jews who are listening to and enjoying the music of Bob Dylan—just as there are nominal, mainline, and evangelical Christians doing the same. Additionally, atheists and agnostics certainly populate the fan landscape; and folks who consider themselves spiritual but outside the religions of Judaism, Christianity, and Islam no doubt count themselves as fans.

But what we *can* know about the hopelessly unpredictable, inscrutable artist behind the many recordings, concerts, and interviews is this: Bob Dylan's spiritual journey remains bent on an unshakeable monotheism.

2

1961–1969: ESCAPING ON THE RUN

Dylan himself ran and ran hard, but for every stride he slipped two steps back toward the altar of Yahweh.

—DAVIN SEAY AND MARY NEELY, 1986

My heart stopped beatin' and my hands turned cold
Now I believe what the Bible told

—BOB DYLAN, 1962

IN 1961, WE SEE A POSING TWENTY-YEAR-OLD DYLAN who (besides spinning tall tales of running away from home to join the carnival) claimed to have already "been there, done that" in the religion department. He hadn't received any satisfaction. "Got no religion," he told Izzy Young. "Tried a bunch of different religions. Churches are divided; can't make up their minds, [and] neither can I. Never seen a god; can't say 'till I see one."[1]

But by the following year, as was evident in songs he composed and recorded, the Judeo-Christian God became a continuing preoccupation. Dylan's self-entitled debut album, released in March 1962, had him in more than one song, staring death in the eye and crooning about Jesus and his dying bed. He sounded like a world-weary soul at age twenty. The lyrics, though, were the work of the gospel bluesmen who came before him. However, in this same year, Dylan penned "Long Ago, Far Away," a song that opened and closed with a reference to the crucifixion of Jesus.

By November 1962, the twenty-one-year-old had written and recorded, for *Broadside* magazine, "I'd Hate to Be You on That Dreadful Day." The song depicts the dilemma of a person who arrives at the pearly gates only to be told that it is too late to make amends for the life he lived on earth. "Shoulda listened when you heard the word down there," Dylan tells the dearly departed through the lyrics (indicating he believed his Maker would be waiting on the other side). For those who had denied or ignored God, the song warned that it would be a dreadful day indeed.

Other Dylan compositions of the early 1960s revealed this same preoccupation with spiritual matters. "Quit Your Low Down Ways" noted the futility of the pretty mama who read her Bible and prayed to the Lord, but just wouldn't quit her ways. The image of death creeping under one's door was on display in "Whatcha Gonna Do?" It wasn't a matter of if the devil calls your card, but when.

"Long Time Gone" with its line, "But I know I ain't no prophet / An' I ain't no prophet's son," was lifted from a passage in the Bible (Amos 7:14), and "Let Me Die in My Footsteps" reflected a familiarity with the words of Jesus: "There's been rumors of wars and wars that have been" (Matthew 24:6).

And who could ever forget the provocative lines from "With God on Our Side," a composition written by a twenty-two-year-old Dylan? Other folks his age might not have had too many dark hours thinking about Jesus being betrayed by a kiss, or whether Judas Iscariot had God on his side. Dylan left it up to the listener to decide. Whatever one might offer as an answer, one thing seemed sure: if the pop song had a coffin, then Dylan certainly drove a few nails into its clunky edifice.

Even though he has generally been the silent type between songs, Dylan did say these words during his 1963 Carnegie Hall gig, just prior to singing his apocalyptic song, "When the Ship Comes In": "Nowadays there are crueler Goliaths who do crueler and crueler things, but one day they're going to be slain, too, and people 2,000 years from now can look back and say, 'Remember when the second Goliath was slayed.'"[2]

As for Jesus, Dylan laid down these weary words in the liner notes to his fourth album, *Another Side of Bob Dylan* (1964): "People pound their chests an' other people's chests an' interpret bibles t' suit their own means. Respect is just a misinterpreted word an' if Jesus Christ himself came down through these streets, Christianity would start all over again."

Besides the aforementioned lyric from "With God on Our Side," Dylan only named the name of Jesus on two other occasions in the 1960s: in "Masters of War" with a tongue-in-cheek (or sincerely damning?) theological overstatement ("even Jesus would never forgive what you do") and in "Bob Dylan's 115th Dream" when some comic dialogue concludes with a character reminding the singer that he is not Jesus. But there is no question that in 1965, Dylan confessed to not having a specific belief in Jesus and even struggled with the relevance of it all:

> Everybody talks about names that strike familiar chords. Jesus Christ. They say, 'Look at all the good he did.' But I ask, 'Where? How? When? For who?' And look at what they did to him. Everybody's talking about how he really felt, but it's such a long time ago, you can't really know. You really just have to believe. And that's a dangerous business, just believing. You have to sacrifice a lot.[3]

In *Dont Look Back* (1967), D. A. Pennebaker's documentary of Dylan's 1965 English tour, the twenty-three-year-old affirmed this dangerous business of faith when responding to a reporter's question of whether he "believed" in something. "No, I don't believe in anything. No, why should I believe in anything?" he asked. "I don't see anything that anybody's offered me to believe in that I'm gonna believe in and put my trust and faith and everything in."

Maureen Cleave, a reporter for the *London Evening Standard*, asked him if he had read the Bible. Dylan shrugged off the question, mumbling that he had "glanced" through it. Cleave later explained why she asked the question in the first place: "I realized he had been reading the Bible because of the line, 'The first one now will later be last,' which comes directly from one of the Gospels," she said. "So that is why I asked the question."[4]

Cleave wasn't the only soul noticing the moral component to Dylan's lyrics. Ralph Gleason, the *San Francisco Chronicle* jazz critic, initially dismissed Dylan as not being a force to reckon with, but by 1965 was calling him "a genius, a singing conscience and moral referee, as well as a preacher."[5] When referring to *Highway 61 Revisited*—the epic album composed in 1965 by a twenty-four-year-old Dylan—another journalist saw it as "Dylan translating the Bible in street terms."[6]

In 1966, Dylan and Nat Hentoff of *Playboy* conspired together for a put-on interview, which was full of delightfully outrageous responses. However, when Hentoff asked the world-famous singer what he had to look forward to, he got the reply "salvation" and "prayer." One wonders if a serious moment had been captured. Shortly thereafter, though, the fun and games continued. When asked if there was anything else he looked forward to, Dylan said that he would like to start a cookbook magazine and that he always wanted to be a boxing referee.

There is no question that after his motorcycle accident of 1966, the Bible became much more than, say, the occasional inspiration gleaned from a glance. The accident short-circuited the fast pace of touring and the onslaught of interviews—and that may have been a blessing in disguise. "He badly needed to disappear," writes author Paul Williams, "and I guess you could say God gave him the cue, the opportunity."[7]

Prior to the motorcycle accident, his longtime friend, Allen Ginsberg, was asked about the acoustic versus electric controversy; did he think Dylan had "sold out"? "Dylan has sold out to God," Ginsberg replied.

"That is to say, his command was to spread his beauty as wide as possible. It was an artistic challenge to see if great art can be done on a jukebox. And he proved it can."[8]

In "Sign on the Cross," Dylan's worrisome outtake from *The Basement Tapes* (recorded in 1967), he picked up where 1963's "With God on Our Side" left off: was Judas Iscariot on God's side? "Sign on the Cross" referred to the sign that Roman Governor Pontius Pilate placed on the cross on which Jesus was crucified—"Jesus of Nazareth, the King of the Jews" (according to the Gospel of John).

"The underlying motif [of the song] is obviously worry, a nagging and disquieting worry about the cross and what it represents," writes John Herdman in his book, *Voice Without Restraint*. "Something is now becoming clearer. Behind Dylan's prophetic utterances of doom directed toward society lies fear, personal fear, fear about his own salvation. Now for the first time, instead of projecting that fear outward in apocalyptic imagery, he begins to examine its source within his own consciousness . . . he suggests, too, in the final verse, that this worry may be a sign of strength rather than of weakness. The song, has, as it is without a doubt supposed to have, a disconcerting, unsettling effect. . . . Dylan is asking, and from a Jewish point of view, the question: was this man really the Messiah?"[9]

In 1967, Dylan also composed (and released) *John Wesley Harding* with its estimated sixty-plus biblical allusions; in fact, this album from which Jimi Hendrix plucked out and popularized one of its songs, "All Along the Watchtower," was the same album Dylan later called "the first biblical rock album."[10] Even a Rolling Stones biographer picked up on the album's biblical feel, likening the songs to "new acoustic psalms."[11] As the so-called Age of Aquarius was dawning upon a nation and world, Bob Dylan was digging into his Bible.

While he acknowledged a passing acquaintance with the Bible in 1965, his mother confirmed that the picture was altogether different by 1967–1968. In an interview with Toby Thompson for his book *Positively Main Street*, Beatrice Zimmerman revealed that there was one book in her son's Woodstock, New York, home that stood apart. "There's a huge Bible open on a stand in the middle of his study. Of all the books that crowd his house, [that] overflow from his house, that Bible gets the most attention. He's continuously getting up and going over to refer to something."[12]

In 1967, Noel Paul Stookey (the Paul from the group Peter, Paul, and Mary) found himself in this same Woodstock home visiting Dylan as the era of Flower Power was in full tilt. "I'm talking about how I'm really blown away by the Beatles. I love what they're saying about love, and I'm wondering if he senses what's happening in their music . . . what does he feel life's all about?" In response, Dylan simply asked, "Do you ever read the Bible?"[13] Stookey had not, but soon would follow Dylan's advice. By the following year, he had a life-changing encounter with Jesus. LSD wasn't the only thing blowing people's minds.

Some of Dylan's friends continued to be surprised by his approach. Take, for example, John Cohen. He attempted to dig beneath the surface, searching for possible roots to the enigmatic—morality saturated—*John Wesley Harding* album. Did the key lie in the parables and paradoxes of Franz Kafka? No, that wasn't it, said Dylan, he was only familiar with the biblical parables. And yes, he read the Bible often. Cohen retorted, "I don't think you're the kind of person who goes to the hotel where the Gideons leave a Bible, and you pick it up." A wonderfully Dylanesque response followed: "Well, you never know."[14]

Following the death of his father on June 5, 1968, Dylan made two trips to Israel, during the summers of 1969 and 1970. Harold Leventhal, who had managed Woody Guthrie and Pete Seeger and promoted an early Dylan gig in New York, suggested that Dylan visit the Holy Land. "After his father died, Bob became quite conscious of his Jewishness," Leventhal said. "He was very excited about Israel when he got back."[15]

When it came to Dylan's 1969 release, *Nashville Skyline*, author Tim Riley saw it as "a straightforward country record, which made him a determined outcast to the counterculture that was blooming in his backyard of Woodstock, New York."[16] While fending off the occasional loonies outside his home, perhaps Dylan was comfortable in the outcast role, lyrically giving thanks to "the Lord" for his woman in "To Be Alone with You." He even joined up with his friend Johnny Cash in what amounted to an outtake from *Nashville Skyline* for a swapping of lines (mostly humming by Dylan) on the time-honored spiritual, "Just a Closer Walk with Thee."

An album entitled *Dylan's Gospel* by the Brothers and Sisters of Los Angeles was released in the same year as *Nashville Skyline.* Consisting of Dylan covers and featuring a picture of a church on the front and back of the album, the compilation included "The Times They Are A-Changin'," "I Shall Be Released," "All Along the Watchtower," "The Mighty Quinn," "Chimes of Freedom," and "My Back Pages." This curious release, produced by Lou Adler and featuring The Los Angeles Gospel Choir, provided further evidence that some of Dylan's songs were hitting folks on a spiritual level, long before any train could be seen slowly chugging on the horizon.

Might it be that the closing song on Bob Dylan's debut album of 1962, "See That My Grave is Kept Clean,"—adapted by the singer to include the declaration, "My heart stopped beatin' and my hands turned cold / Now I believe what the Bible told"—captures a core belief of the singer/songwriter? As the decade of the 1960s vanished, Dylan's spiritual journey would continue.

3

1970–1979: DON'T MIND THE DRIVING RAIN

The Dylan who inspired us to look beyond banal textbooks and accepted ideologies now implores us to turn inwards to the pages of the Holy Bible, a book filled with contradictions, inaccuracies, outrages, and absurdities.

—AMERICAN ATHEISTS PRESS RELEASE, TUCSON, ARIZONA, 1979

Well, the Bible says, "The fool has said in his heart, 'There is no God.'"

—BOB DYLAN RESPONDING IN KIND, TUCSON, ARIZONA, 1979

DID BOB DYLAN, BY 1970, have a personal relationship with God? Whatever the case, there is precious little doubt that he possessed a strong monotheistic bent. During the Age of Aquarius, LSD was serving as a formidable god in its own right, and traditional monotheism was far from hip. "Psychedelics and the brotherly communion of seekers caught up in the pulsing aura of impending nirvana conspired to turn the religious process on its head," wrote Davin Seay and Mary Neely in their book, *Stairway to Heaven.* "Existential doctrines were birthed from the foreheads of the new believers . . . the direst biblical warning had come to pass: Every man was doing what was right in his own eyes."[1]

"Psychedelics never influenced me," Dylan would later say in 1977. "I don't know, I think Timothy Leary had a lot to do with driving the last nails into the coffin of that New York [music] scene we were talking about. When psychedelics happened, everything became irrelevant; because that had nothing to do with making music or writing poems or trying to really find yourself in that day and age."

But the interviewer, Ron Rosenbaum, insisted people were doing just that—finding themselves. "People were deluded into thinking they were something that they weren't," Dylan concluded. "Birds, airplanes, fire hydrants, whatever. People were walking around thinking they were stars."[2]

How did Dylan cope with the changes that were swirling about in that day and age? How did he attempt to find himself? In 1970, when he received an honorary doctorate from Princeton University, perhaps their citation provided a clue:

"Paradoxically, though known to millions, he shuns publicity and organizations, preferring the solidarity of his family and isolation from the world. Although he is now approaching the perilous age of thirty, his music remains the authentic expression of the disturbed and concerned conscience of young America."[3]

This mind-set didn't escape the notice of the late cartoonist Charles Schulz who let one of his Peanuts cartoons capture the zeitgeist. Linus and Charlie Brown, sitting together, pondered the future. "Bob Dylan will be thirty years old this month," said Linus. Charlie Brown gives a distressed look, and with hands on cheeks, declares: "That's the most depressing thing I've ever heard."

Dylan, in 1989, reflected on the 1960s "don't trust anyone over thirty" mantra: "That was false to begin with, that statement," he said. "Look how much play it got. It probably sold a lot of tennis shoes and things people need from the accessory department."[4]

It is an inescapable (and paradoxical) fact that at least part of Dylan's legacy is his lyrical appeal to a moral framework. According to one report, Dylan's mother, Beatrice Zimmerman, circa 1970, said this about her son: "I know people my age [in their mid-fifties] who are listening to his music, and they tell me, 'Did you know your son writes about the Bible? He's really a prophet of our times.' Most people do not understand how deep Bob is. But I don't say to him anymore, 'You're great,' because he doesn't want to hear that."[5]

Dylan himself, in 1970, talked about the tension between his public and private life, particularly following his motorcycle accident in 1966:

"I believe that at certain periods in a person's existence it is necessary, if not vital, to bring about a change in your life so as not to go under. I felt that I needed to stop in order to find something new, in order to create—and then again, I wanted to live part of my life without being continually disturbed for no valid reason. I have children and I want to watch them grow up—to get to know them, and for them to get to know me, and know that I'm their father."[6]

Dylan's concept of a father wasn't limited to the human arena. In "Father of Night," the last song on his album *New Morning* (1970), Dylan acknowledged the God of creation: "the father who built the mountains and turneth the rivers and streams." The song's final line called for solemn praise. Although Moses wrote it down many moons ago this way—"Hear, O Israel! The Lord our God, the Lord is one" (Deuteronomy 6:4, NIV)—there was no mistaking the monotheism in Dylan's lyric.

Just days after the album's release, a twenty-nine-year-old Dylan found himself in the company of two old friends, Scott Ross, a New York deejay, and journalist Al Aronowitz. The three sat together in a balcony at the Fillmore East in New York City, taking in an Eric Clapton concert. Ross had recently become a Christian and, after the concert, they all joined Clapton, piling into a station wagon driven by Aronowitz. Ross recalled Dylan's curiosity about spiritual things:

"I started to tell him the story about what happened with the Lord in my life, and he was intrigued, asked a lot of questions," remembers

Ross. "A lot of earlier conversations in my pre-Jesus days were so spacey; we got into some weird, esoteric, you know, ozone-level kind of stuff. Who knew what we were saying? You thought you were intelligent and profound and deep, but it was just a lot of gobbledygook. . . . So I think what he was hearing in me was something pretty clear, that I had come to some realization of truth that he was intrigued by. At that point, I don't think he called that truth 'Jesus,' but he was certainly interested. God certainly came into the conversation, and I was clear that my conversion was to Jesus."

Before the station wagon ride was over, Dylan mentioned his new album to Ross and had Aronowitz drop by his apartment; after running upstairs and emerging with a copy of *New Morning*, Dylan gave Ross some instructions: "Listen to it. There's a couple of things on there about God."

"And sure enough," said Ross, who still has the album today, "there were some things in there, and they were pretty clear, you know? So I just kept praying for him."[7]

After trips to Israel in the summers of 1969–1970, Dylan was planning another trip, one he would take with his family. He went to great pains to keep it private, but his thirtieth birthday to the Holy Land wouldn't go undetected.[8] Local record executives were apparently tipped off and the following advertisement awaited him in the *Jerusalem Post*: "Happy Birthday Bob Dylan, Wherever You Are. Call us if you feel like it. CBS Records, Israel."

According to biographer Robert Shelton, Dylan simply wanted to visit without a public brouhaha.[9] On May 22, 1971, two days before his thirtieth birthday, Dylan and his wife Sara visited Jerusalem's Mount Zion Yeshiva, a well-known Cabalistic training center. Introduced to the singer by Yoso Rosenzweig, one of the resident rabbis, an American student wondered why Dylan avoided an overt proclamation of his Jewish identity. "There is no problem; I'm a Jew," replied Dylan. "It touches my poetry, my life, in ways I can't describe. Why should I declare something that should be so obvious?"[10]

As fate would have it, on the day of his thirtieth birthday, Dylan visited the Western Wall in Jerusalem and was captured on film—accidentally—by someone who was shooting pictures of tourists. After the UPI-employed photographer realized what he had, the photo was published around the world. So much for the private trip. *Rolling Stone* pitched in their two cents: "Is Bob Zimmerman Really Jewish?" The circus, apparently, was in town.

More seriously, Robert Campbell, writing for *Christian Century* in 1971, saw Dylan gradually being accepted as a poet by the cultural establishment—or he looked ahead to a day when acceptance would come from other circles.

"Perhaps the day will come when the clergy, too, open themselves to Dylan's work," Campbell wrote. "For his music, even apart from its many references to Jesus, God, and the Bible, has a general spirituality about it. This spirituality has endured in Dylan's music because of his determination to maintain his integrity, to continue to make an honest, personal statement about his life."[11]

By 1972, Dylan began composing "Forever Young," a classic song in the Dylan canon that was not without its biblical allusions (reportedly penned for Jakob Dylan, his youngest son). The late Bert Cartwright, in his book, *The Bible in the Lyrics of Bob Dylan*, has noted how the song's opening line—"May God bless and keep you always"—reflects the Aaronic benediction of Numbers 6:24: "The LORD bless you and keep you."

Author Stephen Pickering has said that during the Yom Kippur War—two years after Dylan's 1971 visit to the Holy Land—a member of the United Jewish Appeal sent several telegrams to the singer. He was requesting Dylan's help since he remembered seeing Dylan at the Western Wall and sensed his "profound concern with his own soul."[12]

At the time of this request, Dylan was recording *Planet Waves*, an album that contained the aforementioned "Forever Young" and appeared under his new record company label, Ram's Horn Music. The name of the label is no doubt an allusion to the shofar, the ram's horn that is blown to awaken Jewish souls to their heritage, especially during the High Holy Days.[13]

In fact, during the Yom Kippur War of 1973, Harry Leventhal, a friend who gave Dylan some books and encouraged him to visit the Holy Land, attempted to organize a benefit for Israel at Madison Square Garden. Dylan declined, without publically offering any reason, but Leventhal later discovered that Dylan privately gave a "sizeable amount of money" to Israel.[14]

Another report claimed Dylan's tour proceeds went to assist Israel, accompanied by charges that he was a "Zionist." "Just gossip" is how Dylan responded to the murmuring, along with wondering about the label: "I'm not sure what a Zionist really is."[15]

Even though Dylan has faithfully eschewed the role, the baggage of Dylan-as-Leader was not easily discarded. Perhaps this was nowhere more evident than in January 1974, when Dylan kicked off his first tour since the hair-raising, globetrotting, frenetic days of 1966. The expectations of a return to the stage translated into another peak in the singer's popularity. He made the cover of *Newsweek*; millions of ticket requests were received for the forty-concert tour. In fact, astonishingly, more than 7 percent of the U.S. population had applied for the 658,000 available tickets.[16]

Two weeks into the tour, Richard Rocklin, the rabbi of Temple Israel in Charlotte, North Carolina, received a visit and a gift. He grew up with Dylan and was a family friend. The two were also fraternity brothers at Sigma Alpha Mu during Dylan's brief flirtation with college at the University of Minnesota.

"When Bob came by he left six tickets so I could give them to my confirmation class. It excited the kids, and instead of wanting to talk Jewish philosophy, they wanted me to tell them everything about Bobby," Rocklin remembered. "He'd make one helluva rabbi because he and I both grew up in homes with intense Jewish feelings. . . . You don't necessarily have to be a praying Jew to be a Jew. Bobby never lost his Jewish roots. Israel moved him very much. He was bar mitzvahed like all of us."[17]

The now thirty-two-year-old singer confirmed as much, telling

Stephen Pickering that he had "never forgotten" his roots. "I am a Jew," said Dylan.[18]

Two days after visiting with his friend, Dylan attended what *Rolling Stone* called a "religious rally," an event held at Peacock Park in Miami, Florida. To be more precise, it was an event where the message of Jesus was being preached. Dylan requested (and was granted) a meeting afterward with one of the speakers, Arthur Blessit, a man once known as "The Mod Minister of the Sunset Strip." Blessit had a club in Hollywood called His Place, which catered the gospel message to the countercultural crowd.

Surreal as it may seem, Dylan, in the midst of his 1974 tour, had pedaled up to the event on a ten-speed bicycle. The two men met together, someone happened to snap a photo (which Blessit still has to this day), and Blessit recorded the day's events in his journal.

Just as Dylan had asked questions of his friend Scott Ross a few years earlier after the Eric Clapton concert, he was asking questions of Arthur Blessit. "He asked how did I know Jesus was in my life; how did I know there was a God, and that He really cares; and how did I know Jesus was the right way. Our conversation was all about Jesus, not religion," Blessit remembers. "He was wanting to know if Jesus was really the Way, the Truth, and the Life. I sought to answer the questions he asked as best as I could. The talk was very intense, and he was totally interested in Jesus. I showed him how in the Bible [it says] sinful man needs a Savior, that the Holy God cares and loves us, and that Jesus came to live without sin, do the mighty work, and then die for our sins on the cross. After dying, he arose on the third day, was seen by thousands, then ascended into heaven, and will hear our prayer, and put His Spirit in our hearts, and we can have peace with God."

Blessit and Dylan's chat lasted about ten minutes. "I prayed for him, that he would come to know and follow Jesus. He said he had come to hear me, and see what a real Jesus follower would say to his questions. . . . It was a powerful time," concluded Blessit. "Here was a radical man of music who was talking with a radical follower of Jesus. We understood each other. We did not talk about his music, or my life, just Jesus."[19]

Two days after his encounter with Arthur Blessit in Florida, Dylan's tour rolled on to Atlanta, where he was invited to a party at the governor's mansion. Governor Jimmy Carter's son, Chip, presented Dylan with a coin that was found at an archaeological dig and learned that Dylan was impressed by his father's visit to Israel in 1972.[20] Although Dylan later claimed there was no special significance to his visits to Israel, he did acknowledge that he was interested in "what and who a Jew is." And he knew that, unlike other Semitic people, one thing that distinguished Jews was that they were hated by a lot of people: "There's something going on here that's hard to explain."[21]

As Stephen Pickering waited in line before Dylan's concert in Uniondale, New York, on January 29, 1974, he observed how conversations among "the yarmulked Jews" were "revolving around Dylan's influence upon their souls as Jews." That influence, of course, wasn't limited to Jewish souls. Governor Carter said his understanding of "what's right and wrong" in American society came into sharp focus after listening to Dylan's song, "The Times They Are A-Changin'."[22]

Yet when questioned about the religious images in his music, the notion of religion seemed elusive to Dylan. "Religion to me is a fleeting thing. Can't nail it down. It's in me and out of me. It does give me, on the surface, some images, but I don't know to what degree."[23] According to biographer Robert Shelton, Dylan wasn't ready to say it was "God's will" that propelled him back onto the road in 1974. However, after the Rolling Thunder tour of 1975 commenced, Dylan had changed his tune. "I didn't consciously pursue the Bob Dylan myth. It was given to me . . . by God," he remarked to Jim Jerome of *People* magazine. "Inspiration is what we're looking for. You just have to be receptive to it. . . . I don't care what people expect of me. Doesn't concern me. I'm doin' God's work. That's all I know."[24]

During the Rolling Thunder tours of 1975–1976, Allen Ginsberg remembers Dylan telling him that he would "write better poetry" if only he believed in God.

"Dylan also said he believed in God. That's why I wrote 'Lay Down Yr Mountain,'" explained Ginsberg. "Dylan said that where he was, 'on top of the Mountain,' he had a choice whether to stay, or to come down. He said God told him, 'All right, you've been on the Mountain, I'm busy, go down, you're on your own. Check in later' [Ginsberg laughs]. And then Dylan said, 'Anybody that's busy making elephants and putting camels through needles' eyes is too busy to answer my questions, so I came down the mountain.'"[25]

Here we have Dylan—several years before the events of 1979—revealing an awareness of the words of Jesus:

"Truly I say to you, it is hard for a rich man to enter the kingdom of heaven. And again I say to you, it is easier for a camel to go through the eye of a needle, than for a rich man to enter the kingdom of God" (Matthew 19:23–24).

John Henry "T-Bone" Burnett was in Dylan's band for the Rolling Thunder tours. If readers of Bob Spitz's *Dylan: A Biography* believed his account, then Burnett was indeed one of the guilty men. The scandalous charge? Bringing Bob Dylan into the fold of Christianity:

> The gloom that had surrounded Bob attracted the attention of his guitar player, T-Bone Burnett, whose built-in radar detected the blips of his boss's emotional crisis like an early-warning device. A lanky, raven-eyed Texan. . . . T-Bone moonlighted in the service of the Lord. He was an early disciple of born-again fundamentalism, the type of guy who loved to party and get crazy just like anyone else—up to a certain point. Then, as if some excess had tripped a spiritual circuit-breaker, his personality was driven by a different current and suddenly T-Bone possessed all the spooky religious rhetoric of a Christian missionary.
>
> He was very earnest about his born-again experience and babbled rapturously about the Word of God, righteousness, and the blessing of salvation. Rob Stoner [another Dylan band member at the time] credits T-Bone with Bob's religious recruitment, although his influence was anything but Svengali-like or irresistible. The steady,

low-pressure manner in which T-Bone described things like his "inner light" was persuasive enough, and Bob, vulnerable and open-minded, swallowed the bait like a prize fish.[26]

After being read this excerpt from Spitz's account, Burnett laughed:

It's total fiction. There's not one word of truth in it. Not only is it fiction, but it's bad writing as well. It's yellow journalism and melodrama, cheap melodrama really. How's that for a comment?

First of all, I've been an Episcopalian my whole life, just for starters, and still am. Second, the real story is none of us were really going to church during that period of time and none of us were particularly religious, I didn't think. Or at least I didn't hear any discussions of religion at all. But there was, after the tour, spontaneously, about ten to fifteen people from the tour started going to church, and either going back to church or becoming Christians or something.

I think that's the more interesting story than the idea that Bob was somehow manipulated into some sort of bogus—this is the way the stories have been presented—that Bob Dylan was weak and manipulated into a false religion, the religion of the enemy, in fact. That's the way that story is in the Spitz book. Which isn't the story at all.

Within a year or two after the tour, I think Roger McGuinn and Steven Soles, several of the people were going to church. Girlfriends, girls on tour, guys on tour. I don't know what that was or why that happened. I was just sort of hanging around at the time. I think it's interesting. I think it's a really important thing that something more accurate and true be printed on it. And if someone could come to a deeper understanding.

That Spitz interpretation of the thing, that's real easy, it's all so tidy. It ties the whole thing up and it's also *a la* cliché. It turns it all into a cliché. It's not even imaginative fiction...I just ignored this thing for the last twenty years or however long it's been, but now that it's all on the Internet, I want to go ahead and try to set the record straight.[27]

Dylan has found it difficult to escape certain questions, even from a publication as seemingly innocuous as *TV Guide*. In 1976, when asked how he imagined God, Dylan first chuckled and asked why nobody ever asks, say, Kris Kristofferson the question; then he answered the question in what could be construed as a pantheistic view, saying he could see God in a daisy, at night, and in the wind and rain. However, the fuller context revealed the monotheism that has seemingly been etched into his soul. "I see creation just about everywhere. The highest form of song is prayer: King David's, Solomon's, the wailing of the coyote, the rumble of the earth," he observed. "It must be wonderful to be God. There's so much going on out there that you can't get to it all. It would take you longer than forever."[28]

Here is, arguably, the essence of Dylan's Jewish heritage: a heritage where God is proclaimed as the one and only Creator—an omniscient God, a God entirely aware of the goings on in His creation. Yet just over a year after the interview, Dylan told Ron Rosenbaum of *Playboy* magazine that he wasn't a "patriot to any creed." He said a devout Christian or Muslim could be just as effective as a devout Jew. But notice the monotheistic thread of these three faiths. He sensed a "heartfelt God" but didn't think God wanted him thinking about Him all the time. "He's got enough people asking Him for favors. He's got enough people asking Him to pull strings," Dylan remarked with characteristic wit.

Dylan's most extensive public commentary about Jesus prior to the *Slow Train Coming* era may have been drawn out in this same interview when Rosenbaum asked the question, "Do you think Christ is an answer?"

"What is it that attracts people to Christ?" Dylan asked. "The fact that it was such a tragedy is what. Who does Christ become when he lives inside a person? Many people say that Christ lives inside of them. Well, what does that mean? I've talked to many people whom Christ lives inside; I haven't met one who would want to trade places with Christ. Not one of his people put himself on the line when it came down to the final hour. What would Christ be in this day and age if he came back? What would he be? What would he be to fulfill his function and purpose? He would have to be a leader, I suppose."

It is interesting that Rosenbaum's single question elicited so many questions from Dylan. Why did the followers of Jesus flee when it came down to that final hour?

Dylan's memory also served him well in recollecting an eleven-year-old headline:

"I remember seeing a *Time* magazine on an airplane a few years back and it had a big cover headline, 'IS GOD DEAD?' [incidentally, dated April 8, 1966 and coinciding with Easter weekend] I mean, that was—would you think it was a responsible thing to do?" asked a perturbed Dylan. "What does God think of that? I mean, if you were God, how would you like to see that written about yourself?" Then Dylan delivered the hammer blow that epitomized his monotheistic leanings. "You know, I think the country's gone downhill since that day."

"Really? Since that particular question was asked?" inquired an apparently surprised Ron Rosenbaum.

"Yeah, I think at that point, some very irresponsible people got hold of too much power to put such an irrelevant thing like that on a magazine when they could be talking about real issues. Since that day, you've had to kind of make your own way."

Asked how we were doing in "making our own way," Dylan reminded readers that we are born and we die, and we're concerned with our journey from point A to Z. "But it's pretty self-deluding if you think that's all there is," he concluded.[29]

Jonathan Cott of *Rolling Stone* was another journalist who interviewed Dylan in late 1977. Cott brought along to the interview some photocopied pages from the book, *The Wisdom of the Jewish Mystics*, and first quoted a passage from Rabbi Dov Baer, the Mazid of Mezeritch. After taking it in, Dylan declared, "That's the most mind-blazing chronicle of human behavior I think I've ever heard." Asking how he could get a copy of it, Cott informed Dylan that he brought the photocopy for him. "I'll put it on my wall," said Dylan. "There's a man I would follow. That's a real hero. A real hero."

Cott then quoted from a second text: "Another Hasidic rabbi once said that you can learn something from everything. Even from a train, a telephone, and a telegram. From a train, he said, you can learn that in one second one can miss everything. From a telephone you can learn that what you say over here can be heard over there. And from a telegram that all words are counted and charged."

"It's a cosmic statement," Dylan said. "These guys are really wise. I tell you, I've heard gurus and yogis and philosophers and politicians and doctors and lawyers, teachers of all kinds...and these rabbis really had something going."

After the two reflected on some of these rabbinic words, Dylan made this cryptic observation: "You know, I'll tell you. Lately I've been catching myself. I've been in some scenes, and I say: 'Holy s---, I'm not here alone.' I've never had that experience before the past few months. I've felt this strange, eerie feeling that I wasn't alone, and I'd better know it."[30]

On the one hand, Bob Dylan certainly wasn't a faithful follower of secular humanism, which denied the supernatural, neatly doing away with God. On the other hand, even though his monotheistic tendencies were evident, he didn't seem particularly committed. There was some neutral ground; it wasn't a matter of either "faith or unbelief" as later lyrics would assert.

"This album," writes Paul Williams about 1978's *Street-Legal*, "is our final clue to what was happening with Dylan in the months before he gave himself up to God."[31]

One of the questions Dylan fielded around the time of its release dealt with his spiritual journey in its most basic sense. "Do you believe in God?" asked Philippe Adler of the French magazine, *L'Expresse*. "Let's say, as He shows Himself," Dylan responded.

Fair enough.

Out of the ashes of the Rolling Thunder tours, one newly formed band emerged: the musical outfit known as The Alpha Band. Comprised of T-Bone Burnett, David Mansfield, and Steven Soles, the band's self-titled debut of 1976 was basically immune from accusations of peddling spirituality of the Christian persuasion. But the spiritual contagion found on their last two albums—*Spark in the Dark* (1977) and *The Statue Makers of Hollywood* (1978)—didn't go unnoticed.

The story of Fort Worth, Texas, native T-Bone Burnett in particular and The Alpha Band in general serves as relevant context to the Bob Dylan story of the late 1970s. Burnett, who clearly doesn't want—and has denied—credit for Dylan's "conversion," possessed some theological roots before the wonder of music largely consumed him in his teens and twenties. The man who found himself in The Alpha Band by his late twenties—and has remained a lifelong friend with Dylan—has acknowledged the theological influence of his parents. Although an acolyte in the Episcopal church as a young boy, Burnett didn't get a very clear picture of religion and spirituality from his church leaders—with one noteworthy exception: a certain Sunday school teacher.

Many years later, he recalled a "magnificent" moment when she brought up the idea of Providence: "She started drawing lines on a piece of paper and crossing them in every direction until the piece of paper was just completely black—'That's Providence.' That was a pretty abstract thing to tell a ten year old,' Burnett remarked. This same Sunday school teacher planted another seed that he remembered decades later: "The will of God is like a rubber band that you're attached to. It goes from one spot to another. As you walk along this road, the band will let you go as long as you want to, but God will bring you back at some point.' I don't know if I decided to see how far I could go, or if that rubber band's the way it really is, but that's how my life has been."[32]

For their 1976 debut as The Alpha Band, Burnett, Mansfield, and Soles weren't quite spiritually awakened/re-awakened yet, but the signing of a multi-million-dollar deal may have hastened some worldly revelations: "The pressure was ridiculous. We had a six-million-dollar deal with Arista as an unknown band that had been together for three weeks, and [label head] Clive Davis was saying we were the most important band since the Stones, the Beatles, and Dylan," remembered Burnett. "It's so typical of the disease of the Seventies."[33]

Between the time of growing up in the Episcopal church and The Alpha Band days, Burnett recalled, in 1978, where he had been spiritually coming from: "Well, personally I'd been what you might call a Christian mystic. I'd been raised in the church, but somewhere down the line I'd gotten hold of books like *The Aquarian Gospel of Jesus Christ.* Mystical weird books. I never could finish them, or get serious about them, but I was looking. So I'd been touched by God as a kid, and I'd started looking for Christ, but in my wanderings I had become very mystical. The more I went in that direction, the further I got from personal contact. Then at some point I started returning to a biblical basis for the spiritual search. Right at that stage was when we did that second record" [The Alpha Band's 1977 release, *Spark in the Dark*].[34]

Burnett viewed the album as a "revelation" and said that prior to it, things had looked pretty dark, but, he said, "I turned around to where I could see the spark—the Light." Steven Soles described the album in terms of what James Joyce called epiphany—"seeing past the material aspects of what's going on to a more spiritual realization."[35] The liner notes to *Spark in the Dark* included the declaration that the album was "humbly offered in the light of the triune God." Although rock critic Robert Christgau tipped his hat to Burnett's songwriting prowess, he didn't feel the humility, suggesting that Burnett "doesn't know as much as he thinks he does."[36]

For their final effort—the *Statue Makers of Hollywood* (1978)—The Alpha Band pulled no traditional spiritual punches: the songs were steeped in a Bible-based worldview. The word was out as the pithy Christgau chimed in that although the non-believing crowd tended to view Burnett as shrill, he found "something sweet and reflective beneath his cool, caustic self-righteousness."[37]

Although Burnett seemed to eschew any single "moment of truth" (for him, instead, a personal God met him at different junctures in his journey), he was unabashedly pointing to Jesus as the source of the light.

Besides original compositions, the band's swan song effort included Hank Williams' gospel offering "Thank God." Mansfield recalled the context of their last album as a very good recording experience, and also recalled how his bandmate wasn't exactly bashful when approaching the man responsible for signing them to that multi-million-dollar contract: "T-Bone basically went to Clive [Davis] and said, 'I got the idea for this record, but it's completely non-commercial. It's going to be really weird. If you want to let us out of the contract, please do, but if you don't, I'm not going to make any compromises.' I don't know if T-Bone said it quite that diplomatically either. I'm not sure how he put it, but the message he gave Clive was: 'We're going to do this—take it or leave it. If you want to let us go, and cut your losses now, do so.'"[38]

Mansfield also recalled for interviewer Larry Jaffee his take on what transpired once the green light had been given for *The Statue Makers of Hollywood*: "We went in and in many ways that record was pretty fierce. It was incredibly radio unfriendly. But T-Bone (and Steven Soles in a lesser sense) had this mission having been recently converted to Christianity. Besides being sort of wacky musically on many of the songs, he did this Old Testament jeremiad kind of take on the whole thing. It was his chance to take the moral high ground, to do all the social and political criticism, unexpurgated and un-moderated, to get that all out in the open, out of his system. So it was very intense on both those levels. The lyrics were very confrontational and the music was eclectic to the 'nth' degree. Some of it was, anyway, and after that Arista dropped us."

Burnett biographer Lloyd Sachs offered up a suggestion for the band's failure to catch popular fire: it had less to do with its lack of a signature song (Clive Davis's long-running theory) than its "preachy intellectualism"; however, Sachs also commented that in "all their eccentric, prophesizing glory, the most easily dismissed album, *The Statue Makers of Hollywood*, is one of Burnett's real ear-openers."[39]

A contemporary of Dylan, Burnett, Mansfield, and Soles—and a soul not unfamiliar with eccentric, prophesizing glory—was one Lonnie Frisbee, a twenty-nine-year-old who happened to be in the immediate area when Bob Dylan and his band, which now included the aforementioned Mansfield and Soles, flew into Gothenburg, Sweden, in July of 1978. Like The Alpha Band (and soon, Dylan too), Frisbee also had ties to the early Vineyard church, but he was in Gothenburg under the auspices of the Calvary Chapel church to meet with a large group of Swedish kids for Teen Challenge, a ministry formed by David Wilkerson in 1960 to help with alcohol and drug addiction. (Incidentally, part of Wilkerson's evangelism program included a Texas-based group, Dallas Holm & Praise, who were, by 1978, enjoying great success with Holm's composition "Rise Again"—a song Dylan would soon share a history with.) Unlike Dylan, Burnett, Mansfield, and Soles, Frisbee's calling didn't involve albums and concerts; instead, he directly dealt with matters of the soul via sermons, evangelism, prophesying, healing, and prayer. He could also be found dunking newborn believers in mass baptisms in the surf of the Pacific Ocean. Frisbee, though, like Dylan, was a world traveler and in the summer of 1978, Sweden marked his final stop on a mission trip.

Thanks to Roger Sachs, who was tasked with documenting Frisbee's memoirs, we have an utterly intriguing story from Sweden in 1978.[40] Frisbee witnessed the enthusiastic Dylan crowd outside his Gothenburg hotel window and said the Lord put the following prayer in his head—"Bring down the idol. Save Bob Dylan"—and these words simply wouldn't leave him alone. He biblically cited how even the sleep of kings can be disturbed when God wants someone's attention. So Frisbee walked the streets of Gothenburg for hours the day of Dylan's first concert, July 11, 1978, convinced he would run into Dylan and be able to lead him to Christ in prayer (this was old hat for Frisbee, one of the first-fruits of what became known as the Jesus People movement). Occasionally, people would stop to ask him on the street if he was with Dylan's band; this would encourage him that maybe he was getting close to an encounter. Frisbee was fully aware of how some would view this exercise as odd, pointless, a folly, but he felt it worthwhile because he knew the prayer the Lord had laid on his heart was worthwhile.

After an unsuccessful effort to find Dylan ("Of course, we often naively interpret the will of God," he concluded), Frisbee led his presentation for Teen Challenge by acknowledging many in his crowd would probably prefer to be, instead, across the street taking in the Dylan concert. After delivering his scheduled sermon, he decided to lead everyone in raising their hands toward the Scandinavium (the Dylan concert venue) and in unison they all repeated: "Bring down the idol! Save Bob Dylan!" Frisbee said he was then led by the Holy Spirit across the street where many Dylan fans were gathered outside, unable to get in for the first concert. According to his account, the Lord then led him to where he went through an open door at the venue and walked right into the concert. Frisbee described seeing many in the crowd with their lighters lit—a sight he described as "very ethereal"—and witnessed Dylan, in a black jumpsuit with silver lightning bolts, singing "Forever Young."

That the idea of eternity is reflected in the title of Dylan's then-recent song from the *Planet Waves* album was not lost upon Frisbee. The California native who had made a significant impact on countless lives in his home state and eventually wound his way around the world—seemingly sold out to spreading the Good News of Jesus—would pass away the same year Dylan released his *World Gone Wrong* album. But Lonnie Frisbee would never forget that July 1978 day: "I am convinced that the Holy Spirit of God had a divine purpose in directing me to walk the sidewalks of Gothenburg, Sweden, all those years ago, diligently looking for Bob Dylan. I don't think God led me in vain. There is a spiritual connection. I have been interceding [in prayer] for Bob Dylan for years. He faces pressures that most of us could not imagine. The Lord has poured out tons of grace upon me. Who am I to judge another? Love never fails, my brother, and Jesus is the One who can keep us 'Forever Young' in an eternal kingdom!"[41]

According to Dave Whiting-Smith, who as a young man encountered Lonnie Frisbee in the context of the Vineyard church, there was one story he heard that positively stood out. (With some variation, Whiting-Smith's story here lines up with the preceding account given by Frisbee biographer

Roger Sachs): "Well, Lonnie Frisbee told me that he was asked to speak at a Christian convention in Sweden in 1978, and Bob was playing a big show across the street the night of the convention. Lonnie said the Lord told him to have all the people stand and lift their hands toward the stadium across the street and yell, 'Bring down the idol, and save Bob Dylan!' They all did this and Lonnie, being himself a fan, snuck out of the meeting and walked across the street where Dylan's concert was already happening. He said he found a door, opened it (there was no security), and he walked right up backstage to the side of the stage, fifteen feet from Bob. As Bob was playing 'Blowin' in the Wind,' Lonnie said the Lord spoke clearly to him and said: 'I gave him this song, and he doesn't even know what it means, but he will shortly.'"[42]

During this season of Dylan's life, at age thirty-seven, the singer was not above seeking the counsel of others about spiritual things. While on tour in 1978, one of the other singers, Helena Springs, remembered a conversation with Dylan where the subject of prayer came up. "He was having some problems once and he called me and asked me questions that no one could possibly help with, and I just said, 'Don't you ever pray?' And he said, 'Pray?'. . . I said, 'When I have trouble, I pray.' He asked me more questions about it, he started inquiring, he's a very inquisitive person which is one good thing about him—he's always searching for truth, truth in anything he can find."[43]

Flashback to 1961 when the young singer found himself newly arrived in New York City: "Never saw a God; can't say till I see one," Dylan told Izzy Young. But in the intervening seventeen years, more than a few allusions to the God of the Bible cropped up in songs penned by Bob Dylan. Bert Cartwright, a minister, civil rights activist, and Dylan fan, took on the frightfully challenging task of cataloguing all instances where the songwriter's lyrics alluded to a Bible passage. After resting from his labors, Cartwright published his findings which included the period 1961–1978: "During this period of song composition, eighty-nine out of 246 songs and liner notes contain references to the Bible—36 percent of the total. There are approximately 387 individual biblical allusions that I have identified within these songs."[44] Of this number, Cartwright observed how there was a basic split between the Hebrew Bible and the Christian Scriptures (190 and 197 respectively).

Strangely enough, a significant signpost in Dylan's journey to Jesus may have been in November 1978, in San Diego, when he retrieved a small silver cross that an audience member had tossed onstage. A full year after it happened, Dylan referred to the moment while onstage again in San Diego, and ultimately thanked the person who tossed it his way.

"Now, usually I don't pick things up in front of the stage; once in a while I do, sometimes I don't. But I looked down at that cross. I said, 'I gotta pick that up.' So I picked up the cross and I put it in my pocket. . . . I said, 'Well, I need something tonight.' I didn't know what it was. I was used to all kinds of things. I said, 'I need something tonight that I didn't have before.' And I looked in my pocket and I had this cross. . . . So if that person is here tonight, I just wanna thank you for that cross."[45]

Within two months, Dylan made a request of his girlfriend, Mary Alice Artes, to have someone from the Vineyard Christian Fellowship—in which Artes had become involved—visit him at his home in Brentwood, California. According to Dave Kelly, a personal assistant hired by Dylan in 1979, the relationship with Artes was as follows:

"As far as I know, they were living together and she had come back to the Lord so she knew it wasn't right for them to be living together without being married. I think it was mind-blowing to him and he had to know why. Why can they no longer live together? He had never had anybody that believed that much that it wasn't the right thing to do. She started witnessing to him about her faith."[46]

Soon afterward, Dylan was one of twenty students meeting on a daily basis in Reseda, California, for a three-month session of Bible classes.

It is helpful to remember that Dylan eventually publicly addressed these Bible classes, the visit from the pastors that he initiated, and his thoughts about the experience. He spoke to Robert Hilburn of the *Los Angeles Times*. "I was sleeping one day and I just sat up in bed at seven in the morning and I was compelled to get dressed and drive over to the Bible school. I couldn't believe I was there." Hilburn interjected, "But you had already accepted Jesus in your heart?"

"Yeah, but I hadn't told anybody about it because I felt they would say, 'Aw, come on,'" Dylan remembered. "Most of the people I know don't believe that Jesus was resurrected, that He is alive. It's like He was just another prophet or something, one of many good people. That's not the way it was any longer for me."

When did it dawn on Dylan that Jesus was alive and well, that he was resurrected, and that he wasn't simply a prophet? Apparently, not long after Artes put in Dylan's request for someone to come and talk with him.

"I was willing to listen about Jesus," Dylan said. "I was kind of skeptical, but I was also open. I certainly wasn't cynical. I asked a lot of questions, questions like, 'What's the Son of God, what's all that mean?' and 'What does it mean—dying for my sins?'"[47]

In previous conversations with believers in Jesus—with Scott Ross (1970), Arthur Blessit (1974), and Helena Springs (1978)—we see Dylan did much of the same thing. Larry Myers was one of the pastors who, in 1979, answered questions in Dylan's home. He went on the record for the first time in an interview that was published in 1994. Incidentally, Myers' mandolin work can be heard on "Precious Memories," a song on Dylan's 1986 album, *Knocked Out Loaded.*

"I was one of two pastors (Paul Emond was the other) who went to see Dylan in Brentwood in very early 1979, at the request of Bob Dylan who extended the request through Mary Alice Artes. There we met a man who was very interested in learning what the Bible says about Jesus Christ. To the best of my ability, I started at the beginning in Genesis and walked through the Old Testament and the New Testament and ended in [the book of] Revelation. I tried to clearly express what is the historical, orthodox understanding of who Jesus is. It was a quiet, intelligent conversation with a man who was seriously intent on understanding the Bible. There was no attempt to convince, manipulate, or pressure this man into anything. But in my view, God spoke through His Word, the Bible, to a man who had been seeking for many years.

Sometime in the next few days, privately and on his own, Bob accepted Jesus and believed that He was indeed the Messiah. After yet more time and further serious deliberation, Bob was baptized. . . . Dylan then studied in the school of discipleship under Kenn Gulliksen and at least four other competent pastor-teachers, including myself. . . . Bob attended the intense course of study along with other students for three and one-half months."[48]

Dave Kelly was another witness and remains convinced that Dylan's experience was genuine:

> There's no question about it in my mind that Bob had an absolutely bonafide, real conversion. He had an epiphany. He had an experience where he recognized that Jesus was the Messiah, the Jewish Messiah. No question in my mind that it was real. It was not fake, and it was not a game. It was as real as could be. Again, you wouldn't want to risk death every day for a game. You would not do that. Then he would've changed his tune; he would've said, 'Wow, I don't want to be too zealous' and he could justify toning down the message and everyone would've loved it and supported it, but he didn't do that.[49]

After hearing the news that Dylan had been baptized, and was studying and praying with a community of Christian believers in 1979, Martin Grossman has noted how some of Dylan's Jewish fans regarded it "as the most shocking act of apostasy since Shabtai Zvi, a messianic pretender of medieval times who converted to Islam and left millions of followers in despair."[50] According to author and journalist Larry Yudelson, one Washington area rabbi "painfully excommunicated Dylan from his record collection when the singer converted."[51]

Besides attending the Bible classes taught by Larry Myers and others, in 1979, Dylan also attended a Bible study held in the Beverly Hills home of Al Kasha. A songwriter who won two Academy Awards for his musical scores to *Poseidon Adventure* and *The Towering Inferno*, he originally met Dylan in the early 1960s at Columbia Records. A fellow Jew who became a believer in Jesus in 1978, Kasha recalled inquiries from the media: "There were a few people who called us on the phone and wanted to interview us, but we didn't do any interviews. We said that coming to Christ was a very personal thing. They would ask me if Dylan was still Jewish, and I said, 'Like myself, you don't leave that, but he's a Jewish believer.'"[52]

Terry Botwick, a Jewish believer in Jesus since the mid-1970s, was one of the teachers at the Vineyard's School of Discipleship and taught one of the classes Dylan attended. Botwick was also the pastor of a small church located in Point Dume in a public school's auditorium that the Vineyard rented out. For a season, Dylan was among the fifty or sixty people that attended this Vineyard church in Malibu, California. Dylan also briefly attended the much larger (original) Vineyard church until press reports prompted some "fans" to show up for worship services, ulterior motives in tow.

"I knew Dylan and interacted with him and taught the Bible to him but I do not claim any sort of credit for his faith. However, I have no doubt in my mind that he was sincere," Botwick said. "He was a sincere and honest seeker trying to understand and learn. What struck me about him was how deeply interested he was. My only frustration was keeping up with his questions. I'd go over five to six subjects each week, an Old Testament book like Isaiah 28, and he would've read ahead to like chapter 43."[53]

Dylan's publicist, Paul Wasserman, was at a loss for how to handle the situation once word leaked out that his client had apparently gone loopy:

"I remember Keith Richards [of the Rolling Stones] saying to me, 'And you thought you had problems with me.' I've always had more than a few clients, but like, well, it's like this: I handled the Rolling Stones, I handled U2, and royalty know each other. Keith Richards was always calling Bob Dylan; uh, Bono was calling Dylan. Dylan was calling Bono, Dylan was calling Keith and Mick Jagger, you know, so it was all part of the same royal entourage.

"But yeah, the people, the musicians, were talking about it [Dylan's experience with Jesus], like 'What's going on here?' And everyone gossips about everybody. I would get calls from, you know, like Linda Ronstadt, like 'What is going on with him?' Things like that. You know, everyone was mystified. I wish I knew. You just kinda were at a loss."[54]

But the "born-again Bob Dylan" didn't suddenly isolate himself from people who didn't share his beliefs. Jerry Wexler, the legendary producer—and the man whom Dylan chose to co-produce his first batch of songs after his experience with Jesus—proudly wore the "Jewish atheist" label, but this didn't prevent the two from bonding in their own unique way. Dylan attempted to engage Wexler in the Bible. "I'm a sixty-two-year-old card-carrying atheist," Wexler proclaimed, "and so that was the end of the discussion."

For his part, Wexler cannot recall a time when he did not disbelieve: "Including when I was going through Reformed Hebrew Sunday School [when] you're learning all about the religion, and the Bible, and the stories. I can't remember ever believing in a God, ever. And when I was bar mitzvahed, and I was standing, you know, I was standing there giving this speech and going through all the rigmarole [and] inside, I'm sorta laughing at the whole thing, because to me it was a mockery."[55]

But in that small studio in Sheffield, Alabama, where *Slow Train Coming* was birthed, one man remembers more of an exchange between the two than simply Wexler saying he was an atheist and that was the "end of the discussion."

"Every time they slowed down they discussed Scripture; I have a photograph of Bob taking notes from Jerry, about chapter and verse [from the Bible]," remembers Dick Cooper (an assistant to co-producer Barry Beckett). "But Jerry is not a religious person by any stretch of the imagination. I mean, one of the things that really cemented our early relationship was the fact that Jerry liked to go to this restaurant that had these great breakfasts with country ham, you know, so he's certainly not Orthodox. But Jerry and Bob, they definitely went through some discussions; that was their leisure activity, discussing religion. And neither one could convert the other."[56]

Jerry Wexler's son, Paul, who was in charge of mastering duties for the album, would say this about Dylan's creation: "The strength of *Slow Train Coming* is the passion. Dylan's Jewish fans may have cringed, his free-thinking anarchistic followers may have retched, but there was passion in Dylan's Christian convictions, passion in his view of the Crucifixion, passion in his born-again beliefs."[57]

The late Barry Beckett, who assisted Jerry Wexler in the production of the album, remembers the closing song as a favorite:

"Well, 'When He Returns,' that one was just him and the piano. I thought that was great. I don't know how many takes it took, but I don't think it took that many. I think it was an early take. But it was something, you know, it was the first time I really got into his style because I was literally backing him up as an artist by himself. And it was the first time I really realized what his singing was about, how much soul he had. So it was quite a revelation for me."[58]

Micky Buckins, an active player in the Muscle Shoals music scene, was called in to play sparse bits of percussion on the album. It was a dream come true for Buckins who greatly admired Dylan and enjoyed covering his songs: "Well, I knew I played some congas and bongos and tambourines and shaker stuff. I can tell you this: it was a thrill to be on a Dylan record, man, because I was one of only two Shoals players that got on the record, you know."

Years later, Buckins ran into Jerry Wexler at a symposium and wanted to thank him for the opportunity: "I said, 'Man, you know, you could have hired anybody in the world,' and he's worked with all the best percussionists in the world, [but] he said, 'Man, I hired you because you got the feel.'"[59]

As August 1979 approached, the feel of a new Dylan was indeed in the air; some murmurings in the press helped things along. In early August, just prior to the release of *Slow Train Coming*, Dylan chatted with journalist Jon Bream at the Orpheum Theater, a Minneapolis establishment owned by Dylan's younger brother David. The singer had attended a Twins baseball game and several movies with his children and had been on his farm in Minneapolis. Dylan asked Bream if he had been to "the Jesus People Church," a church across the street from the Orpheum; he also told the journalist that he might "play some concerts this fall—no formal tour, no big arenas, just maybe bars or clubs here and there."

As to the much-awaited album, Dylan had this to say: "We finished it in April. The single was supposed to be out in June. I don't understand why it isn't out yet. I hope the album is out by Christmas." The previous week Dylan had taken in "Beatlemania" at the Orpheum, the musical tribute to the Beatles. As Bream chatted with Dylan in the lobby, some of the theatergoers approached Dylan; he took time to shake their hands and listen.[60]

When *Slow Train Coming* was finally released, it served to confirm the rumors that had been circulating for months: somehow Dylan had embraced Jesus. Dylan gave specific instructions about what he wanted for his album cover art. "The in-house art director at the label came up with a design and Dylan rejected it," remembers freelance artist Catherine Kanner. "They were desperate to get something he'd approve, because he kept rejecting everything. He described the image he wanted: he wanted a train and a pickaxe with a symbol of the cross. I was Jewish and he was, so it was a little weird, but how often do you get an opportunity like that?"[61]

Nick Saxton, who provided the back cover photo for *Slow Train Coming*, remembers the context of the photo selection: "At the time, you know, Dylan was going through that Christian change and at that particular time, I was heavily involved in a secret Bible study of my own, and Tony Lane [art director for Columbia Records] was also picking up on that. And I mean, of course, it's a big thing for a Jewish person to embrace Jesus."[62]

Despite perceptions to the contrary, Dylan didn't become the fearsome figure some might have dreamt up in their worst nightmare. He would not join the ranks of the Rev. Jerry Falwell inspired "Moral

Majority." He would not pay a visit to the television studio of Rev. Pat Robertson's *700 Club*; and he would endorse neither President Jimmy Carter who professed to being a "born-again" Christian nor the soon-to-be president Ronald Reagan who enticed many "born again" voters with various pledges.

Journalist Dan Wooding, when interviewed for A&E's biography on Dylan, made this observation: "Here was Bob Dylan—who was the main representative of the counter-culture—in the eyes of his fans selling out to the Religious Right, which he never did. He accepted Jesus as Messiah, but he didn't join the Religious Right. He still was very much a prophet, a revolutionary."[63]

Writing of the spiritual renaissance that seemed to be sweeping the country by the late 1970s, Dylan biographer Bob Spitz concluded with an issue that some found troubling: the inherent problem of Dylan's embrace of Jesus in the face of his Jewish heritage.

"A lot of them were people just like him, children of the Sixties who'd turned their back on God and conducted their spiritual search through the ministries of psychedelic drugs and the free-love movement," wrote Spitz. "But that faith, the hippie faith, had failed, and after slogging through the decadence of the early Seventies, these same people had found something new to believe in. But . . . Jesus? Jesus was a concept for the Gentiles. He was their Son of God, their Messiah. He walked on water and raised bodies from the dead. Jews weren't supposed to believe all that hocus-pocus."[64]

Uri Geller reflected back on what was a troubling season for many Dylan fans: "When Dylan became a Christian evangelist in the late 1970s, one fan I knew, an accountant in Los Angeles, threw out all his albums. He had everything the singer had released since 1961, some of it autographed, and he heaved the whole collection into a skip. I told this man, Milton, he was acting like the Bible-belt fundamentalists had when they burned Beatles LPs in protest at John Lennon's 'we're bigger than Jesus' ad-lib. Milt wrote to me. . . . Re-reading Milt's letter has made me think hard about what fans expect from their heroes. Dylan did not write his songs as a soundtrack for Milt's adventures—he wrote them for himself. So it was unreasonable for Milt to hold his idol to his personal code of conduct. I believe Milt could have kept listening to *Blonde on Blonde* and *Freewheelin'*, without turning Christian—and without the right to insist that Dylan stayed a Jew."[65]

Although Dylan was clearly in a small minority among his fellow Jews, he certainly wasn't alone. As for Jews who do happen to believe in Jesus, author Michael Brown has noted that the worldwide figure of 150,000 to 200,000 is "probably a conservative estimate." He says that that this minority group includes "American Jews, Russian Jews, South American Jews, and Israeli Jews. Many of them are highly educated, and some are ordained rabbis," Brown writes. "Jews do believe in Jesus, and their numbers are growing by leaps and bounds."

In 1995, *The Jewish Press* reported on a conclusion drawn by the Task Force on Missionaries and Cults: "From Chicago to Moscow, from Israel to the Ukraine, the so-called Hebrew-Christians are capturing Jewish souls at a rate never before 'witnessed' in the 3,500 year history of the Jewish people."[66]

Back in late 1979, though, following the release of *Slow Train Coming*, no one was really sure how Bob Dylan was captured. Even one of Dylan's employees, his publicist (of all people), was taken aback.

"The whole press was printing the Christian story and I said, 'Bob, I got to have a meeting with you. I mean, I have so many problems [with this], I don't know how to handle it,'" remembers Paul Wasserman, who had been with Dylan since 1974. "I went and had a meeting with Bob and he said, 'Well, what's your problem?' I said, 'Alright, I don't know how to deal with the press who ask me questions about you and religion.' He said, 'Give me an example.' Well, Bob, are you a born-again Christian? And he looked at me and said, 'What do you mean [by] born again?' You know, that's a typical Dylan way of answering you, by asking you another question."[67]

How Dylan's personal assistant, Dave Kelly, was hired in October 1979 makes for a fascinating story.

I was approached by Michael Canfield who attended the Vineyard and he said, 'Bob needs someone to work with him that understands the music business, isn't put off around celebrities, and he also needs someone who is a true believer.' I had been in my group Ark at that time but Mike knew I was on a hiatus and that Bob needed someone to work for him.

So he took me to Bob's studio and it was an incredible place. This big, muscle-built guy, like a bodyguard type, took us to the back where there was a record-listening room, because it was all vinyl and there were records wall-to-wall and to the ceiling. It was crazy; it seemed like every record you could imagine was there. And on the turntable was my Ark album [*The Angels Come*] that had just been released. I thought, 'Oh, no, I'm going to lose the job before I even get it.' Bob Dylan listening to my record? But he knew what I was doing musically.

Ark was way ahead of our time—there was no real market for us. No one knew what to do with us. Our album *The Angels Come* was one of the first Christian rock albums. But we were a secular group, signed to the Beatles' label and then Warner Brothers, and we weren't really aware of the Christian music industry. We were just making a secular album except we were sharing the Gospel so we didn't really have a home.

So Bob said to me, "Good to meet you; thanks for coming down. Look, I need someone to talk to the guys, the crew and the band. Right now I don't want to defend my faith; I don't want to have to explain to them what's going on. So I want someone to be there and if need be, explain to them what's going on." [laughs] He shook my hand; it was very strange, a very gentle handshake, and not like someone gripping your hand. I squeezed but he didn't squeeze back. Bob was like that, though, maybe just being different to catch you off guard.

Within five minutes of meeting him, and right after my record being on his turntable, he said, "Let's go into the kitchen, there's someone I want you to talk to." And of course I'm thinking "Who's he going to introduce me to?" So Bob sat down next to me in the kitchen at this table and there's Baboo, this guy who's a great percussionist and a famous Rastafarian. Bob says, "Why don't you tell Baboo what we believe." [laughs] And I'm thinking, "Okay, here's my audition and I'm going to fail when I just got the job." [laughs again] I'm thinking Bob's going to get up and go away and leave me with Baboo, but he doesn't. He sits right next to me and puts his elbows on the table and his fist on his chin, you know, like he's intent on listening.

So then I said, "Baboo, you're a Rastafarian and as I understand it, Haile Selassie, King Haile Selassie of Ethiopia, you see him as the Messiah," and he said "Ya, ya." "So what you do is you study the Old Testament and Babylon and all that stuff, but what Bob's got into is the other book you need to read, which is the New Testament."

I knew this amounted to a rival Messiah to him but he was probably aware that he had to be on his best behavior because he wanted to play with Dylan; so he was gracious enough to listen to what I was saying and he did say, "Yeah, I'll check it out."

So I guessed I passed the audition [relieved laughter], but it was nerve wracking. Now, I spent a good portion of my musical life, prior to [moving to] America, in London and London has a big Jamaican community. So I knew about Reggae and Ska and Jamaican music and had Jamaican friends. But can you imagine if I had never studied Rastafarianism? So I was prepared by the Lord and knew a fair amount about it as a religion, which is bizarre since it's pretty obscure.

I found out that Dylan's assistant was Arthur Rosato, who used to work for the Rolling Stones. He was the one indispensable person around Dylan during this time. It seemed most people after three or four months got fired. I don't think Dylan likes having people around a long time. He likes to keep it fresh with new people. But Arthur was always with him. And Arthur was one of the people Dylan wanted me to talk to. Arthur didn't understand what was going on, or what to do with it. He thought it was something silly or a game. So I would talk to him a bit about Dylan's faith.[68]

Dylan's faith was being manifested in some significant ways, including the lead-up to his November 1979 shows at the Warfield Theater. Another one of Dave Kelly's roles included making some phone calls on behalf of his new boss. Kelly picks up the story:

> While we were in Santa Monica prepping for the two weeks [of concerts] in San Francisco, Bob asked me if I could call the churches in San Francisco. He'd seen we had a youth group and an outreach group at the Vineyard so he basically said:
>
> "Why don't you call the churches and talk to the pastors and organize it so the groups come out to the shows. They could stand outside and give them literature and talk to them about the church and invite them to their church because I'm just going to be there and then gone. It'd be great if some of these people that are interested in knowing about the Gospel could be invited by these youth groups back to their churches and services; they could do the follow-up. Every night I'm going to preach the Gospel to these people and some of them are going to want to follow up. So why don't we have the church groups sit outside, stand outside, and some of them we give free tickets, but mainly we want them out there when we finish so they can talk to people and recruit them for their denomination and we can give them all a fair share."
>
> So I said, "Okay, but churches don't quite work like that.' And he said, 'How many are there?" I said there's probably at least fourteen major denominations and he said "Well, give each one of them a night; each church gets their own night."
>
> So it was like give the Baptists Monday; give the Presbyterians Tuesday; give the Pentecostals Wednesday, etc. So I called them up and I got through to several churches. I talked to a Pentecostal church, a Baptist church, a Presbyterian church, and, I think, a Lutheran church. And none of them wanted to do it if any of the others were going to be doing it; that was the most common thing. I think it was the Pentecostal church, the Assembly of God in San Francisco, and the first thing out of their mouth was "Well, isn't Dylan going to be

> here for two weeks?" I said, "Yes," and they asked, "So, who's doing the other nights?" And I told them the other denominations. "Oh, oh, well, no, I think we'll just pass on that, but thank you very much."
>
> And none of them wanted to do it unless they were the only ones doing it; they didn't want to have just one night. They didn't want to share with other churches. It was a terrible testimony to Dylan. It was devastating to him, really. He was disgusted by it. He could not believe that they would really think like that because that's so un-Christian. He couldn't believe they would leave these kids unattended because of their ego or their own sense of they were right and those other guys were wrong. It was the clearest I've seen of denominational separation, of how deadly it is. I'd seen a bit of it before but I'd never seen as much as that. It was really bad.
>
> And so, you know, the half of it was, instead, every cult that ever made San Francisco its base, and most cults have made San Francisco their base, had their group standing outside. I mean, they were going to be there anyway, I'm sure, but there were no Christian groups out there.[69]

Kelly also vividly remembered a particular night in late October 1979, just before the San Francisco gigs commenced:

> I can remember when we went to San Francisco for the fourteen concerts there, and the first night when we arrived we met Bill Graham, the promoter. Bob was supposed to have dinner with George Harrison, who was in the same hotel. But what we found out was he had literally just checked out. It was the first time that they would've been able to talk in a while and you figure that George is going to talk to Bob about his newfound faith. But apparently George had very quickly checked out right before Dylan arrived which was very, I thought, symbolic of how everybody was treating him—even people that he knew and loved and had been his friend for many years and had admired him. And from George's perspective, almost semi-worshipped Dylan, but he was not about to have that meeting and talk about that stuff

> because maybe he was too afraid of what might happen.
>
> I remember Bob saying, 'He was supposed to meet with me here tonight, to have dinner, and he checked out early.' I think Dylan took that as pretty much an insult and at the same time, like a 'Why is he afraid to meet with me? What's he scared of?' kind of thing. I never heard any follow-up, like there was an emergency at home or anything, so it just seemed very fishy.[70]

Around the same time as the Harrison incident, Kelly also recalled his first impressions of the San Francisco shows' promoter:

> When we arrived at the Warfield, I remember that when I first met Bill Graham he was down on his knees in the front foyer of the theater, paintbrush in hand, touching up some woodwork that had been overlooked by the main painters. Right after that, he began organizing a way to keep a handful of Jewish protesters who were parading outside the Warfield with large placards from following Bob back to the hotel.[71]

In typical Dylanesque fashion, no interviews were granted when the bombshell event of his two-week concert stint at the Warfield Theater in San Francisco was announced. Dylan's own publicist, the press and his fans would soon realize how serious the singer was about his new direction. When he took his recently penned compositions from *Slow Train Coming* (and from the not-yet-released *Saved* album) and sang them on stage in November 1979, the eyebrow raising and head scratching officially began.

Author Paul Williams published his legendary treatise on the matter, *Dylan—What Happened?* not long after the two-week run of shows ended. There is no account from this period that even comes close in trying to honestly grapple with Dylan's art. "Still, one can't help wondering why twenty-four songs out of twenty-four are about the glory of the Lord God Jesus," wrote Williams after taking in one of seven nights. "Why has Bob Dylan, of all people, turned in this particular direction?"

Yet Williams acknowledged that the songs were "authentically humble," "beautiful," and "heartfelt," and even offered this up: "I have to admit, when I hear 'Hanging on to a Solid Rock' [from the *Saved* album] I believe in Dylan's God. I can't help it."

Paul Williams foreshadowed what the *Slow Train Coming* period would thrust upon Dylan fans for years to come:

"One thing that is striking about Bob Dylan's conversion is the way that it has brought up the subject of religion, born-again Christianity, the place of God in our lives," wrote Williams. "Dylan has a power—not merely the superficial power that comes from being a symbol of an era, but a power inherent in the living strength of his art...and it moves people collectively as well as individually; ultimately it affects the public consciousness, what people share and talk about. It may not entirely offset the hypnotic drivel of the daily newspapers, but it serves as a vital balancing force, a voice from the heart to cut through the mindlessness of daily chatter."[72]

The chatter of the daily newspapers and magazines was in full swing after the August 1979 release of *Slow Train Coming*, but especially so with the accompanying November concerts. From the West Coast to the East Coast of the United States—and even overseas to England—here is a sampling of the headlines from this heady season:

"Amazing Chutzpah" (*New West*);

"Bob Dylan: The Rebirth of Wrath" (*Washington Post*);

"Self-Righteous Dylan" (*Washington Post*);

"Bob Dylan Turns On the Brimstone" (*Melody Maker*);

"Dylan Tour Off to a Shaky Start" (*Rolling Stone*);

"Bob Dylan: His Born-Again Show's a Real Drag" (*San Francisco Examiner*);

"Bob Dylan's God-Awful Gospel" (*San Francisco Chronicle*);

And to fittingly conclude:

"Looking for the Old Bob Dylan" (*San Francisco Chronicle*).

But on opening night at the Warfield in San Francisco, before any song had been sung, before any gospel concert had been delivered, there was a fascinating backstory involving Dylan's decision-making. One of Dylan's backup singers, Regina McCrary, picks up the story:

> Carolyn [Dennis], Helena [Springs], and I had rehearsed about five or six songs to open up Bob Dylan's show. We rehearsed every day, getting those five to six songs together. And Bob said that his show was ready. When we got to San Francisco for the first time, I realized how big Bob Dylan was. I didn't, you know, it still hadn't registered to me who he was or what he was about. But when we got off that van at Market Street to go inside of the auditorium we were overwhelmed by all the people that were screaming and hollering; women were crying and people were reaching for him. I realized then that I was singing with somebody who was very, very, very important to a lot of people.
>
> We walked in and we did a sound check. It was about twenty minutes before it was time to go on stage when he said he thought something was missing. He didn't know what, just something was missing. He really didn't feel right about the beginning; the opening of the show. We were all in the dressing room putting on makeup and I was acting silly when he came into the dressing room to talk to all his backup singers. He said something just didn't feel right, something was missing that he needed to open the show 'cause he didn't want people to think his music was just a gimmick. He wanted them to know that he was for real about confessing that Jesus Christ was his Lord and Savior. He wanted people to know that this was not a fad, or a phase he was going through. It was for real.
>
> So, I've always been silly, I love to laugh, act silly, and have fun. I turned to him—and I was acting silly. I was not serious at all—and I said, "Okay, look this is what I'm gonna do. I'm gonna walk out on the stage and I'm gonna tell this story about this old woman trying to

get on the train." She's trying to get on this train because her son was hurt in the war and they said they didn't think he was gonna make it. She got this letter from him saying, "Mama, come and see me, I don't think I'm gonna make it." The woman didn't have any money. She got on her knees, she prayed to God, and an angel appeared and told her to go to the train station. She went down to the train station. I went on and I told the whole story about when she got on the train:

The conductor saw her and he walked to her and asked her if she had her ticket. And she said, "No, I don't have a ticket." And he told her, "I'm sorry, old woman, I'm gonna have to put you off." He put her off the train and the woman started to sing as she stood next to the railroad train, "Father, I stretch my hands to Thee, no other help I know." Meanwhile, the conductor was pulling on the string for the train to start but it wouldn't move. The woman kept singing and praising God, "Father, I stretch my hands to Thee, no other help I know."

And when the conductor looked out, he saw the woman praising God and singing. He looked at the woman and he realized that she was the reason the train wasn't moving. So he went to the old woman and he told her to come and get back on the train. She got on the train, and the train slowly started to move.

I said to Bob, "Now after I finish telling that story, then I'm just gonna go into 'If I got my ticket, Lord, can I ride?'—because that was the first song that we were opening up with anyway." Bob Dylan looked at me like I had lost my mind and he left out of the dressing room! I was laughing, and the other women were laughing, we were all laughing. We went on back to getting our makeup on and getting dressed.

Bob came back in the dressing room a few minutes later and he had Spooner Oldham, Fred Tackett, Jim Keltner, and Tim Drummond with him [Dylan's band]. I'm looking out the corner of my eye like, "What's up?" And he said, "Tell them that story." Now I'm looking at him kind of funny 'cause I'm thinking, "I was just playing and having fun with him!" But I go on and I tell the story again, anyway. Then he looked at me and he said, "That's how we're gonna open up my show." And I said, "Oh, uh, I was just playing. I was just *playing*. I can't do that. I don't . . . uh-uh. No. I can't do that." And he said, "You are a professional. Yes, you can."

Fred Tackett's wife is an actress and she was there. I became very nervous and I said, "Look, what do I do? How do I do this?" She said, "Well, you play all the characters on stage—you be the narrator, you be the old woman, you be the son's voice when the letter's being read. You just do it." But I still wasn't feeling good about it. I mean, I was nervous.

So I called my father long-distance. And I told my daddy, "Daddy, you know how you always told me I was gonna get in trouble with my mouth? Well, guess what?" I asked him. "I was playing and acting silly and now Bob Dylan says that's how we are gonna open up the show. And I can't do this!" My daddy said, "Yes, you can." I said, "Daddy, I'm not a preacher. I can't tell that story." And he said, "You already told it. Now what you need to do is pray before you walk out on that stage and then, if you get nervous, look into the spotlight. Inside of that spotlight you're going to find the Spirit of God. And you're gonna feel my spirit. I'll be there."

So with very little planning and no rehearsal, I walked out on that stage and I told that story. The women stayed off the stage while I was telling the story. As I got to the part where the conductor told the old woman to get back on the train that's when the other women started to slowly walk out and get into position. By the time the old woman says, "Conductor, you said if I didn't have a ticket I couldn't get on the train." And the conductor says, "Well, Jesus got your ticket. Come on and get on board."

By that time, the keyboard player [Terry Young] was making a brroomp, brroomp sound with the piano like the wheels of the train beginning to move. Then I say, "The old woman got on the train and the train started to move," and I'd start singing "Yes, I got my ticket Lord." And the women were already in position at the mic and they came with "Can I ride?"[73]

McCrary summed up their part of Bob Dylan's gospel concerts: "The beginning of the show was his way of giving us an opportunity to showcase our talent and also to be able to sing the anointing of the Holy Spirit into the room. And there were many times that people would pay that money to come hear Bob Dylan do 'I ain't gonna work on Maggie's Farm no more,' and they got 'Slow Train Comin.' Some people that were there came in high, ready to just rock 'n' roll and they ended up being saved."

Dylan was not unaware of McCrary's background with her father being a well-known singer within gospel circles. In fact, according to McCrary, the story about the woman and the train had family roots:

> The first time I heard the story was in church. My father, Reverend Samuel H. McCrary was a pastor. They called my father 'the singing preacher' because he was one of the original, famous Fairfield Four, a quartet group. He traveled on the road with the Fairfield Four, and he also was our minister. As a little girl and growing up to a woman I would hear him at different times tell a story about this woman who had faith in God in spite of her circumstances—she didn't have money to visit her son who had been hurt at war.[74]

Paul Wasserman won't soon forget the Dylan concert run at the Warfield Theater; he recalls when singer Maria Muldaur, who had also recently embraced Jesus, was hanging around with Dylan. "Every night after a show, Bob would be going with her, as she came in with gospel types . . . these are my words, you know, and she was bringing them backstage," remembers Wasserman. "There's a Hebrew Yiddish word for Christian called 'Goy,' and my line at the time was, 'Well, we got another Goy backstage.'"

Joel Selvin, the *San Francisco Chronicle* writer who wrote the review "Bob Dylan's God-Awful Gospel," remembers Wasserman being banned from going backstage; according to Selvin, Dylan called Wasserman an "infidel" and prompted this protest from his own publicist: "That's ridiculous, you've got to fire me because I can't do my job." Dylan replied, "I can't fire you, Paul, you're the best in the business."[75]

"But I also knew at this period, which made it confusing, there were all these very religious Jews in the background too, who had come in and were hanging out," said Wasserman. "And I speak a little Hebrew and I had an Orthodox upbringing, so I knew what was happening, and you know, they would come in and visit and then Dylan would also study the Torah with them [at his office in Santa Monica and at their homes]. He went to synagogue too, you know."

As for Dylan calling Wasserman an "infidel," Dylan's former publicist (1974–1983) remembered it this way:

> I think what he meant was I had a closed mind, you know; like there's an expression in AA [Alcoholics Anonymous] about practicing contempt prior to investigation. And there is, I don't remember what the Hebrew equivalent of it is, but there's a lot of old Hebrew in AA, and when he said, "infidel," I'm sure he meant I have a closed mind—[that] I practice contempt prior to investigation.[76]

One man who arguably needed to have an open mind about Dylan's run of shows at San Francisco's Warfield Theater was Bill Graham. Although the legendary promoter tried to get his friend to play something besides the brand-new songs, Dylan remained steadfast, only singing the songs that reflected his newfound faith.

As for the media coverage, as has been implied, there would be hell to pay.

"Well, they brutalized him; they were all pissed off because he wouldn't sing the old songs [laughter]. It was nuts," remembered Dylan's bass player Tim Drummond. "And I mean, Bill Graham came up to us, and said, 'Please'—I was standing right there with Bob—when Bill said, 'Please, Bob, just sing one old song.' And Dylan wouldn't. And then Bill said, 'Oh, I don't care, I'm going to retire anyway.' It was a funny scene [laughter]. But I mean, Bob stuck to his guns. I told him that I'd stay with him until the t--- fell off the Statue of Liberty, after seeing what he went through. They were one degree short of buying fruit off the sidewalk and throwing it at him, throwing it at the stage."[77]

The rowdiness mainly occurred at the beginning of the fourteen-concert stint. During the first few shows there was some booing (and some cheers), but certainly the occasional report of large numbers booing or walking out was fictitious. According to *Rolling Stone*, there were a few who sold their tickets after realizing the format of the shows, but most wanted to see what was going on—whether they agreed with Dylan or not. Musically, there is no question that Dylan supported himself with one of his best bands, and the passion in his singing was evident.

"After the first three nights the rebels either didn't come back or accepted it," keyboard player Spooner Oldham remembered. "It calmed down, and everybody seemed to enjoy it more. It was sort of enjoyable even when it was weird, because it was challenging to face that kind of audience. You knew the music and message was nothing but good news, so you couldn't be bothered by that."[78]

On Sunday evening, November 4, 1979, Dylan and his band would be performing their fourth gospel gig in a row at the Warfield. Meanwhile, in the nation's capital, not too long before the concert, some of the same songs would be played by Jimmy Carter. The president of the United States was playing host at his residence, and Wesley Pippert, a UPI journalist who covered the White House beat, remembers well what happened after dinner:

> Then Carter suggested we go into the den across the grand hallway, and he played Bob Dylan's new record, *Slow Train Coming*. Carter had remarked during the meal that Dylan had become a Christian and he wanted him to perform at the White House (which never occurred). As the record played, Carter nuzzled the little boys [his grandchildren, Jason, and James Earl IV] and softly sang the words to "Man Gave Names to All the Animals." And whenever they got to the part, "I think I'll call it a pig" or "I think I'll call it a sheep" they laughed with glee.[79]

Meanwhile, back in San Francisco, not everyone agreed with the commander in chief. Lead guitarist Fred Tackett remembered one audience member holding up a sign that read, "Jesus Loves Your Old Songs Too." "People were surprised by Bob's religious songs because Bob did not fit the stereotype of a Christian fundamentalist," remarked Tackett. "Bob Dylan was a whole other world. He represented the intelligent, the literate. He was East-Coast hip, but he was completely sincere in everything he sang and said."[80]

Peter Barsotti, an employee of Bill Graham Presents, remembers the stint well:

> Most of the songs were just blowing my mind and they were especially blowing my mind from the point of view that I was raised Catholic. "Okay, here we are, now Bob's doing this Christian stuff." All these biblical references were there and a lot of them from the New Testament. It just killed me, you know, the songs were crafted so cool and his singing was so heartfelt and the band was so good, that I was just knocked out. Well, I was in the minority, I guess. Most of the people were like, "Hey, man, we're getting gypped; we're getting gypped here. We just paid whatever and this is bulls---."[81]

Although he may have longed for a gem from the 1960s, Graham was still amazed by what he was witnessing: "From night to night, the show keeps getting stronger. It is awesome. I am a Jew, and I am deeply moved by what this man is doing. It's a very profound public display of personal convictions."[82]

While Dylan was performing onstage at one of the shows, Graham heard the personal convictions of another fellow Jew, Mitch Glaser, who was at the Warfield Theater passing out gospel tracts every night on behalf of the San Francisco–based Jews for Jesus. Early one evening, Glaser was approached by a man who wanted to know more about what he was doing at the Warfield and why. He asked Glaser to sit with him in his Rolls Royce so they could talk. Glaser then realized that the man he was talking to was Bill Graham.

For the next two hours, the pair sat and talked about Graham's background and his financial support of Jewish causes. Glaser shared the gospel with him. Finally, Graham told Glaser that Dylan was "pushing this stuff down my throat" and asked how he could get him to stop. "I said, 'Well, that answers my question about Dylan being sincere,'" Glaser recalls. "Graham said, 'He's sincere.'"

Strangely enough, Glaser's presence at the Warfield was apparently instigated, behind the scenes, by Dylan himself. In late October of 1979, a man who claimed to work for Dylan called the offices of Jews for Jesus and asked if they would be willing to hand out tracts during the concerts, which were scheduled to begin a day or so later. Unconvinced that the call actually came from someone in the singer's entourage, Glaser decided to put the caller to the test, requesting that eight tickets be left at the will-call window for their ministry. "We went to the theater, and they were there. I couldn't believe it. We walked in and listened to the concert; it was one of the high points of my life," Glaser said. "Then we stayed up the entire night and wrote a tract called 'Times They Are A-Changin'. We presented the gospel through the lyrics of Dylan's songs, but not his Christian songs. . . . I was there every single night."

One concertgoer who met Glaser on the first night of the Warfield run was a Jewish man who expressed significant bewilderment at Dylan's songs about Jesus; later on he agreed to meet with Glaser on a regular basis and the two would talk about Jesus, the Bible, and being Jewish. According to Glaser, eventually the man came to believe in Jesus as the Messiah.[83]

Dave Kelly won't soon forget his role at the Warfield shows of November 1979:

> At the San Francisco shows, one of my jobs was two-fold: to collect all the books, pamphlets, documents, and papers that people would either leave on the stage or offer outside of the theater. My job was to collect it all and bring it back to the dressing room and we'd go through it.

There were New Age bibles, books on aliens, The Urantia Book was a common one, and all kinds of odd things, a large group of them. Ken Kesey was there and came to the shows and he would be backstage a few times. He had a new UFO/alien-type book he was pushing. Besides being famous for his book *One Flew Over the Cuckoo's Nest*, he was part of the San Francisco music aristocracy, along with Bill Graham. So Kesey was there and he had his books and some of his fellows were in the audience and they'd be putting books up about aliens visiting the planet and such. So we had that whole array of New Age themes and false gospels. So I'd gather this stuff up and take it into the dressing room where it was just me and Bob.

Bob would sit there and unbeknownst to me he had a big garbage can behind him, over his shoulder. He'd lift up one of these books I had collected and say, "What's this?" To the best of my knowledge, I'd explain what it was. And he'd typically say okay and then throw it over his shoulder into the garbage can. The first time he did this the book made such a loud clang; I didn't even know the garbage can was there, you know, this big, heavy book hitting it as it went in. I remember thinking, "Oh my gosh, I gotta be careful with what I say because he's throwing it away based on what I say." But then again, I'm sure he had his own instincts and I was just confirming or denying. So when he heard from me a little bit more knowledge about a book, he'd make a decision. He wouldn't do it based on somebody like me saying anything. I'm sure he did that because he already felt that.

Another one of my jobs after the shows was to go out there and engage in the conversations. There'd be little clusters of people with pamphlets and things and I'd take one from each of them. I'd look at what they were doing and what they were talking about. I'd hear them as they made their presentation. I remember one night someone in a group was saying, "Hey, you know what Bob was talking about? That's what we're into, so come on with us." And I had to go, "No, Bob's not into that; that's not what Bob was talking about."

I had my Dylan backstage pass thing so the people could see I

> worked for him. It was pretty hairy. Some of them didn't like me saying what I said but that's what he wanted me to do, to make sure they didn't take any of these people home. You know, to make sure they don't convince anyone that he's believing the same thing they believe. So I found myself in the front of the theater and breaking up conversations and trying to stop some of these people. But man, I was thinking, "I need a crew of people; I can't do this just myself."
>
> I remember one night I touched one guy on the shoulder because he was really coming on strong to this young girl and she looked really frightened. When I touched him on the shoulder to just move him aside a little bit to say, 'Brother, just leave her alone; you know, that's not what Dylan was talking about,' it turned into one of those moments like that character in *The Exorcist* movie. He lurched back like I hurt him when I simply touched him on the shoulder. He looked at me with these big, fierce eyes. And then this voice came out of him that terrified the girl that he had been talking to. Suddenly, this deep, horrible voice came out of nowhere. It made the hairs on the back of my neck stand up.
>
> From a Christian perspective, it was a great place of spiritual warfare; there was a lot going on. There were wars going on backstage, under the stage, outside the theater, around the hotel. There was so much going on during the Warfield period. I didn't appreciate it at the time, but I was in the eye of the storm, really.[84]

Tim Charles, Dylan's sound man from 1978 to 1981, also remembered the shows:

> With the born-again thing, Bob was out there, it was like a man in a small life raft. There's a scene at the end of the movie *Perfect Storm*, it's just a guy in a small life raft in a big ocean . . . and you know the outcome. With Bob, he actually survived, but Bob was in a small life raft, man. You know, here's a guy who had a million songs and he could only do the ones, he only had these ones, he had to stand or fall with these songs on the record.

> He made a really good record and then he was going out there to sell it, you know. Above all, he was going out there to put this over. I mean, because he believes in it. If everybody walked out, still, that would be a different deal, but he believed in it and he was going out there. In other words, I think people sometimes mistake, [they] think Bob's being lazy or something, but Bob's behind all this stuff, you know. He goes for it. And he didn't disappoint me, man. He didn't disappoint me. I loved it, I loved the born-again shows. I thought they were cool and had energy.[85]

Dave Kelly remembered some of the disappointments that came with the territory—even Christian territory:

> I think Bob was let down by the Church all over. I think it started with the churches not wanting to support the concerts in San Francisco. I think it was then followed by an article that came out where someone was interviewed and one of these big Christian bookstore chains said they were not going to stock his records until they were absolutely convinced he was a real Christian because they didn't think he was. . . . It was really shocking. And that was something he actually read; that wasn't something someone told him about. He read it to me himself, and showed it to me. I think it was a head of a record chain. Had he ever heard the songs? He couldn't have heard them; he must've just read things or been told things by people.
>
> You know, some saw Bob as a wolf in sheep's clothing; that was the common thread I seemed to pick up on. They thought if we let him in, he could be the wolf in sheep's clothing. But I also think there was a lot of ego within the Christian music industry and they were threatened by a real, serious professional coming in.[86]

Speaking of threats—in an entirely different context—according to Kelly there were death threats galore when Dylan began to publicly proclaim the name of Jesus:

I don't think Bob could believe that article where that Christian bookstore guy was quoted. I think he was absolutely astounded that they would actually think he wasn't a Christian. I mean, because think about this: this was a man who basically got a death threat every day of the tour. And then some in the press are saying he's not a real Christian. Well, what non-Christian would be threatened with death for mentioning the name of Jesus onstage? None of these guys were ever being threatened to be killed constantly for spreading the Gospel. Only him. You know, I think he's the only Christian artist that's been threatened to be killed for spreading the Gospel. The death threats were common—all the time. I particularly remember it happening all the time during the San Francisco shows.

We had an accountant that was traveling with us from this accounting firm Gelfand, Rennert, and Feldman. I think it was Marty Feldman. He was like white as a ghost; he was constantly in fear that someone was going to blow us up in the hotel, or blow up the van, or blow up the theater, or shoot Bob while he was around.

A number of people were really aware of the death threats so they were really scared. I don't know if he had any security, but, honestly, I don't remember there being any security. He had a tour manager but it was not like today where you would have security. Dylan never did, I don't think. He would get on buses; he would get on planes on his own. I never saw a bodyguard. Even at his studio in Santa Monica, I don't think the muscle-built guy that used the gym downstairs was a bodyguard. I think he just used the gym in return for looking after the place.

Bob laughed at the death threats. I mean, they didn't even remotely frighten him. And it wasn't like he didn't believe they were potentially real. It's just like he basically said, "Hey, I'm in the Lord's hands. I don't care. They can do what they want to do. They'll be allowed to do what they're allowed to do, so that's fine." Bob knew all the prophets had been pretty much killed, so he figured if he's going that way, so be it.

What I specifically remember about the death threats were that

> they were "You can't mention the name of Jesus; you mention the name of Jesus tonight and you're dead." Can you imagine how many Christians put in that situation would pass that test and how many would fail? The threats were faxed; some were notes stuck on the wall of a theater. The one I was quoting that I remembered specifically was a fax. But everyone knew about them.
>
> When we went to dinner we took a limo; when we went to the theater we had a bigger van, a ten-seater or whatever and so some people were sitting there thinking, "I don't normally sit near Dylan; I wonder if tonight they're going to blow us up." Because some crew wouldn't go in the limo because they weren't part of his personal crew; they were part of the bigger crew like the lighting guys or the sound guys and the only time they'd be with Bob was in the van. So they'd be terrified, you know, that maybe this was the time someone was going to hit him with an RPG or something. They didn't know, but they took it seriously.[87]

The sincerity of Dylan's convictions, as vouched for by the likes of his guitarist Fred Tackett and his promoter friend Bill Graham was, on occasion, also seen by a member of the media. Take Harvey Kubernik, a writer for *Melody Maker*, who saw one of Dylan's four gigs in Santa Monica, California, in November 1979:

> I may not agree with the content of most of his new material, and his religious ramblings between songs seemed forced ('there's a man who died on the cross for us, and it's time that you recognize that if you want to be saved'), but as the night unfolded it was very clear that this man is honest and sincere. . . . There were times in the Dylan performance when any jerk, including myself, could realize that he wasn't faking. I laugh at music critics like Greil Marcus who doubt the sincerity of Dylan's new direction.[88]

At the final concert in Santa Monica, Mona Lisa Young, one of Dylan's singers, would sing a song entitled "God Uses Ordinary People." But not before Dylan spoke at length to his audience about the origins of Passover. His comments revealed his perceived connection between a covenant in the Hebrew Scriptures and a covenant found in the Christian Scriptures. This is significant because not a few fans assumed Dylan was abandoning his Jewish heritage; but from these comments onstage in Santa Monica in 1979, it is evident that Bob Dylan had no problem connecting his Judaism with the new truths he was discovering in Jesus. Although he had been saved "by the blood of the Lamb" and was hanging on to that "solid rock made before the foundation of the world," he had not forgotten Moses nor the theological significance of the Torah.

The late drummer Bruce Gary enjoyed the shows at the Warfield so much that he also found himself in Santa Monica (through an invitation from Dylan's drummer and friend, Jim Keltner). "I think that that period in his career is extremely valid and potent—those religious albums were probably the greatest testament—I mean, I'm Jewish, but those albums had such an effect on me. I drove up to those shows at the Santa Monica Civic and got to go backstage."[89]

Bruce Gary wasn't suspicious of Dylan, but this seemed to be the exception to the rule when it came to people approaching Dylan—whether Jew or Gentile. According to Jim Keltner, Dylan's drummer from 1979 to 1981, a notable sense of suspicion surrounded the gospel tours.

"What I found to be really amazing was the amount of people who mistrusted Bob. There were so many Christian people that mistrusted him, saying, 'This is not for real. He's a phony.' [And] people in the Jewish community mistrusted him," Keltner told biographer Howard Sounes. "They were offended or mistrusted whether he was for real with it. Bob [was] offending everyone. And at the same time I know, from being out there with him, and talking with certain people, that a lot of people's lives were changed forever. In the Christian world, they say 'saved.' I know for a fact that happened to a lot of people."[90]

When Dylan's tour of 1979 concluded with two concerts in Tucson, Arizona, there was yet another group feeling the need to express mistrust for the thirty-eight-year-old singer. A local chapter of the American Atheists organization distributed leaflets in protest of the "new Dylan." Dylan was informed of their presence during his interview with Bruce Heiman of KGMX-Radio in Tucson.

"Are they against the doctrine of Jesus Christ, or that he died on the cross, or that man is born into sin? Just what exactly is it they're protesting?" Dylan wondered.

"Well, the atheists are against any sort of religion, be it Christianity—" but then Dylan interjected, "Well, Christ is no religion. We're not talking about religion. . . . Jesus Christ is the Way, the Truth, and the Life." Dylan also responded to the claim that religion is repressive, and to the notion of religions based on good works.

"Well, religion is repressive to a certain degree. Religion is another form of bondage which man invents to get himself to God. But that's why Christ came. Christ didn't preach religion; He preached the Truth, the Way, and the Life. He said He'd come to give life and life more abundantly. He talked about life, not necessarily religion...Well, a religion which says you have to do certain things to get to God—they're probably talking about that type of religion, which is a religion by works: You can enter into the kingdom by what you do, what you wear, what you say, how many times a day you may pray, how many good deeds you may do. If that's what they mean by religion, that type of religion will not get you into the kingdom, that's true."[91]

On December 7, 1979, a well-researched article appeared in Dylan's home state of Minnesota where it was clear that one Steve Berg of the *Minneapolis Tribune* did some prodigious digging in Hibbing:

> It would be overblown to portray Bob Dylan's hometown as rocked and shocked over his apparent embrace with Christianity. Jews here don't clutch their bosoms, shake their heads, and talk about how the boy has gone wrong. And Gentiles don't walk the streets with smirks on their faces telling each other that Bobby Zimmerman has finally seen the light...the talk was more of Hibbing High's chance for a good hockey team this winter than about Dylan's religious preference.[92]

However, as Berg quickly acknowledged, the story was not about hockey. He quoted Mark DeMillo, an employee at Erickson's, a music store in Hibbing. DeMillo said people in their fifties were requesting *Slow Train Coming*, including some who had never even bought a Dylan record before.

Berg observed how there was caution in discussing the matter among the Jews he interviewed. It was a sensitive story and no one wanted to hurt the Zimmerman family. Dylan's uncle, Max Edelstein, briefly remarked, "I don't suspect the family is taking it too well."

Hibbing clothing store owner Kopple Hallock was surprised and wondered if what he had heard was true. He initially thought it could be a publicity stunt, but knew that didn't ring true. Hallock was at a young Bobby Zimmerman's bar mitzvah and recalled seeing him in school at the synagogue. "I know his great grandfather, Mr. Edelstein, would flip over in his grave if he heard the news," he remarked. But Hallock concluded that religion was something each person had to contend with individually.

Another Jewish businessman had a similar philosophy. "This doesn't mean we're not still proud of him. I admire anybody who has a religion. Jesus is supposed to be the Son of God. They worship him. We worship the Father. It's all the same family. If Jesus comforts you, that's fine with me. We have a melting pot here in this town. We always had to get along."

DeeDee Seward, who introduced Dylan to his old high school flame, Echo Helstrom, heard the news of Dylan's new direction through an evangelist at her church. The news didn't come as a surprise to her; she had been hoping and praying that Dylan would accept the Lord. "God gave him a fantastic talent and I think He'll bless him seven-fold," she said. But back in high school, the blessings of his peers (at least musically speaking) were conspicuously absent, when, according to Seward, Dylan was treated "shabbily" and "no one would accept what he was doing. They didn't understand."

Fast-forward to 1979. Déjà vu?

John Perry Barlow, lyricist for the Grateful Dead, spoke out on why he thought some folks were upset at Dylan in 1979. "Oh God, I like just about everything on *Slow Train Coming*. I'm not a Christian, but I didn't have the same kind of adverse reaction to it that other people did. I thought there was a fair amount of religious intolerance that greeted that series of records. And I thought the music was great."

So why did so many Dylan fans give their hero such a hard time? "Well, because most of his fans were not Christians," said Barlow. "Christians have created a fair amount of animosity among non-Christians by virtue of their own intolerance so that there's a knee-jerk response in a lot of people, especially Bohemian people, to any manifestation of devout Christianity. I personally take the view that the solution to intolerance is certainly not more intolerance. It seems to me that if you want to do something about intolerance the first order of business is to tolerate those that would not tolerate you."[93]

Journalist Al Aronowitz told an A&E audience that he was crazy enough to think that the Dylan of the 1960s was "the new Messiah"; however, by the late 1970s, after reflecting on his old friend's experience with Jesus, Aronowitz could only muster that Dylan "had taken too much heroin."

As 1979 became quite the blip in the Dylan chronology, the national magazines were drawing their respective conclusions on the wall. "Dylanologists are shocked and saddened by Dylan's apparent conversion to Christianity," reported *Rolling Stone*.[94]

"There is something terribly ironic about the brooding anti-idealogue taking shelter from the storm in evangelical pieties," opined *Newsweek*. "But the times they are a-changin'—and so, once again is Dylan."[95]

Stephen Pickering's words from 1975 further illuminate the tension and irony of the 1979 controversy: "Dylan has shared with us, in all of his released (and unreleased) poetry, perspectives of his spiritual path as a Jew, but he has not (as no poet can) given us 'directions' for our own paths."[96]

But by November 1979, Dylan was doing just that. The seemingly honest worry he expressed in 1967's "Sign on the Cross" had now, apparently, translated into joy—but not without a good dose of prophetic Dylan wrath. Maybe biographer Robert Shelton got it right when he said, "I think the born-again phase for him solved a lot of problems for himself, did things for him rather than us. He has a talent to disturb. Bob Dylan is a disturber of the peace, if not ours, then his."[97]

With the Age of Punk flourishing, it seems cosmically funny that Dylan's career would come to this. "Who would have ever thought in the age of the Sex Pistols and punk rock that the most controversial issue in rock would be religion," wrote Robert Hilburn in 1979, "and that Bob Dylan would be at the center of it?"[98]

Even Dylan's own mother would eventually chime in on the controversy: "What religion a person is shouldn't make any difference to anybody else," she told Fred Bernstein. "I'm not bigoted in any way. Rabbis would call me up. I'd say, 'If you're upset, you try to change him.'"[99]

According to the Gospel of Luke (chapter 15), the angels in heaven rejoice more over one sinner repenting than over ninety-nine righteous persons who need no repentance. As the 1970s drew to a close, the world of rock 'n' roll didn't quite know what to do with one repentant sinner: Bob Dylan.

4

1980–1989: RING THEM BELLS, YE HEATHEN

Dylan's trio of straightforward evangelical albums, *Slow Train Coming* (1979), *Saved* (1980), and *Shot of Love* (1981) caused a kind of identity crisis within the rock establishment itself. Had Dylan led them down so long and scenic a road only to deposit them at the foot of the cross?

—DAVIN SEAY AND MARY NEELY, *STAIRWAY TO HEAVEN*, 1986

You'd never hear me saying that stuff [the 1979-1981 albums] is "religious" one way or the other. To me, it isn't. It's just based on my experience in daily matters, what you run up against and how you respond to things. People who work for big companies, that's their "religion." That's not a word that has any holiness to it.

—BOB DYLAN, *USA TODAY*, 1989

ROCK AND ROLL MADE IT THROUGH THE SEVENTIES, but not without its casualties. The bleak horizon bore testimony to many a shooting star, as drug and alcohol abuse often lurked in the shadows. The season reeked of that smell which Ronnie Van Zant so skillfully wrote and sang about just before his plane crashed into Mississippi ground, devastating the family of Lynyrd Skynyrd.

A number of well-known musicians died in the first few years of the

1970s, in what should have been the prime of their lives: Jimi Hendrix, Janis Joplin, Jim Morrison, Ron "Pigpen" McKernan of the Grateful Dead, and Gram Parsons of the Byrds and Flying Burrito Brothers. After all of this tragic loss, it seemed Elvis Presley was an elder statesman when he died in 1977 at the age of forty-two. The following year, The Who's drummer Keith Moon died of an overdose.

Although initially rebelling against the rock 'n roll scene and its seemingly stereotypical conclusions, Sid Vicious of the Sex Pistols apparently couldn't resist the forces already set in motion; he died of a heroin overdose in 1979, at the age of twenty-one. Journalist Al Aronowitz suggested the seeds were planted in the previous decade: "The '60s was one of the greatest binges of self-destructive genius or creativity in history"; and Aronowitz noted the trend continued into the '70s: "They started dropping like flies. They started destroying themselves."[1]

As the 1980s dawned, there was, to some among the rock faithful, a living casualty. Thirty-eight-year-old Bob Dylan had embraced Jesus. Perhaps the singer was acutely aware of his peers who had fallen. By his own admission, he had come close to the edge; yet he survived. Dylan audiences in early 1980 were hearing "Saving Grace," his song of thanksgiving to God, which included lyrics that referred to escaping death on repeated occasions—and living now by the saving grace of the Lord.

Author Paul Williams, who wrote his book *Dylan—What Happened?* on the heels of having witnessed seven Dylan concerts in November 1979, added this insane fact to the mix: "Dylan read *What Happened?* at the beginning of 1980 (and had his secretary order 114 copies from me), and apparently because he liked the book he allowed Sachiko [Williams' wife] and I to spend several hours with him backstage after four of the November 1980 shows."[2]

So how did Dylan describe his encounter with Jesus? "Let's just say I had a knee-buckling experience," he told Paul Vitello of the *Kansas City Times*. He referred to the disillusionment he felt with writing and performing prior to his experience. "Music wasn't like it used to be. We were filling halls, but I used to walk out on the street afterward and look up in the sky and know there was something else. A lot of people have died along the way—the Janises and the Jimmys. . . . People get cynical, or comfortable in their own minds, and that makes you die, too, but God has chosen to revive me."

The influence of the Bible (both Testaments) on Dylan's worldview was apparent. "Everything that's happening in the news today is prophesied in the Scriptures. It's all in the book of Daniel and the book of Revelation. The anti-Christ will bring peace to the world, first. That's right; he'll be the biggest deceiver of all time. I believe in the Bible, literally. Everything in it, I believe, was written by the hand of God. And I believe Christ will come again. In this generation. And no, He's not gonna be on television."[3]

In this same year, *No One Here Gets Out Alive*, a biography of Jim Morrison, made the *New York Times* nonfiction bestseller list, a rarity in the world of rock and roll books.[4] Meantime, Bob Dylan, in 1980, was losing a multitude of longtime fans for his troubles.

Author John Ledbury interpreted Dylan's spiritual discovery in terms of astrology, penning his booklet *Mysteriously Saved: An Astrological Investigation into Bob Dylan's Conversion to American Fundamentalism* in 1980. For Ledbury, the God of *Slow Train Coming* and *Saved* was no different from the God of Dylan's 1963 composition, "With God On Our Side": "They are in fact the same, constant, authority-God of American nationalism, indeed of Dylan's Jewish upbringing and of his father, Abraham. It is the Jupiter Patriarch."[5]

By rounding up Dylan's birth chart, Ledbury had it all figured out: "What is Dylan singing about at the moment? An absentee (Pisces) god (Neptune) who can be thought of in tangible, anthropomorphic terms (Mars in two; Mercury in Gemini; Neptune in Virgo) and who is due back on the scene soon (balsamic moon) to smite the unbeliever (Mars square sun, in conjunct Pluto, opposite Neptune) and set up some kind of world government (moon/Saturn). Astrologically the script fits, right down to the willing suspension of disbelief of Neptune square Mercury."[6]

After this handy-dandy script, Ledbury left precious little mystery to ponder. For Dylan, though, it seems that the Almighty Creator cannot be written off with such a skillful flick of the wrist.

In January 1980, Dylan's three-night stint at Denver's Rainbow Music Hall included a visit from his old friend Allen Ginsberg. Arriving from the Buddhist-oriented Naropa Institute in Boulder, Colorado, Ginsberg and some friends had traveled to the Mile High City to lodge a friendly protest of sorts.[7] After gaining backstage access on opening night, Ginsberg talked of a forgiving God, to which Dylan retorted, "Yes, but He also comes to judge."[8]

Even though Dylan's response arguably represented a biblically balanced view, some prefer steering away from (or overlooking) any notion of judgment—a concept that is certainly found in both the Hebrew and Christian Scriptures.

Four nights after the visit from Ginsberg, Dylan was on stage in Omaha, Nebraska, in the heartland of America, dashing any hopes for the "old tunes." "Shan't be hearing any old songs tonight, so anyone who wants to leave better leave right now," Dylan advised. "Might be somebody outside who wants the seat." And in one of the most telling statements to his public, he offered up this bitter pill to the crowd in Omaha:

"Years ago they used to say I was a prophet. I'd say, 'No, I'm not a prophet.' They'd say, 'Yes, you are a prophet.' 'No, it's not me.' They used to convince me I was a prophet. Now I come out and say, 'Jesus is the answer.' [And now] they say, 'Bob Dylan? He's no prophet.' They just can't handle that."[9]

During this same tour of the Midwest, Larry "Ratso" Sloman was invited to come along for the ride. (He had recently published his *On the Road with Bob Dylan*, a chronicle of the Rolling Thunder tours of 1975–1976.)

"I did a little 'On the Road' with Bob then," he said, "when he was playing in the Midwest, in little theatres, and preaching the Gospel," Sloman confided to journalist Robert Levinson.

"It was amazing. There was something so pure about it, and that's in the face of everyone saying Bob's gone *mehshugahnah* [Yiddish for 'crazy'], why is he doing this? But those times were among the most passionate I've ever seen him on stage; the music was unbelievable, and it still holds up, very well, in fact. And those songs from that period are among some of the best spiritual songs ever written."[10]

On an irony-filled evening in February 1980, Dylan received his first Grammy Award for the very song that was associated with his unpopular embrace of Jesus: "Gotta Serve Somebody" won Best Male Rock Vocal. When it came to old friends and acquaintances, not everyone was as charitable as Sloman. After the Grammy show, the place to be was Chasen's Restaurant in Hollywood. Harold Leventhal (former manager of Woody Guthrie, Cisco Houston, and Pete Seeger) was one of those at Chasen's who likely subscribed to the *mehshugahnah* school of thought.

"I helped him once before when he wanted to visit Israel," he told biographer Howard Sounes. "I lent him books so I felt a sense of betrayal." That sense of betrayal would manifest itself at Chasen's when Leventhal approached Dylan.

"This is ridiculous, what are you doing here? What have you got this cross dangling around you for?" he asked. Dylan was "taken aback, and suggested they have lunch together to talk about it. Sure enough, Dylan called Leventhal the next day to arrange the lunch, but Leventhal was not available."[11]

The awkward encounters were not limited to Hollywood restaurants. During one of his trips home to Minnesota, Dylan visited his lifelong friend Howard Rutman, who was now a dentist. Rutman was an old buddy from the summer days of Camp Herzl (a Jewish camp in Webster, Wisconsin, that Dylan attended in the 1950s).

Biographer Howard Sounes picked up the story in the dentist's office:

"As he was working on Bob's teeth, Rutman noticed Bob was wearing a heavy gold cross. It was encrusted with rhinestones. 'Bob, what's up with this?' 'Howard, I'm looking for the one truth.' 'Bob, you're Jewish,' said Rutman. He then invited Bob to his house for lunch, and the singer duly arrived with one of his Christian girlfriends. 'My ex and myself were there and we had lunch for him and we talked and everything and then [Bob's girlfriend] was talking to my ex about Christianity and all that kind of stuff. And my ex is major league Jewish,' says Rutman.

"'We kept kosher, the whole thing. So they were going back and forth about justification [the theological concept that one is justified before God by faith in Jesus alone] and all that. You know, they look in the New Testament for justification for why Jews should be like Christians and all that kind of stuff.'

"Rutman was utterly bemused by his friend's change of faith. 'He's a Jew, you know, a Jewish guy. And his soul, too. He's really Jewish.'"[12]

Was his famous friend, who sat in that dental chair, and later shared a kosher meal with him, really any less Jewish than he was back when he canoed, swam, and banged on the piano at Camp Herzl in Webster, Wisconsin, in the 1950s? Sure, Dylan made an unpopular move, but can ethnicity and cultural identity be stripped away because of personal beliefs?

By March 1980, Dylan had befriended fellow singer Keith Green and contributed harmonica to "Pledge My Head to Heaven" (a song that appeared on Green's album *So You Wanna Go Back to Egypt?*). Before his experience with Jesus, the Jewish-born Green—who was thirteen years younger than Dylan—read the New Testament, something he called an "odd combination." But he was soon at peace with the label "Jewish Christian."

This was during the season when Dylan was mingling with people at the Vineyard, the church he was associated with in 1979–1980. Keith Green, incidentally, was intimately involved with the same church. "Bill Dwyer, Paul Emond [two Vineyard pastors], and Michelle Brandes [Green's secretary and friend] all told me Bob was very curious about how you can be a Christian and be Jewish, what the relation was/is," remembered Dave Whiting-Smith, who attended the Vineyard church in 1980. "Michelle said Bob had a long talk with Keith Green about this, as Keith was Jewish too, and he had problems with his family after his embrace of Jesus; I guess Keith's family wasn't too thrilled about it."[13]

By May 1980, Dylan embarked upon what we now know to be his final gospel-only concerts. In Hartford, Connecticut, musician and writer Peter Stone Brown (whose brother Tony played on *Blood on the Tracks*) attended one of these Dylan concerts, a concert he would not soon forget:

> I saw only one "all gospel" show at Hartford in 1980. It was perhaps the strangest Dylan show I ever saw. I knew full well what the show was going to be, but given that, it was still weird. At the entrance to the (small) hall, people were handing out religious tracts. For some reason, these people had a demonic air about them, reminding me of Harry Dean Stanton in [the movie] *Wise Blood*.
>
> The show itself did not move me at all. *Saved* was not yet released (for the record, I loved *Slow Train Coming*). The only song I remember liking was "Ain't Gonna Go to Hell for Anybody." But Dylan did not seem into it [the show], and he did not convince me. I began to suspect that this [the whole Christian thing] might turn out to be another phase. He delivered a few of the now-famous raps, the major one was before "Solid Rock" where he talked about "iniquity in San Francisco." Coming from the man who wrote "Chimes of Freedom," I found this rap despicable.
>
> After the show, we were hanging out outside the hall. Arlo Guthrie was there and so was Larry "Ratso" Sloman, who was at the time [I believe] editor of *High Times* magazine. All of a sudden these doors at the side of the theater burst open and out comes Bob surrounded by about eight rent-a-cops who march him to his tour bus, followed by the backup singers. After a few minutes Sloman got on the bus, which kind of surprised me.[14]

Karen Hughes was the first journalist to conduct an extensive interview with Dylan after his experience of 1979. In May 1980, Dylan reflected back on his journey. "At every point in my life I've had to make decisions for what I believed in. Sometimes I've ended up hurting people that I've loved. Other times, I've ended up loving people that I never thought I would."

He was disarmingly honest with Hughes about his sense of God's call:

> I guess He's always been calling me. Of course, how would I have ever known that, that it was Jesus calling me? I always thought it was some voice that would be more identifiable. But Christ [Messiah] is calling everybody, we just turn Him off. We just don't want to hear. We think He's gonna make our lives miserable, you know what I mean? We think He's gonna make us do things we don't want to do; or keep us from doing things we want to do. But God's got His own purpose and time for everything. He knew when I would respond to His call.

Dylan was clearly embracing who he thought was the living God. "See, Christ is not some kind of figure down the road," he told Hughes. "We serve the living God, not dead monuments, dead ideas, dead philosophies. If he had been a dead God, you'd be carrying around a corpse inside you."[15]

When Dave Kelly served his time as Dylan's personal assistant from October 1979 to November 1980, he recalled the presence of rabbis on occasion—and specifically a rabbi of great note:

> It started during *Saved.* I don't think it came to anything for another year but they turned up, about three or four rabbis, including Rebbe Menachem Schneerson. Of course, Schneerson's pretty famous; anybody who lives in New York knows him. I remember them visiting a couple of times: once in the Santa Monica studio and once while we were out on tour. The way I understood it was that Bob had to compromise because they felt he had taken the time to study Christianity because he had gone to that school [the Bible classes at the Vineyard's School of Discipleship]. So their position, as I understood it, from picking up different things that Dylan had said, was that they felt like he should give them a chance.
>
> You have to understand the record company bosses were

> Orthodox Jewish in name only, kinda like a lot of people say they're Catholic but they're really not. They only know so much about what the Catholic Church teaches; they go to Mass maybe three times a year. Well, there's a lot of that in the music business, a lot of Jewish Orthodox people that really are only nominally religious, but they have to be seen going to the synagogue. It's a very small club. So they're having pressure put on them by the Lubavitchers to pressure Dylan. Do you see how the politics work? So they're putting pressure on the leaders of CBS.
>
> The record company guys don't care as long as they're making money. They saw they could get a Grammy and make money so they did it. It's simply business. But then the rabbis started hounding the record company guys so now the record company guys have to come to Bob and say, "Listen, Bob, you gotta be fair to Israel; you gotta be fair to our Jewish faith. You studied at this church and studied Christianity and their teachings but you never really officially studied Judaism. You did it privately so it's only fair that you should at least give them a chance. Sit at their feet and listen to what they have to say." And so this was the consensus of opinion that I came away with after working with Dylan, that he was going to at least give them a chance by listening to what they had to say. Or go somewhere and study under them.[16]

When *Saved* was released on June 20, 1980, record buyers were confronted with Dylan's most controversial album cover. Per Dylan's request, an artist painted the original cover, which depicted a huge, bloody hand reaching downward as smaller hands reached upward. If the pickaxe Dylan requested for the album cover of *Slow Train Coming* was a subtle reference to the cross of Jesus, then the *Saved* cover was the rhetoric of the redemptive blood that flowed from it.

"I guess the record company changed it at the earliest opportunity [in 1985]. They always hated it. Hated it," said Tony Wright, the artist who painted the cover. "They were waiting for it—the record was ready—then, when I finally took everything in, they were so rude, so nasty about Bob Dylan and said how they weren't going to promote this record, another gospel record. . . . I was just astonished to hear these people, high-up people at CBS, talking about this man as if he were just someone . . . a 'f--- him' kind of attitude. They hated the sleeve, too. It was really depressing."[17]

Wright also shared why Dylan wanted the cover in the first place:

> Apparently when he was doing the previous album, *Slow Train Coming*, in Muscle Shoals, he'd had this vision of Jesus, of the hand coming down and these hands reaching up. And he said that at the same time he had this vision, he saw the whole album too—all the songs, everything, the whole thing was there. And he said, "What you've drawn here was exactly what I saw."[18]

Those who purchased the *Saved* album would also notice that Dylan chose to include a passage within the record sleeve from the Hebrew Scriptures: "Behold, the days come, saith the Lord, that I will make a new covenant with the house of Israel, and with the house of Judah" (Jeremiah 31:31).

Like the onstage rap he gave in Santa Monica, California, in November 1979 about the origins of the Passover, Dylan was, once again, linking the two Testaments together. Jews who believe in Jesus will commonly cite this verse as a foretelling of the alleged new covenant, through Jesus, that God made with the house of Israel.

Not everyone was thrilled with this theological arrangement. Kelly remembers a strained relationship between the artist and his longtime label:

> I think CBS put a lot of pressure on him. I don't think they liked having the album *Saved* come out. I don't think they wanted to put it out. Seems like I remember at one point they weren't going to release it. I think the Grammy Bob received [for "Gotta Serve Somebody" in February 1980] helped a lot. But by the second album they were like, "Oh no, you're going to continue this Jesus stuff? Not at all. Not going to work."

Bob and I had a lot of time to talk, just him and me. Frequently it was just me and him and no one else in the room. It was kind of a weird thing. I always used to think, "Well, why am I here? There's gotta be a ton of people more qualified than me to be here, but I was there."

I would talk. I would listen. I would ask questions and sometimes the question he'd be willing to answer and sometimes he would look at me like I was out of my mind. But I understood the record business and the record company business. Warner Brothers and CBS were very similar in their corporate structure and how they treated people. They had a lot of control whether he'd make a record or not. He couldn't go somewhere else and make another record. He was signed to the label and he wasn't going anywhere. If they didn't release a record, no record came out.

Bob talked to me like someone from the old school. Stevie Wonder was the same. I worked with him too. He tried to leave Motown in '75 or '76 and they stopped him from doing it. These guys from the old school era, they really believed the record company owned them, controlled them. If you said, "Why don't you just leave?" they'd look at you like you're out of your mind. They couldn't conceive it was possible. Even though they're superstars, they were locked into this mindset, almost like you had a Mafia family running your record company or something. They had the kind of attitude of "You can't leave."

Bob was very frustrated with his record company because they were trying to control him, what he sang about, what he recorded, and he wasn't about to have that happen. But, at the same time, he knew he could record it and they wouldn't necessarily release it. I think one of the things he said to me was just that: "I can record it but they don't necessarily have to release it, but I'm going to record the album I want."

Everyone at the record label really hated the *Saved* record. Everyone, period. They hated him doing this stuff. He didn't have any support from any direction I could see. Everybody was deserting

> him. I do think Bill Graham tried to play arbiter and explain the business perspective, but Bob's a pure artist and any restriction on his work is not acceptable [laughs]. So Bob was not happy at all with how he was treated.[19]

By the fall of 1980, Dylan recorded what would become one of the masterpieces in the Dylan canon—"Every Grain of Sand." Jennifer Warnes, who happened to be dating Leonard Cohen at the time, sang backup vocals on the track (which eventually found its home on *The Bootleg Series Vol. 3*, 1991). "Leonard used to wander around the house, wringing his hands saying, 'I don't get it. I just don't get this. Why would he go for Jesus at a late time like this? . . . I don't get the Jesus part,'" Warnes told biographer Howard Sounes. "Leonard felt a certain kind of brotherhood with Bob because he was a Mr. Zimmerman and Leonard is so Jewish. I think it seriously rocked his world."[20] However, Cohen told Martin Grossman that he was not devastated by the news and never thought of it as a "conversion." He simply thought Dylan had been touched deeply by the figure of Jesus.[21]

In fact, Cohen greatly appreciated the music that accompanied his friend's experience. "Dylan, to my way of thinking, is the Picasso of song," he told a journalist in 1985. "People came to me when he put out his Christian record and said, 'this guy's finished. He can't speak to us anymore.' I thought those were some of the most beautiful songs that have ever entered the whole landscape of gospel music."[22]

Dave Kelly's stint as Dylan's personal assistant concluded during the second run of shows at the Warfield Theater in late 1980. Before Kelly departed, he was the recipient of a generous offer from his boss:

> When I left Dylan in November, it was to do my second record [a solo album entitled *Crowning of a Simple Man*]. Bob persuaded me to do that record. He gave me his band for the recording, including Jim Keltner, Tim Drummond, Terry and Mona Lisa Young, and his backing singers. Bob asked if he could come in and play harmonica on my solo album, but I just never got around to doing it. I also just

> felt uncomfortable asking him to do it even though he offered to do it. I felt kind of embarrassed asking him. But the second song on the album would've been perfect for him to do. To this day, I wish I had done it.[23]

In November 1980, Dylan would return to the scene of the crime—the tiny Warfield Theater in San Francisco where he debuted his songs from *Slow Train Coming* and *Saved* a year earlier. Things had changed though. For the first time in two years, Dylan fans would get the privilege of hearing some of the "oldies" as the thirty-nine-year-old singer included a greater variety of his songs. Biographer Robert Shelton has noted that these Warfield shows began a "part of the healing process between Dylan and his fans."[24]

And unlike the previous year, Dylan granted interviews, so the press even received some salve for any wounds that might have occurred. But there was an exchange when Dylan was interviewed by Paul Vincent of KMEL radio, which showed that his beliefs remained intact:

> VINCENT: Some critics have not been kind as a result of the past two albums, because of the religious content. Does that surprise you? . . . For example, they said you're proselytizing. Is Jesus Christ the answer for all of us in your mind?
>
> DYLAN: Yeah, I would say that. What we're talking about is the nature of God, and I think you have to, in order to go to God, you have to go through Jesus. You have to understand that. You have to have an experience with that.[25]

Musically speaking, though, after some soul searching, Dylan was at peace in bringing back his older songs. "Those songs weren't anti-God at all," he told Robert Hilburn of the *Los Angeles Times*. "I wasn't sure about that for a while. . . . I love those songs. They're still a part of me."

What is interesting here is that, contrary to some speculation, Dylan's decision to sing only his gospel material from November 1979 through May of 1980 was not the decision of the Vineyard Church. In fact, Larry Myers, the pastor who visited Dylan's home in early 1979 (and who was invited on tour in 1979–1980) urged Dylan to sing his older material.

In Myers's view, God had given Dylan a gift in songwriting and many of those older songs were "truth songs"; therefore, he should feel free to sing them. However, as Dylan told Hilburn, he wasn't sure initially if they were anti-God or not, and he personally decided to only sing the newly penned gospel material. "I didn't mean to deliver a hammer blow. It might come out that way, but I'm not trying to kill anybody," Dylan said to Hilburn. "Anybody can have the answer I have. I mean, it's free."

Even as far back as 1964, when discussing his epic, "With God On Our Side," Dylan was—if not a bit tongue-in-cheek—perhaps circumspect. "There must be some people somewhere that don't believe God is on their side," he remarked to *The Daily Princetonian.* "Do Communists believe in God? How could He be on their side if they don't believe in Him? I can't put God over anyone's head; I can't force anyone to believe in God. If I did that, I'd be a cop or a Communist."[26]

As to his new songs and his approach to his audience, by November 1980, there was this declaration:

"I've made my statement and I don't think I could make it any better than in some of those songs [on *Slow Train Coming* and *Saved*]. Once I've said what I need to say in a song, that's it. I don't want to repeat myself." Dylan encouraged following Jesus and offered this definition as to who the real preachers were. . . .The basic thing, I feel, is to get in touch with Christ yourself. He will lead you. Any preacher who is a real preacher will tell you that: 'Don't follow me, follow Christ.'"

In what amounted to one of the most in-depth interviews he gave after his experience of 1979, Dylan apparently felt comfortable talking to Hilburn. The journalist also inquired about how the experience had affected his life. Dylan's response indicated that he did not think overt statements were still necessary; his beliefs were his beliefs, and his season of articulating them to the public was drawing to a close:

"It's in my system. I don't really have enough time to talk about it. If someone really wants to know, I can explain it to them, but there are other people who can do it just as well. I don't feel compelled to do it. I was doing a bit of that last year on the stage. I was saying stuff I figured people needed to know. I thought I was giving people an idea of what was behind the songs. I don't think it's necessary anymore. When I walk around some of the towns we go to, however, I'm totally convinced people need Jesus. Look at the junkies and the winos and the troubled people. It's all a sickness which can be healed in an instant. The powers-that-be won't let that happen. The powers-that-be say it has to be healed politically." [27]

Meanwhile, onstage at the Warfield in 1980, a number of guests graced the stage to play with Dylan during the two-week run: Carlos Santana, Michael Bloomfield, Jerry Garcia, Maria Muldaur, and Roger McGuinn. Dylan himself, from the stage, thanked others, including Elton John, Bruce Springsteen, and Captain Beefheart, for stopping by.

The night before Bloomfield's appearance, Dylan visited his old friend who was there by his side at the storied Newport Folk Festival of 1965 when Dylan plugged in. Bloomfield, who, in the words of Jerry Wexler, was "the Jewish Chicago boy with a wicked Muddy Waters guitar style,"[28] also lent his guitar skills to the 1965 masterpiece, *Highway 61 Revisited*. On the evening of November 14, 1980, though, Dylan made a house call. Biographer Bob Spitz picked up the story (which was recounted by eyewitness Maria Muldaur):

> It had been years since the two men had last seen each other, and now they hugged and clapped each other on the back like a couple of long-lost camp buddies. They visited for a half-hour . . . before Bob got up to go, Mike faced him squarely. "So I hear you're a Christian now," he snickered. "*Oy gevalt*!" Bob took the kidding good-naturedly. "Listen pal, wait here a minute, I've got something I want to give you." Bloomfield disappeared into another room, and when he returned, he was carrying a Bible wrapped in an ornately engraved silver cover. "Here," he extended it to Bob. "I want you to have it. My grandmother

> gave it to me. It's been in the family for over a hundred years, but Lord knows I'll never read it." Bob seemed almost embarrassed to take it, but Michael insisted. "Put it to good use, *boychick*," he grinned and pushed his friends out the door.[29]

The next night Bloomfield joined Dylan and his band for memorable, scorching versions of "Like a Rolling Stone" and "The Groom's Still Waiting at the Altar." It would be, tragically, the last public performance for Bloomfield; three months later he died of a drug overdose.

On the closing night of the twelve-concert run at the Warfield, Dylan gave thanks to his promoter friend Bill Graham for not pulling the plug on the shows when the press was so relentless the previous year:

"Bill Graham's gonna get a lot of credit because we did the same thing last year. We came in here with a show and the newspapers, they . . . I don't know, they distorted it and slandered it and lied about it, whatever they did, and that's enough for most promoters in the business just to cancel out the rest of the shows. But Bill didn't do that. He deserves a lot of credit."[30]

Dylan also addressed the Bay Area press when he gave a radio interview to a San Diego deejay who said he was anticipating Dylan's upcoming concert. "Well, I hope so, because, uh, we get a lot of bad publicity up here in San Francisco. . . . There's a couple of writers up here, for some reason, they did this to us last year . . . they did it to us this year . . . I mean, they . . . as far as I think . . . they should . . . I'd like to see their licenses revoked, you know, in writing about me, anyway. . . . Because they don't seem to be up to no good at all. . . . And San Diego people picked up one of those articles and it tends to throw a dark shadow over the show . . . in saying it is something that it's not."[31]

The oft-perceived dark shadow of 1979–1980 seemed to lift a bit as Dylan took a break from the road for over six months. After reminiscing about Dylan's younger days—leaving Hibbing, Minnesota, for college and collecting folk songs instead—Dolores Barclay, writing for the Associated Press, issued this summation:

"He's a long way from those days now. His music has changed, his religion has changed, his old fans are now corporate executives, busy parents, and members of the power elite. And Dylan has grown older. He spent his thirtieth birthday at the Wailing Wall in Jerusalem, reaffirming and celebrating his Judaism. Now he's a born-again Christian. The reclusive, elusive hero of the '60s refused to be interviewed on the occasion of his fortieth birthday. . . . *Newsweek* did a cover story [in 1974], and Dylan was asked if he would once again become the voice for a new generation. His reply: 'I am not looking to be that new messiah. That's not in the cards for me. That's all over, that's in the past'. . . . And now Bob Dylan is forty; no longer an idol. 'Idols are old hat,' he once said. 'They aren't people, they're objects. But I'm no object.'"[32]

When he resumed what was largely a European tour in the summer of 1981, Dylan wasn't unwilling to answer questions about the last two albums. There was this exchange with Neil Spencer of *New Musical Express*:

> SPENCER: Do you feel the only way to know the Creator is through Christ?
>
> DYLAN: I feel the only way . . . let me see. Of course, you can look on the desert and wake up to the sun and the sand and the beauty of the stars and know there is a higher being, and worship that Creator. But being thrown into the cities, you're faced more with man than God. We're dealing here with man, y'know, and you have to know what God would do if He was a man. I'm trying to explain to you in intellectual mental terms, when it actually is more of a spiritual understanding than something which is open to debate.
>
> SPENCER: You can't teach people things they don't experience for themselves.
>
> DYLAN: Most people think that if God became a man, He would go up on a mountain and raise His sword and show His anger and wrath, or His love and compassion with one blow. And that's what people expected the Messiah to be—someone with similar characteristics,

> someone to set things straight, and here comes a Messiah who doesn't measure up to those characteristics and causes a lot of problems.[33]

Knowing that Dylan had visited Israel between 1969 and 1971, Spencer asked this question. "You were interested in Judaism at one point. You visited Israel and the Wailing Wall in Jerusalem. Do you feel that your interests at that time are compatible with your present beliefs?"

"There's really no difference between any of it in my mind," Dylan said.

Dylan may not have perceived a conflicting message between his Jewish heritage and his belief in Jesus, but Harvey Brooks, who toured with Dylan in 1965, and helped record *Highway 61 Revisited* (1965) and *New Morning* (1970), was living in Atlanta, Georgia in 1981, and was clearly struggling with his old friend's new ways:

"I was a studio manager and producer in Atlanta, and he came to tour [on November 15–16, 1981]. He had just converted to Christianity, and I called up and got passes for the show, but to be honest, I had problems with his confusion and I just couldn't bring myself to go. It led to my own confusion."[34]

Apparently, Brooks assumed Dylan's acceptance of Jesus was the result of confusion. If so, where did the confusion lie? Probably in the idea of the coming of the Messiah. Orthodox Christians are not confused about the matter: Jesus was/is the Messiah, and He will return. But Orthodox Jews aren't confused about the matter either: Jesus was not the Messiah. Messiah is yet to come.

Despite the theological left turn Dylan had taken, friends like Lou Kemp and Larry "Ratso" Sloman were not excluded by Dylan. The two traveled with the entourage at different points in 1979–1980. Another example would be Larry Kegan who, like Lou Kemp and Howard Rutman, had attended Camp Herzl with Dylan. Kegan was also invited to travel, in 1981, on a ship that so many were jumping off of. He graced the stage on two occasions on the last leg of the '81 tour, for the final encore song, singing Chuck Berry's "No Money Down" while Dylan accompanied on tenor saxophone. For the record, Kegan was also in Dylan's first band, The Jokers (along with Rutman), who performed at the camp and on occasional weekend jaunts to the Twin Cities between 1956 and 1958.

Author William McKeen looked back and saw it this way: "Though Dylan never renounced Christianity, he apparently remained a Jew throughout the gospel years, seemingly able to find some accommodation between the two faiths."[35]

Finding accommodation between the faiths was one thing, but what about the art? Leonard Cohen and Larry "Ratso" Sloman thought Dylan's gospel work was solid, but what about those in more formal critical circles? "For a literary critic to take a serious interest in the lyrics of Bob Dylan is still an unusual thing, and is likely to become more so," wrote Imre Salusinszky. "The political climate in our universities hardly encourages the study of an artist who is a white, male, Zionist, Christian, American millionaire."[36]

Journalist Michael Long reflected on the gospel era by observing Dylan's propensity to not pander to the crowds or critics:

> Already notorious for going his own way, Dylan committed what to many seemed to be professional—and creative—suicide: He became a born-again Christian, had the nerve to actually tell people about it, and began to write music about Jesus. . . . For a time, Dylan even renounced his catalog and began playing concerts in which he performed only religious songs. He also added an ordained minister [Larry Myers] to his road crew and began preaching sermons—interesting, Dylanesque sermons, but sermons nonetheless—at his shows. Fans abandoned him in droves. Dylan, however, plowed on. . . . Yet during this period of depressed record sales and critical spitballs, Dylan produced some of the greatest songwriting and recording of his career.[37]

Less than four months after Dylan's final concert of 1981—a concert whose encore included "It Ain't Me, Babe" and "Jesus Is the One"—an issue of *New York* magazine hit the newsstands with an article entitled "Dylan Ditching Gospel?"[38] Because of its newsy revelations, the article was promptly picked up by the *Washington Post*, one of the nation's most widely circulated newspapers. An unidentified source in *New York* asserted the following: "The evidence is that his Christian period is over. In a sense, he never left his Judaism. My interpretation is that the New Testament and Jesus were a message he thought he got, but that he was still testing."

An anonymous source giving an interpretation was not the stuff of journalistic legend, but it made the rounds nonetheless. Implicit in this interpretation, of course, is the assumption that Dylan embraced Jesus and therefore abandoned his Jewish heritage. Although this may be a perfectly logical and reasonable conclusion to arrive at, from the evidence we have seen, Dylan himself didn't think along these lines. He gave his onstage rap about the origins of the Passover during one of his gospel-era concerts. He included a passage from Jeremiah on the inside sleeve to his *Saved* album. He continued to hang out with fellow Jews who did not share his beliefs. And he said he didn't see any difference between his current beliefs and his interest in Judaism and visits to Israel a decade earlier.

Furthermore, the source in the *New York* article that claimed "the evidence is that his Christian period is over" only proffered one piece of evidence: the fact that Dylan would not be presenting the gospel song of the year in New York. Instead, he would be in California attending one of his son's bar mitzvahs (presumably Samuel Abram, Dylan's third child, who was thirteen at the time). But is this evidence at all? Would presenting an award to a likely stranger at some ceremony be the more "godly" thing to do than being at your own son's bar mitzvah?

The anonymous source also claimed Dylan "never formally committed to Christianity." But this is a red herring because Dylan never said he committed to the religion of Christianity; however, he did say, repeatedly, that he had a very personal experience with Jesus, which, to him, wasn't the same thing as "religion" or "Christianity."

Terms like "religious," "Christianity," "conversion," and "fundamentalist" were virtually absent from Dylan's vocabulary, but his personal experience, as described by outsiders was—and is—constantly framed in these terms.

More to the point, Dylan's 1979 interview with Bruce Heiman (KMGX-FM radio, Tucson, Arizona); his 1980 interviews with Paul Vitello (*Kansas City Times*), Karen Hughes (*Dominion*), Robert Hilburn (*Los Angeles Times*), and Paul Vincent (KMEL-FM radio, San Francisco); and his 1981 interviews with Neil Spencer (*New Musical Express*) and Dave Herman (WNEW-FM radio, New York) more than adequately serve as testimony from Dylan himself about his personal experience. He said as early as November 1980 that he had made his "statement" and he didn't like to repeat himself.

True to form, Dylan didn't grant any interviews to confirm or refute the rumors that were sparked by the *New York* article. After his statement in song, stage raps, and interviews, perhaps he saw nothing to be gained by any further explanation; no words needed to be said.

In 1982, besides a year of no interviews, there was no album release, nor any tours. However, tragedy struck when two people close to Dylan died in 1982—a longtime friend and someone he had just become friendly with: Howard Alk and Keith Green, respectively.

Alk toured with Dylan in the mid-1960s and helped edit Dylan's first film, *Eat the Document* (1966), as well as the *Renaldo and Clara* film over a decade later. He could also be found in the shadows of the 1981 tour, filming some of the concerts as he traveled with the entourage. Alk was the victim of either a drug overdose or suicide shortly after New Year's Day. "That's kind of when Bob decided to stop touring for a while," said Arthur Rosato, Dylan's assistant at the time. "He told me he wasn't going to go out [on tour] until '84. . . . He was upset, and he talked a little bit. He wanted to know if I was going to be okay. . . . But he shut down the [Santa Monica] studio then and there."[39]

Less than seven months later, Keith Green, whom Dylan had befriended through the Vineyard church, died in a plane crash along with eleven others, including two of Green's children, Josiah and Bethany.

Dylan's only performance of 1982 took place some seven weeks before Green's death, when he was a surprise guest at the Rose Bowl in Pasadena, California, for a concert promoting nuclear disarmament. He joined Joan Baez for the setting-appropriate "With God on Our Side," an age-appropriate "A Pirate Looks at Forty," and his time-honored classic "Blowin' in the Wind."

Baez was later asked about their collaboration and if Dylan had mentioned anything about his "current religious posture." "He didn't bring it up," she replied, "and I'm not interested in hearing about it."[40] Incidentally, Baez had recently penned "Children of the '80s," a song inspired by letters from her younger fans. One of its lyrics succinctly illustrated the apathy of the season: "We don't care if Dylan's gone to Jesus / Jimi Hendrix is playing on."[41]

On the lighter side of things, by late 1982, Dylan had written a batch of songs and was in search of a producer and an attentive ear. Author Michael Gray picks up the rather bizarre story of how the search led Dylan to the home of a legendary musician:

> In December [1982], Frank Zappa got an interesting visitor, who turned up at his house unannounced. Zappa said later: "I get a lot of weird calls there, and someone suddenly called saying, 'This is Bob Dylan. I want to play you my new songs.' Now I've never met him and I don't know his voice, but I looked at the video screen to see who was at the gate, and there, in the freezing cold, was a figure with no coat and an opened shirt. I sent someone down to check, to make sure it wasn't a Charles Manson, but it was him. . . ." Zappa told Karl Dallas, "he played me his eleven new songs and I thought they were good songs. He seemed like a nice guy. Didn't look like it would be too hard to work with him. I asked him if it had any Jesus in it. I said, 'Do these songs have the big J in them?' and he said no. When I took him upstairs to give him a sandwich, my dog barked at him. I told him to watch out, my dog doesn't like Christians. And he didn't laugh. But maybe he's not supposed to."[42]

No one, it seemed, knew what Dylan was supposed to do. From

dogs that barked at him to those who thought he had embarked on an errant theological journey, Dylan had succeeded in mystifying many people. With an apparent fondness for tweaking those who were troubled by the mystery, Dylan, in 1983, began studying with the Lubavitchers, the Orthodox Jewish community whose world headquarters were in Brooklyn, New York.

So how did he wind up there, and what did it mean? Unlike the visit he initiated when the Vineyard pastors came to his Brentwood home in early 1979, Dylan has never publicly addressed his studies in Brooklyn (though we've heard Dylan assistant Dave Kelly's take). According to Rabbi Kasriel Kastel, it was Manis Friedman, the Minneapolis-based rabbi, who had the most contact with Dylan and provided much of the Judaism teachings.[43]

Affirming Dave Kelly's account, Dylan's former publicist reminds us that even in 1979–1980, Dylan had interactions with rabbis. "I know rabbis did come, [they] came often to Dylan. I remember one rabbi, I forget where we were playing, but a rabbi was at the show and came backstage," recalled Paul Wasserman. "And he was welcomed, you know, no one said, 'Keep him out,' or anything like that. Yeah, we were all joking, 'Thank God, a Jew.'"[44]

"He's been going in and out of a lot of things, trying to find himself and we've just been making ourselves available," Rabbi Kasriel Kastel remarked in 1983. "As far as we're concerned, he was a confused Jew. We feel he's coming back."

"I don't think he ever left his Jewish roots," said Paul Emond, when asked about Dylan's attending his sons' bar mitzvahs and studying with the Lubavitchers. Emond was one of the two Vineyard pastors who visited Dylan in 1979, and said that the 1983 meetings took place at the request of the Lubavitchers. "I think [Dylan] is one of those fortunate ones who realized that Judaism and Christianity can work very well together because Christ is just Yeshua ha' Meshiah [Jesus the Messiah]. . . . They can't take the fact that he was able to come to the discovering of his Messiah as being Jesus. Jews always look at their own people as traitors when they come to that kind of faith . . . when one of their important figures is 'led astray,' they're going to do everything they can to get him back again."

Kastel, however, denied the Lubavitchers were taking advantage of Dylan: "We don't want anyone to feel that he's being used in any way, which he's very sensitive to. So we're keeping this very, very low key."[45]

It is entirely unclear who interviewed both Kasriel Kastel and Paul Emond for *Christianity Today* in 1983, but once the above comments were out, the situation seemed anything but low-key. Years later, Rabbi Kastel clarified his organization's mission:

"We are an educational group, with an educational message for Jews. Judaism has a message for non-Jews—to keep the seven Noahid Laws of basic humanity—but we do not have a message for them to convert to Judaism. We're coming up with all kinds of educational programs to make things easier for Jews to be able to become more observant and know what they believe . . . and so Bob Dylan was just as good a candidate as anybody else."[46]

Bryan Styble, editor and publisher of *Talkin' Bob Zimmerman Blues* (the first Dylan fanzine in the U.S.) offered up his perspective on the situation:

"Some people have found it odd that Dylan maintains his contacts with Judaism as a Christian. Actually, this has been quite natural. His ex-wife Sara and five children are observant Jews, and Dylan has always valued his close family ties."[47]

What looked like a sharp dichotomy between the two camps—presumably the Vineyard Christians and Lubavitch Jews—didn't necessarily exist for Al Kasha, a Jewish believer in Jesus. Kasha hosted a Bible study in 1979 that Dylan attended. "Lubavitchers are like Hasidic Jews . . . [like] Jesuit priests," Kasha told author Mark Joseph. "They're very much intellectuals . . . into the Kabbala, but they're spiritual, they're in constant search of the scriptures. I go into a Hasidic synagogue sometimes to listen to the teachings since they're very good rabbis and good teachers."[48]

It is not surprising that Dylan might gravitate to this branch of

Judaism considering the seriousness with which their adherents view the Scriptures. Additionally, the Hasidic tendency to separate from the rest of society is conspicuously absent in Chabad circles. The 250-year-old Chabad-Lubavitch movement derives its name from the Russian city of Lubavitch (meaning "city of brotherly love"). The Hebrew word "chabad" is an acronym consisting of three words meaning *wisdom, comprehension*, and *knowledge*. The linking of the two terms signifies the group's commitment to responsible and compassionate living.

"Those who follow Dylan primarily through rumor or the press often ask if he hasn't gone back to being a Jew, but the question is wrong," concluded James Earl. "After the first flush of his rebirth he rediscovered and reabsorbed his Jewishness in new and personal ways."[49]

Dave Kelly, the man Dylan hired, in part, to speak on his behalf in 1979–1980, had his interpretation of the events:

> So the only thing the rabbis could do was teach him more and more about the Old Testament and his heritage because all they could do is say that the Messiah has not come yet. Because that's what they believe. All they could do is say, "No, we don't think Jesus was the Messiah because of this, this, and this." I don't see how this could ever possibly make Bob think, "Oh, you're right, Jesus wasn't the Messiah" because he had a serious spiritual conversion proven to him that He was, so there's no risk in him studying with the Lubavitchers. I know I've studied with them and some of their group myself, but there's no risk.[50]

After studying with people at the Vineyard a few years prior and then later with the Lubavitchers, there is no doubt that Dylan literally believed what the Bible said; it was, for him, the Truth. In the summer of 1983 (at the conclusion of mixing sessions for the forthcoming *Infidels* album), journalist Martin Keller inquired about the rumored search for his Jewish roots:

"I ain't looking for them in synagogues with six-pointed Egyptian stars shining down from every window, I can tell you that much," Dylan replied. Three years earlier, during the gospel tours, Dylan made some similar (seemingly flippant) remarks about the physical structure of a church during an onstage rap in Buffalo, New York:

"As I was walking around today I noticed many tall steeples and big churches and stained glass windows. Let me tell you once again: God's not necessarily found in there. You can't get converted in no steeple or stained glass window. Well, Jesus is mighty to save, if He's in your heart, He'll convert you."[51]

Although this was a rare instance when Dylan used the verb "convert," the context revealed his "conversion" wasn't from Judaism to Christianity; rather, it was a revelation that amounted to him being brought out of darkness and into the light, a very personal experience which he had expressed through his lyrics, onstage raps, and interviews.

Bob Dylan's spiritual journey may not have been confined to structures with "six-pointed Egyptian stars hanging down from every window," or structures with "stained glass windows" and "tall steeples," but his biblical sensibilities were evident during this 1983 interview with Martin Keller:

> My so-called Jewish roots are in Egypt. They went down there with Joseph, and they came back out with Moses—you know, the guy that killed the Egyptian, married an Ethiopian girl, and brought the Law down from the mountain. The same Moses whose staff turned into a serpent. The same person who killed 3,000 Hebrews for getting down, stripping off their clothes, and dancing around a golden calf. These are my roots. Jacob had four wives and thirteen children, who fathered thirteen children, who fathered an entire people. Those are my roots too. Gideon, with a small army, defeating an army of thousands. Deborah, the prophetess; Esther the queen, and many Canaanite women. Reuben slipping into his father's bed when his father wasn't home. These are my roots.
>
> Delilah tempting Samson, killing him softly with her song. The mighty King David was an outlaw before he was king, you know. He had to hide in caves and get his meals at back doors. The wonderful

> King Saul had a warrant out on him—a 'no-knock' search warrant. They wanted to cut his head off. John the Baptist could tell you more about it. Roots, man—we're talking about Jewish roots, you want to know more? Check up on Elijah the prophet. He could make [it] rain. Isaiah the prophet, even Jeremiah, see if their brethren didn't want to bust their brains for telling it right like it is. Yeah, these are my roots I suppose.[52]

Amid this long line of biblical prophets, for Dylan to include John the Baptist was not insignificant. Chronologically, he is the last Jewish prophet Dylan mentions. According to the New Testament, the prophetic role of the Baptist could be summed up by these words he reportedly uttered when he saw Jesus: "Look, the Lamb of God who takes away the sin of the world."[53]

Dylan himself, back in 1979, told an audience in Tempe, Arizona, as much: "You know when John the Baptist saw Jesus coming down the road, he said, 'Behold the Lamb of God which taketh away the sin of the world.' Did you know that? That's right, that's what he said."[54]

Some six weeks before *Infidels* was released, Dylan was in Jerusalem for the bar mitzvah of his eldest son Jesse. Dylan's mother and son were visiting the Holy City when the possibility of a bar mitzvah came up; before long, Jesse's father flew in to join them. The story of how this event became public in the first place is intriguing, and the subsequent rumors were highly predictable.

"Within a few years of Dylan's conversion, he announced, on the occasion of his son becoming a bar mitzvah, that he had returned to Judaism,"[55] wrote James Carroll in 2001. His matter-of-fact statement piggybacked on rumors through the years, but ultimately amounted to a stellar example of sloppy research.

Carroll's use of the word "announced" in connection to Dylan's alleged return to Judaism invited imagery of an urgent press conference, a laughable image to even a casual follower of Dylan's career. Dylan never "announced" his return to (or departure from) Judaism; the only reason the bar mitzvah occasion of 1983 was even made public was because a photographer basically invaded the family's privacy. This same photographer later sold one of his photos to the Associated Press, a photo that was subsequently published around the world. Inevitably, it fueled further speculation of a Dylan waving goodbye to Jesus.

Fred Bernstein, who interviewed Dylan's mother a few years later, wrote this account:

> Beatty's son, Bob Dylan, joined his son and mother in Jerusalem. Also there, but not invited, was a photographer who insisted on taking a shot of Jesse praying. "I begged him not to do it," recalls Beatty. "I said, 'Can't you just leave this boy alone? Doesn't he have a right? Do you have to do this, just to make a few dollars?' But he took the picture anyway, and he wired it to New York, and it made all the papers. So then the whole world knew Bob Dylan's son had been bar mitzvahed."[56]

The photographer in question, an unrepentant Zavi Cohen, says he actually honored her request and also denies he invaded the family's privacy.

"At the time, I told her I would not be taking any pictures. However, this was after already taking all the pictures I needed! I was very respectful of their private/public moment. After all, this is the Wailing Wall, a sacred place to all Jews, but a very public place. I even ignored the incident with the two bodyguards who manhandled me outside the inner area. They, of course, had no right whatsoever to do that. I was not interested in creating an incident, but a public bar mitzvah of a public persona (incognito and all) is news. I offer no apologies."[57]

So how was Cohen aware of the fact that it was Bob Dylan and his family? At the time, he was just one of many photographers who were making money from tourists by snapping shots in Jerusalem; that is, until he got the unexpected tip. "A local friend of one of the photographers approached us and pointed to a small group of people by the [Western] Wall and said that Bob Dylan was there. . . . I excused myself and said I was going to take a look. I was really excited. What would Bob Dylan be doing by the Wailing Wall, the Western Wall of the ancient Israeli holy temple? I knew that Robert Zimmerman was born to a Jewish family. I also knew that he converted to Christianity at some point."[58]

A more recent Dylan biographer, Howard Sounes, covered the 1983 event in this fashion:

"In fact, Jesse was on vacation in Israel with his grandmother, Beatty, when they discovered a bar mitzvah could be conducted quickly and easily at the Wailing Wall and Bob simply flew in to play his part. He still believed Jesus Christ was the Messiah, and kept a broadly Christian outlook, although he had not maintained regular contact with the Vineyard Fellowship since the early flush of his conversion."[59]

Sounes, citing an "impeccable, confidential source" for the bar mitzvah story, has said he cannot be more specific.[60] Although Dylan may have still believed in Jesus as Messiah, it seems Sounes's characterization of the event that Dylan "flew in to play his part" is unfair. Although he has publicly acknowledged that the bar mitzvah was his mother's idea,[61] the fact that Dylan followed through on the idea does not seem surprising at all. Even Mitch Glaser, the man who distributed gospel tracts for Jews for Jesus at Dylan's 1979 shows in San Francisco, wasn't disturbed by Dylan's presence at such a special event:

> Well, first of all, the fact that he attended, or paid for, or encouraged his son's bar mitzvah, this would be normal for a Jewish dad. The fact is, there's a real bad presumption in all this: and that is that when you become a believer in Jesus, you don't have a bar mitzvah. And that is really, for the most part, false. I mean, I had a bat mitzvah for my daughters, and I would say lots of Messianic Jews [Jewish believers in Jesus] have bar mitzvahs for their kids. And so that's not disturbing at all.[62]

Just before the release of *Infidels* on November 1, 1983, Dylan granted an interview to Robert Hilburn of the *Los Angeles Times*. When asked if he viewed himself a "born-again Christian," Dylan said this:

"First of all, 'born-again' is a hype term. It's a media term that throws people into a corner and leaves them there, whether people realize it or not; all those political and religious labels are irrelevant."

What *was* relevant? Although Dylan acknowledged that the season of his preaching had passed, he obviously didn't have any qualms about the message he communicated in 1979–1980. "I don't particularly regret telling people how to get their souls saved. I don't particularly regret any of that. Whoever was supposed to pick it up, picked it up."

Hilburn wondered if any *Slow Train Coming* songs would appear in future tours. "Yeah, I'll do probably a few of those. I get letters from people who say they were touched by those shows. I don't disavow any of that. . . . That was all part of my experience. It had to happen. When I get involved in something, I get totally involved. I don't just play around on the fringes."[63]

Although Dylan's *Infidels* album didn't have the angle of *Slow Train Coming* or *Saved*, it was comical that some press reports characterized it as a "secular" album (considering there was not a single song without a direct biblical allusion). There were some no-brainers: "Neighborhood Bully" was a pro-Israel song if there ever was one; and although the images in "Man of Peace" were classic Dylan, its conclusions about "Satan" were plucked right out of the New Testament.

What is interesting here is that Dylan's biblical worldview had dramatically shifted since 1979. We know that Dylan was familiar with the Bible long before 1979, but by 1980, he acknowledged that he formerly viewed the Bible as only good literature, but "that's not the way it was anymore for me." Witness his 1983 Jewish roots rant to Martin Keller: he was recounting the history of the Bible and unabashedly assuming its truthfulness.

Singer and friend Joni Mitchell recalled a conversation they had during the Rolling Thunder days of 1975–1976, and then a subsequent conversation the two had, around the time of the gospel tours. "I asked Dylan one time, 'What do you mean by 'God,' 'cause if you read the Bible, I can't tell God from the Devil half the time! They seem to me to act very similarly.' And Dylan said, 'Well, it's just a word that people use.' I said, 'Yeah, but when you use it, what do you mean?' And he never answered me."

Then, not long after 1979, Mitchell remembered this conversation:

"He came up to me and said, 'Remember that time you asked me about God and the Devil? Well, I'll tell you now,' and he launched into this fundamentalist crap, and I said, 'Bobby, be careful. All of that [Bible verse] was written by poets like us; but this interpretation of yours seems a little brainwashed.' 'Poets like us,' he said. He kind of snickered at that."[64]

Ironically, the next time Dylan and Mitchell toured together,[65] many years later, Dylan opened his sets with his famous composition that invoked God, the Devil, and mankind—"Gotta Serve Somebody"—a song whose message many did, indeed, equate with "fundamentalist crap."

Many, though, did not view Dylan's songs from the late 1970s and early 1980s in such simplistic, crass terms. "The songs on *Infidels* reveal that even as Dylan sings prophetically of Israel and America and life in general from his biblical worldview, he is still searching for greater clarity concerning the personal significance of that biblical outlook for his own life," wrote Bert Cartwright in his book *The Bible in the Lyrics of Bob Dylan*:

"For him that search is not a matter of rejecting Christ or accepting Judaism, but understanding more fully the whole Bible—Old and New Testaments alike—and grasping the meaning of its story of God dealing with His people."[66]

As questions still lingered, in some circles, as to where he "stood" spiritually, Dylan shared this provocative nugget with Martin Keller during a summer 1983 interview: "People want to know where I'm at because they don't know where they're at." Within a few months of the *Christianity Today* article (which featured the aforementioned quotes from Rabbi Kasriel Kastel of Chabad and Paul Emond of the Vineyard), Dylan sat in a café in New York City and chatted with Kurt Loder for an interview.

LODER: You're a literal believer of the Bible?

DYLAN: Yeah. Sure, yeah. I am.

LODER: Are the Old and New Testaments equally valid?

DYLAN: To me.

After asking if he belonged to any church or synagogue ("not really" was the answer) and finding out that Dylan believed the end of the world would be at least another 200 years, Loder still wanted more theological meat.

LODER: When you meet up with Orthodox people, can you sit down with them and say, 'Well, you should really check out Christianity'?

DYLAN: Well, yeah, if somebody asks me, I'll tell 'em. But, you know, I'm not gonna just offer my opinion. I'm more about playing music, you know?[67]

The subsequent tour of 1984 did reflect a more musical than theologically driven approach, but crowds still heard about Jesus "on a cross" in "When You Gonna Wake Up?" and echoes of the Nazarene's words at nearly every show via "Every Grain of Sand" ("sparrows falling" and "every hair" being numbered).

As for the "oldies" (which received prominent attention in 1984), an interesting development occurred with the 1963 composition, "Masters of War." Its original line, "Even Jesus would never forgive what you do" was dropped and—to this day—has *never* been uttered in a performance of the song. "Dylan knows it is not biblically correct," asserts author Ronnie Keohane, "because all sins that a man can commit are possible for God to forgive."[68]

Some may view Keohane's interpretation as a stretch, but Dylan's response to journalist Mick Brown's question in 1984, on whether he believed in evil, seemed to bring it right back home.

"Sure, I believe in it. I believe that ever since Adam and Eve got thrown out of the garden, that the whole nature of the planet has been heading in one direction—towards apocalypse. It's all there in the book of Revelation, but it's difficult talking about these things to most people because most people don't know what you're talking about, or don't want to listen."[69]

"Israel interests him from a 'biblical point of view,' but he had never felt that atavistic Jewish sense of homecoming," wrote Brown who heard Dylan's above screed on the apocalypse.

Although Dylan did give a few one-off performances in 1985—Live Aid, Moscow's International Poetry Festival, and Farm Aid—it was, like 1982 and 1983, a non-touring year. In fact, 1985 is the last year, to date, that Bob Dylan has stayed off the road. During this year, Dylan was chatty with the media. This manifested itself through an extensive interview arena that included television, radio, magazines, newspapers, an interview for a book on songwriters, and an interview which produced a booklet and liner notes to *Biograph*, a two-decade compilation of Dylan songs.

Although the time to preach onstage may have passed, these interviews became downright preachy at times, and revealed the center from which Dylan's spiritual view of the world emanated. "The Bible runs through all of U.S. life, whether people know it or not. It's the founding book; the Founding Fathers' book, anyway," Dylan remarked to Bill Flanagan during the mixing sessions for his 1985 album, *Empire Burlesque*.

"People can't get away from it [the Bible]. You can't get away from it, wherever you go. Those ideas were true then and they're true now. They're scriptural, spiritual laws. I guess people can read into that what they want. But if you're familiar with those concepts they'll probably find enough of them in my stuff. Because I always get back to that."

One of those concepts Dylan embraced—which found its way into his songwriting—was the premise of original sin, a premise which can arguably be found in both the Hebrew and Christian Scriptures. The following quote left no wiggle room as to where the forty-three-year-old singer stood.

"We're all sinners. People seem to think that because their sins are different from other people's sins, they're not sinners," he observed.

"People don't like to think of themselves as sinners. It makes them feel uncomfortable. 'What do you mean a sinner?' It puts them at a disadvantage in their minds. Most people walking around have this strange conception that they're born good, that they're really good people—but the world has just made a mess of their lives. I had another point of view. But it's not hard for me to identify with anybody who's on the wrong side. We're all on the wrong side, really."[70]

Dylan took his new batch of songs from the not-yet-released *Empire Burlesque* and sought input from an old friend, Allen Ginsberg. Raymond Foye was at Ginsberg's apartment when Dylan dropped by with the cassette tape. Foye, co-founder of Hanuman Books, would later publish some of Ginsberg's work and also *Saved!: The Gospel Speeches of Bob Dylan*, an unauthorized compilation of Dylan's stage raps from 1979 to 1980. As the tape of *Empire Burlesque* played that day, Foye recounted this playful exchange between the two friends in 1985 who, although sharing a Jewish heritage, didn't exactly share the same spiritual worldview.

"At one point Ginsberg thought he detected a quasi-religious overtone [in one of the song's lyrics]. 'Aha!' he said sarcastically, 'I see you still have the judgment of Jehovah hanging over our heads!' 'You just don't know God,' Dylan replied, twice as sarcastic. 'Yeah, I never met the guy,' Allen said, ending the exchange."[71]

"He always seemed to me to be seeking some ultimate, eternal truth," Ginsberg told interviewer Wes Stace in 1985. "It might have been expected that he'd have a visionary experience, which he did, and it might not have been expected that he would have solidified it into the symbolism of born-again Christianity. Well, why not? It might have been expected that he'd evolve out of it as something closer to his natural Judaism.

"In the conversation we had when he visited a couple of weeks ago, there was a great deal of judgmental Jehovaic or 'Nobodaddy'—'nobody daddy up in heaven'—a figure of judgmental hyper-rationality. There's this judgmental Jehovaic theism in his recent work, and he said, 'Allen, do you have a quarrel with God?' and I said, 'I've never met the man' and he said, 'Then you have a quarrel with God.' And I said, 'Well, I didn't start anything!' So he still has a fixed notion of divinity, and I think that's a mistake, as a non-theistic Buddhist, that any solidification of the ideal God like the ancient Jews warned against—naming the name of God—is a mistake. It's a psychological error on a simple point."[72]

In the same year that Ginsberg perceived some "judgmental Jehovaic theism" in Dylan's work, Dylan had this to say to Cameron Crowe:

"The Bible says, 'Even a fool, when he keeps his mouth shut, is counted wise,' but it comes from the Bible, so it can be cast off as being too 'religious.' Make something religious and people don't have to deal with it, they can say it's irrelevant. 'Repent, the Kingdom of God is at hand.' That scares the s--- out of people. They'd like to avoid that. Tell that to someone and you become their enemy. There does come a time, though, when you have to face facts and the truth is true whether you wanna believe it or not, it doesn't need you to make it true. . . . That lie about everybody having their own truth inside of them has done a lot of damage and made people crazy."[73]

Students of the Good Book will likely recognize Dylan's biblical allusions in the above quote. He paraphrased a bit of wisdom from the book of Proverbs in the Hebrew Scriptures, and repeated the scandalous declaration that, according to the Gospels, Jesus uttered.

In 1985, there was also an intriguing interview with Scott Cohen of *Spin* magazine.[74] After a charming description of his 1954 bar mitzvah, Dylan said he discovered his rabbi was of the "Orthodox" persuasion, although it seems unlikely he was unaware of this at the time. Whatever the case, Dylan certainly used it as an opportunity to tweak the conventions of religious labels: "Jews separate themselves like that: Orthodox, Conservative, Reform . . . as if God calls them that. Christians, too: Baptists, Assembly of God, Methodists, Calvinists. God has no respect for a person's title. He don't care what you call yourself."

Cohen also heard Dylan's take on the biblical notion that a prophet is often rejected by his own people:

"Whenever anybody does something in a big way, it's always rejected at home and accepted someplace else. For instance, that could apply to Buddha. Who was Buddha? An Indian. Who are Buddhists? Chinese, Japanese, Asian people. They make up the big numbers in Buddhism. It's the same way with Jesus being a Jew. Who did he appeal to? He appeals to people who want to get into Heaven in a big way."

Cohen and readers of *Spin* were also privy to Dylan's long-winded exposition on the Messianic Age. Whether one agrees or disagrees with his interpretation, there is no doubt that its origins were embedded in both the Hebrew and Christian Scriptures, and reflected a time-honored theme in many a Dylan song—including the sentiments of "This World Can't Stand Long," a song Dylan unearthed years later.

After a year filled with interviews, Dylan took to the road in 1986, touring New Zealand, Australia, and Japan with his support band, Tom Petty and the Heartbreakers (and later with the Grateful Dead). This is when the seeds were planted for what is now called the "Never-Ending Tour."

Cover song surprises like "Across the Borderline," "I'm Moving On," "Lonesome Town," and "That Lucky Old Sun" became staples and an occasional curve ball was tossed in—like the traditional "House of the Risin' Sun" or "We Three," the Ink Spots' song. A good cross section from Dylan's own career was included with songs like "Blowin' in the Wind," "Like a Rolling Stone," "Knockin' on Heaven's Door," as well as a generous smattering of songs from recent albums such as *Infidels* and *Empire Burlesque*. In the post-gospel tour era, biographer Clinton Heylin has noted how one of the staples seemed to stick out.

"Not only was the final song of each night's main set 'In the Garden,' hardly a song an apostate could have brought himself to sing, but he chose to preface the song with a rap that would also figure as the opening sequence in an hour-long concert special from Sydney, broadcast on HBO in June."

The stage rap to which Heylin referred had Dylan offering up these words to crowds in 1986 before singing "In the Garden" from the *Saved* album:

"This last song now is all about my hero. Everybody's got a hero. Where I come from, there's a lot of heroes. Plenty of them. John Wayne, Clark Gable, Richard Nixon, Ronald Reagan, Michael Jackson, Bruce Springsteen. They're all heroes to some people. Anyway, I don't care nothing about those people. I have my own hero. I'm going to sing about him right now."[75]

After the overseas tour and just before his first U.S. tour since the gospel tours of 1979-1981, Dylan granted an interview to Mikal Gilmore. At one point, the *Rolling Stone* journalist alluded to critics who charged that songs like "Slow Train" and "Union Sundown" amounted to a Dylan moving a bit "to the right."

"Well, for me, there is no right and there is no left. There's truth and there's untruth, y'know? There's honesty and there's hypocrisy. Look in the Bible: you don't see nothing about right or left," he insisted. "I hate to keep beating people over the head with the Bible, but that's the only instrument I know, the only thing that stays true."

Not giving up on the political/religious dynamic, Gilmore also asked Dylan if it disturbed him that there seemed to be an abundance of preachers who claimed that a good Christian must also be a "political conservative."

"Conservative?" asked Dylan. "Well, don't forget, Jesus said that it's harder for a rich man to enter the Kingdom of Heaven than it is for a camel to enter the eye of a needle. I mean, is that conservative? I don't know, I've heard a lot of preachers say how God wants everybody to be wealthy and healthy. Well, it doesn't say that in the Bible. You can twist anybody's words, but that's only for fools and people who follow fools."[76]

In mid-summer after the first of three nights at New York's Madison Square Garden, Dylan's bandmate Tom Petty sat down with journalist Bill DeYoung for an interview, the only one Petty agreed to do for the tour. There was this intriguing exchange about a certain song Dylan had just played. DeYoung: Bob was out there tonight pulling these Jesus songs out of the hat. Petty: And rightfully so! DeYoung: Right after your second set, after Ronnie Wood [of the Rolling Stones] came out for "Rainy Day Women," then there was a Jesus song ["In the Garden" from *Saved*]. I could feel the momentum dive. Petty: Yeah, but see, you're still talking about it. You know what, the Beach Boys wouldn't-a done that. They'd have probably just steamrollered that baby to the end like Bruce Springsteen. But that's not what this is about. He had something to say at that point. This ain't show business, man. This ain't show business. That's Bob Dylan. He had something to say at that point. He had something to say about Jesus right then. He sang "Like a Rolling Stone," right? He'd already done that [in the set list, right before "In the Garden"]. Listen, man, you gotta dig that there's a lot of great songs about Jesus. David Lee Roth might not want to do that. But I admire a man that's confident enough in himself to do that. And I tell you what, nobody left.[77]

Near the end of the 1986 summer tour, Dylan arrived in Mountain View, California, and during a rehearsal sound check recorded and videotaped a version of Fred Rose's song, "Thank God" (a song Hank Williams recorded, as did Dylan's friends in The Alpha Band some eight years earlier). The following month, the videotape of this gospel song was given to the Lubavitchers for their annual charity telethon. Martin Grossman has pointed out that Dylan "dropped the verse that specifically mentions Jesus,"[78] but the dropped verse does not even contain the name of Jesus in it, anyway. Jesus is obviously implied throughout this old gospel song which makes it all the more curious and odd (and subversive?) as to why Dylan donated it to the Lubavitcher telethon in the first place.

"From the standpoint of the traditional Jewish law and custom that they [the Lubavitchers] observe," remarked Laurence Schlesinger, a rabbi who has written on Dylan's spiritual journey, "it is almost inconceivable to believe that these Jews, in particular, would actually showcase someone whom they and their audience considered to be an out and out *mumar* (apostate)."[79]

While Schlesinger and others have viewed Dylan's association with Chabad as reasonable evidence that Dylan no longer maintains his faith in Jesus, it is worth noting that at the very Mountain View gig from which "Thank God" was pulled, Dylan included "Gotta Serve Somebody," and "In the Garden."

"His support for Chabad is not at all disturbing because a lot of us support Jewish causes. It's not like we became Christians and all of a sudden we're no longer Jews," observed Mitch Glaser. "We're very much Jews . . . but it wouldn't matter to Chabad [if Dylan still believed in Jesus], that would not keep them from inviting him. They're not like that. They would be very confident that doing anything with Chabad would be a mitzvah. Mitzvah means a commandment. You know, that Dylan would be fulfilling a commandment to God and that God would only bless him for doing that, and it would be a way to get him back into his Judaism."[80]

Dylan also videotaped a public service announcement for the Chabad ministry, lending his support for their drug rehabilitation and education programs. However maddening it might be for some fans, Dylan's belief in Jesus and his Jewish heritage didn't pose a problem.

Like 1986, Dylan's touring in 1987 included a number of gigs with Tom Petty and the Heartbreakers and a brief stint with the Grateful Dead. Robert Hilburn of the *Los Angeles Times* was there to cover Dylan's first concerts in Israel, in Tel Aviv and Jerusalem, respectively. His report, following the Tel Aviv concert of September 5, 1987, touched on the controversy of the singer's biblical faith—a faith that looked to both Testaments, and manifested itself through song:

> The evening's big surprise was "Go Down, Moses," a traditional [song] built around the line, "Let My People Go," one of the most emotional phrases in the Jewish culture. . . . Though many in the audience were touched by the inclusion of "Go Down, Moses," it wasn't enough to those interviewed after the concert to erase the disappointment of the evening [Dylan's alleged lackluster performance]. Some also felt the inclusion of 'In the Garden,' one of the songs associated with Dylan's born-again Christian period, sent a mixed signal about his current religious stance.[81]

"The personality of Jesus of Nazareth stands as an enigma in Jewish history. Hailed by millions as a Savior and giver of life, his name has been used to condemn the Jews and as an excuse to take Jewish lives," wrote theologian Arnold Fruchtenbaum. "As a result, except for a few references in the Talmud and in Jewish legends, Jesus was largely ignored by the Jews."[82]

In typical contrarian fashion, Dylan wasn't one to ignore Jesus. Just penning the lyrics to "In the Garden" in 1979—some eight years before presenting it to a Tel Aviv crowd—was an attempt to get to the root of the truth, cutting through centuries of evil deeds and falsehoods uttered by professing Christians, and ultimately return to the first-century sources, the Gospel accounts. These same accounts were written by Jewish men who (according to the New Testament) were convinced that Jesus was the Son of God.

Two days after Tel Aviv, a crowd in Jerusalem saw Dylan close his main set with "Gotta Serve Somebody." For the encore, Dylan launched into "Slow Train" only to have it interrupted by unforeseen circumstances. "The oddest moment came," wrote Calev Ben-David, "when he chose to end his Jerusalem concert with his evangelical Christian song, 'Slow Train Coming,' and the sound system suddenly and mysteriously short-circuited, prematurely ending the show."[83]

Glenn Frankel of the *Washington Post* wondered if divine intervention might not have been a factor:

"The song that seemed about to lift the concert off the ground, the gospel 'Slow Train Coming,' was cut off two-thirds of the way through when the sound system failed. Dylan stood strumming in disbelief for a moment, then dropped his guitar to the stage floor and stormed away. End of levitation, end of concert. It was as if the Almighty had suddenly caught a glimpse of what this occasional disciple was brewing in His city and decided to call a halt to the proceedings before things got out of hand."[84]

Nothing seemed off limits when it came to the religious connotations of the Israeli sojourn. Take, for example, Robert Hilburn sharing this bit of intrigue after learning of Dylan's trek to Egypt before the gigs in Israel:

"Dylan, who avoids explaining his actions or reflecting on others' interpretations of him, shifted uneasily on his chair when asked if people should interpret his visit [to Israel] in Big Statement terms. Though he expressed warmth for Israel, he said simply that he is willing to play anywhere people want him: 'I'd like to play Egypt. You know the Jews and Arabs have the same father. They're brothers. Basically, there shouldn't be a problem between them. They're both Semitic people. If someone is anti-Semitic, they're anti-Arab as much as anti-Jew. The problem is politics. I felt right at home in Egypt. I wasn't surprised because Egyptland is in all our blood. I didn't go to see the Pyramids. I wanted to see the prison where Joseph was in, and the place Abraham took Sarah."[85]

According to biographer Heylin, two weeks after Israel, while in Helsinki for a concert, Dylan visited the only synagogue in Finland. True to form, after the synagogue visit, Dylan had no problem concluding his next gig with his *Saved* offering, "In the Garden."

A week later, Dylan celebrated Rosh Hashanah with an Israeli dignitary in Rome.[86] His concert set in Rome also ended with "In the Garden." For all of his supposed unpredictability, Dylan's embrace of his Jewish ethnicity and his Jesus-centered songs was becoming more and more predictable.

By January 1988, Dylan found himself in New York City giving an acceptance speech for his induction into the Rock & Roll Hall of Fame. On the heels of a heartfelt speech by Bruce Springsteen, the poet from Minnesota took the podium. Dylan said hello to Muhammad Ali, and acknowledged and thanked Little Richard and Alan Lomax for their help in forming his career (All three men were in the audience). At the conclusion of his speech, Dylan issued this admonishment:

"And I want to thank Mike Love for not mentioning me. I play a lot of dates every year too. And peace, love, and harmony is greatly important indeed, but so is forgiveness, and we've got to have that too. So thanks."

Why did Dylan feel the need to refer to one of the Beach Boys by thanking him for the non-mention? Love had given a speech earlier in the evening where, according to author Tim Dunn, "the absence of Paul McCartney and Diana Ross [The Beatles and the Supremes were also inductees] brought rancorous comments from Beach Boy Mike Love, who also labeled attendee Mick Jagger 'chicken-s---' for good measure."[87]

Leave it to Dylan to bring up the theme of forgiveness in a speech at a Rock & Roll Hall of Fame ceremony. This foreshadowed a lyric from the Traveling Wilburys' song "End of the Line," released later in the year: "Best you can do is forgive."

Coinciding with the end of Dylan's 1988 tours was the conclusion of a tour sponsored by Amnesty International, the organization defending human rights around the globe. When Dylan played his October 14 gig in Upper Darby, Pennsylvania, he said this before a song that appeared late in the set:

"There's this Amnesty tour going on right now. Last year they also had an Amnesty tour. I was really honored when they used a song, a Bob Dylan song, to close the Amnesty show last year, the song, 'I Shall Be Released' . . . This year, they, to my surprise, they chose another song called 'Chimes of Freedom' to close this year's show. I'm hopin' next year they might choose this song."[88]

What song was Dylan referring to? Once again, "In the Garden" from his *Saved* album received special attention. Why did Dylan want to refer the Amnesty world—a world that was ultimately protesting how we treat one another—to a song that amounted to a narrative about the arrest, crucifixion, and resurrection of Jesus?

"Rock at its best makes you feel free, and that's what Amnesty does," asserted Bruce Springsteen, explaining why he joined their tour. Meanwhile, on October 16, 1988, a day after the Amnesty tour ended, Dylan was only a subway ride away from Amnesty headquarters. He repeated his plea before "In the Garden" while playing the first night of a four-night stint at Radio City Music Hall in New York.

On the second evening at Radio City, Dylan added this commentary before singing "In the Garden": "Next year the Amnesty tour, I think, they're gonna use 'Jokerman.' Anyway, I'm trying to get them to change their mind, trying to get them to use this one!"[89]

The following evening Dylan once again included "In the Garden," trying to persuade anyone who might be listening: "I'm trying to get them to change their minds. I'd like for them to use this one if they would."[90] At the final Radio City gig he made the same plea. It almost seems perverse that Dylan would, amid the publicity of the Amnesty tour, offer up his Bible-thumping number from the *Saved* album.

Among the attendees at Radio City was Dylan's longtime friend Allen Ginsberg. It would have been interesting to hear Ginsberg's take on Dylan's rumblings before "In the Garden." When the famous poet cited a handful of personal favorite Dylan songs, in 1985, he included "In the Garden" and said he thought it was "a great song."[91] Perhaps even more odd was that, years later, Rabbi Manis Friedman (Dylan's longtime friend from the Lubavitchers) also acknowledged that "In the Garden" was "a good song."[92] That a non-theistic Buddhist like Ginsberg and an Orthodox Jew like Friedman could appreciate a song like "In the Garden" suggested a tolerance that many refused to grant Dylan.

In 1988, filmmaker Jean-Luc Godard gave an interview to *Actuel* and revealed an affinity toward the Dylan of the late 1980s: "I have a great deal of sympathy for him when I read critics who eviscerate him, who call him a 'has-been.' Sometimes I read *Rolling Stone* to get news of him. I want to see whether he's on the charts. I tried to get him to act in who-knows-what film, a project in the United States, and then all of a sudden he turned toward Christ and I said to myself, 'That will happen to me too.' I forgot all about it, but when I made *Hail Mary*, I remembered: 'Look, Dylan warned me.'"

New Yorker writer Richard Brody informed readers that Godard got a bit of his chronology mixed up: The movie Godard wanted to enlist Dylan for was actually *King Lear*. *Hail Mary* had already been released when Lear was commissioned.[93]

Incidentally, by including Dylan's song "When He Returns" (from the *Slow Train Coming* album) on two of his films' soundtracks from the

'80s (*Grandeur et de'cadence d'un petit commerce de cinema;* and *Puissance de la parole*), Godard will likely go down in cinema soundtrack history without an equal. The song is equally naked in its theology and pathos, and an intriguing selection.

On September 13, 1989, Edna Gundersen of *USA Today* recalled how the press dubbed Dylan as "born-again" a decade earlier. "If that's what was laid on me, there must have been a reason for it," Dylan replied.[94] "Whatever label is put on you, the purpose of it is to limit your accessibility to people." This remark dovetailed with his 1983 comment to Robert Hilburn of the *Los Angeles Times* where he called the born-again label a "media hype" term that "threw people in a corner and left them there."[95]

Gundersen also heard his take on what she called the "religious content" of *Slow Train Coming* (1979), *Saved* (1980), and *Shot of Love* (1981). Not surprisingly, Dylan eschewed the labels, but affirmed his experience.

As the decade of the 1980s ended, the Berlin Wall crumbled in Germany, an event that fostered hope in a world that seemed—as Dylan wrote back in 1961—to be "sick, hungry, tired, and torn."[96] In the latter days of 1989, Dylan found himself revisiting his old stomping grounds in New York's Greenwich Village. Biographer Howard Sounes picks up the story:

"Bob called at the apartment of his old friend Dave Van Ronk. 'He was in the neighborhood and, on impulse, he rang the bell,' says Van Ronk. 'You know, he really hadn't changed all that much'. . . They talked about songwriting. Bob complained that young performers did not know traditional music. He added gloomily: 'The Devil is the lord of this world.'"[97]

By bucking the fashionable trend of ignoring traditional music, supporting a religious organization such as Chabad, and singing the provocative "In the Garden," Dylan, by the end of the 1980s, seemed unwilling to go gently into the night.

5

1990–1999: MURMURS OF PRAYERS

Bob Dylan is the perfect lyric poet and maybe the greatest poet this half of the century, and certainly better known than me, incidentally. I'm not the most well known American poet, I'd say Bob Dylan is, and he's a respectable poet too.

—ALLEN GINSBERG, 1994, NEW YORK, NEW YORK

What kind of artistry is equal to the silver glisten on a river, or a sunset, or lightning in the sky? What kind of man's artistry can compare to the great artistry of creation?

—BOB DYLAN, 1990, LINCOLN, NEBRASKA

AS A NEW DECADE DAWNED, a forty-eight-year-old Bob Dylan may not have been enjoying one of his peaks in popularity, but he continued to do yeoman's work, touring and recording. The so-called Never-Ending Tour showed no signs of letting up. Dylan spent the early days of January 1990 in a recording studio and these sessions, along with subsequent ones, yielded his much-maligned album, *Under the Red Sky*. The album's cover featured Dylan kneeling down on the soil in Israel.

During one of the recording sessions in southern California, co-producer David Was remembered lending something to Dylan. "I was planting books on him I thought he might find interesting. I had a book called *The Bible as History* by an Oxford historian," Was recalled for John Bauldie, the founder of one of the first Dylan fanzines. "He devoured the book. He took it with him and then appeared in the studio with it rolled up in his back pants pocket, which I forgave, given that it was him. It ruined the book, but what the hell!—but he just ate it up."[1]

While in Paris for a run of concerts in February 1990, Dylan met up with an old friend in a café:

"Poet and singer Leonard Cohen was miffed about Bob Dylan's slump in popularity. He had had dinner with Dylan a few nights earlier and was still talking about it," remarked Tom Chaffin, a writer for the *Atlanta Journal-Constitution.* "Dylan's '80s embrace of evangelical Christianity and a series of albums of religious songs had troubled many longtime fans. Cohen thought the reaction unfair, and he told me he was particularly galled by a recent review in which a critic had taken Dylan's album *Shot of Love* [1981] to task because it included 'only one masterpiece'—Dylan's poignant hymn 'Every Grain of Sand.' 'My God!' Cohen exclaimed. 'Only one masterpiece? Does this guy have any idea what it takes to produce a single masterpiece?' Beyond that, Cohen added, 'I think anything he does merits serious attention.'"[2]

As for Dylan's faith in 1990, some relevant content could be found in a letter he penned and sent to Jamie Brown,[3] who was the editor and founder of *Sister 2 Sister*, a magazine for black female executives in the music industry. In this published letter, we catch a glimpse of Dylan the troubadour, traveling the world over while contemplating life, time, and God.

> Dear Jamie,
>
> Life on the road is not what it used to be. But what used to be may not have existed anyway. All of Europe used to be a desert. What they say about shifting sand is not unfounded.

Everything is happening by the clock. Without clocks there wouldn't be any useful idea of time. My soul is unaware of any time; only in my mind. My poor mind—which is so bombarded with dates, calendars, and numbers—has been deceived into believing there is such a thing as time, woe is me.

Hasn't everybody, at some point in their life, asked, "What time is it?" It's no time. The sun comes up and the sun goes down. That's what time it is. That's why it's taken me so long to write you this letter.

Anyway, Jamie, we say things like, "Gee, was that a year ago?" or "Was that ten years ago?" or "Look at those fields that were so familiar to me as a child, where now skyscrapers stand." All of us can tell the story, "It was just the other day when this or that happened." That's only our minds talking.

Anyway, traveling around makes you think of these things, including my thoughts to drop you a line. Reflecting on this, brainwork brings you to the realization that this earth is truly God's footstool and until the entire world believes and obeys the same God, there can be no truth or justice or peace for anyone. The soul never dies and neither does it know time. Okay, Jamie, until the next moment. God bless you much, good luck, and say hello to the boys.

P.S. Congratulations on your second year.

Bob Dylan

This letter makes sense when looked at in context: during the course of 1990, Dylan's audiences frequently heard "Gotta Serve Somebody," "I Believe in You," and "In the Garden," songs from Dylan's so-called "Christian period," which invoked the divinity represented in *Slow Train Coming* and *Saved.*

Implicit in Dylan's 1990 letter to *Sister 2 Sister* is the monotheistic viewpoint that naturally comes against the multitude of "gods." In Dylan's 1989 composition, "Ring Them Bells," Saint Peter—whose naked confession Jesus founded his Church upon (at least according to the Christian Scriptures)—is ringing them bells where the four winds blow, so the people will know. Dylan sings that "the sun is going down upon the sacred cow." No leap of faith is required to safely assume the "sacred cow" here alludes to the time-honored biblical metaphor for all false gods.

As for Dylan's reference in the letter to "God's footstool," this is another biblical concept. For example, in the Hebrew Scriptures the Psalmist writes, "Exalt the Lord our God and worship at His footstool; He is holy."

In the so-called Sermon on the Mount, Jesus affirmed these very words when he addressed the issue of vows and oaths: "I say to you, make no oath at all, either by Heaven, for it is the throne of God, or by the earth, for it is the footstool of His feet, or by Jerusalem, for it is the city of the great king."

Additionally, the prophet Isaiah penned these words:

> Thus says the Lord, 'Heaven is my throne, and the earth is My footstool. Where then is a house you could build for me? And where is a place that I may rest? For My hand made all these things, thus all these things came into being,' declares the Lord. 'But to this one I will look, to him who is humble and contrite of spirit, and who trembles at My word. (Isaiah 66:1–2, NASB)

Not too many months after penning his letter to *Sister 2 Sister*, Dylan chatted about issues of morality and music with Edna Gundersen of *USA Today*. "People say music is intended to elevate the spirit. But you've got a lot of groups and lyrics projecting emptiness and giving you nothing—less than nothing—because they're taking up your time," said Dylan. "It's not difficult to get people throbbing in their guts. That can lead you down an evil path if that's all they're getting. You gotta put something on top of that."

When pressed further about the subject of art, Dylan fired a few rhetorical questions: "What kind of artistry is equal to the silver glisten on a river, or a sunset, or lightning in the sky? What kind of man's artistry can compare to the great artistry of creation?"[4]

Dylan's album release in the fall of 1990, *Under the Red Sky*, included "God Knows," a song that alluded to this great Artist of creation. It might be easy to overlook the thrust of this rocking blues song simply because its title summons up the casual shrug-of-the-shoulders cliché. But the song's lyrics serve as an antidote to anything casual or vain. "God Knows" speaks of the God of Scripture, one who is omniscient—a God who knows, literally, everything. One of its lines, "God knows the secrets of your heart," owes a debt to the psalmist who declared, some 3,000 years ago, that "If we had forgotten the name of our God, or extended our hands to a strange god, would not God find this out? For He knows the secrets of the heart."[5]

The lyrical hook to this song off the 1990s *Under the Red Sky*—"God knows there's gonna be no more water, but fire next time"—may well be one of the grand apocalyptic moments in songwriting history. What other single line could sum up such apocalyptic sentiments? Paying homage to a theme he's been preoccupied with from the start, Dylan borrowed the line—consciously or subconsciously, take your pick—from any number of old familiar gospel songs. This doesn't require a stretch of the imagination. The traditional "Hold On" (Dylan's adaptation became "Gospel Plow," a song appearing on his debut album of 1962) included the following lyric: "God gave Noah the rainbow sign / No more water, but fire next time."

The Charles Johnson composition, "It's Gonna Rain," also included this very lyric, sung by Dylan's female singers during the tours of 1979–1980. "O Mary Don't You Weep," the Inez Andrews song, has the lyric as well. And when the Louvin Brothers eerily crooned out Bill Monroe's song, "Sinner You'd Better Get Ready," it included this amendment: "Oh God gave Noah the rainbow sign / The time's a comin' when the sinner must die / It won't be by water / Be by fire next time."

Whatever the source, the lyrics to "God Knows" ultimately relied upon biblical passages; there was no getting around it. The Hebrew Scriptures (Genesis 9:8–17) and the Christian Scriptures (2 Peter 3:3–10) combined to pack the lyrical punch. Although theologians might take a book or three to expound on the details, whoever originally wrote the line captured God's promise to Noah and the promise given to Jesus disciple Peter who referred to the fire next time: "But the day of the Lord will come like a thief, in which the heavens will pass away with a roar and the elements will be destroyed with intense heat, and the earth and its works will be burned up."

As to the subject of Dylan's spiritual roots, author Larry Yudelson has said this: "Dylan has, if only from the ironic sideline, taken part in—and sung at—the deepest spiritual crises of his generation of American Jews: the drama of the civil rights struggle, the comforts and exoticism of the Jewish homeland, and the spiritual excitements of Lubavitch. He also became a Christian—the one leader he followed—and never really looked back and renounced it—because, like many a *Hasid*, he found God through the music. And in America, the roots of the music are Christian."[6]

Did this mean Dylan had abandoned his Jewish heritage? Not hardly. By the end of 1990, he had endorsed Rabbi Manis Friedman's book *Doesn't Anyone Blush Anymore?* with these words: "Anyone who's either married or thinking of getting married would do well to read this book."

The book set forth a defense of traditional Jewish customs of sexual modesty. Dylan's son-in-law also commented on the book. "Drawing on the accumulated wisdom of over three thousand years," writes Peter Himmelman, "master storyteller Rabbi Friedman offers startlingly practical advice into nearly every facet of human existence." The Reverend John D. Gilmore of the St. Paul [Minnesota] Area Council of Churches had this to say: "Friedman is an excellent communicator and a prophet for an ethic-sick generation."

Although a decade had passed since the tumultuous gospel tours, Dylan's heart still seemed to be set on the apocalypse in biblical terms. Biographer Clinton Heylin interviewed Cesar Diaz (Dylan's rhythm guitarist at the time) and wrote this account of the plane ride over to Europe for the start of the 1991 tour: "Dylan and Diaz had talked 'about

Armageddon and biblical things,' and Dylan had told Diaz that he did not think it was yet time."[7]

Audiences in 1991 still heard Dylan perform some of his songs from *Slow Train Coming* and *Saved* and even make the occasional onstage comments about them. He seemed to be reminding his crowds—through some revealing stage raps—what these songs meant to him. For example, prior to singing "In the Garden" in Glasgow, Scotland, he offered up this: "Alright, this is one of my lesser known songs, but it's still one of my favorites."

At a second concert in Glasgow, the following night, he informed the crowd that "Gotta Serve Somebody" was one of his "gospel songs." A few months later, back in the States, Dylan told a Boston crowd that "In the Garden" was one of his "anti-religion songs," and, a few nights later, another crowd in Massachusetts heard that "Gotta Serve Somebody"—besides being a gospel song—was also an anti-religion song. During the course of 1991, he would repeat these assertions on a number of occasions.[8]

But how could songs so closely associated with Dylan's experience with Jesus be labeled both "gospel" and "anti-religion"? At first, it seems nonsensical. However, there is precious little doubt that he was debunking the common misconception that he had merely turned to religion in 1979–1981. In an interview he gave in 1979, Dylan shared with journalist Bruce Heiman what he thought were crucial distinctions between Jesus and religion: "Religion is another form of bondage which man invents to get himself to God. But that's why Christ came. Christ didn't preach religion, He preached the Truth, the Way, and the Life. He said he'd come to give life and life more abundantly. He talked about life, not necessarily religion."[9]

In 1983, Dylan was singing the same tune, telling journalist Martin Keller that he still felt the word "religion" had connotations to bondage. This supported the idea that Dylan never trusted in a "religion" or what the word itself, in modern terms, conjures up: "Religion is a dirty word. It doesn't mean anything. Coca-Cola is a religion. Oil and steel are a religion. In the name of religion, people have been raped, killed, and defiled. Today's religion is tomorrow's bondage."[10]

In 1991, as Dylan circled the globe and offered up his anti-religion antidotes in songs like "Gotta Serve Somebody" and "In the Garden," he certainly wasn't enjoying the attention (and often ridicule) he received a decade earlier when the gospel tours were in full swing. In fact, when interviewed by Joe Queenan in 1991, Dylan reflected on the backlash:

"People didn't like those tunes. They rejected all that stuff when my show would be all off the new album [*Slow Train Coming*]. People would shout, 'We want to hear the old songs.'"[11]

How many other rock stars would even consider such a move? An old friend, English folk singer Martin Carthy, made this observation:

"I really do think he's the bravest of the lot, and he really doesn't mind risking everything. . . . No one can accuse him ever of selling out. To stand up and do two weeks of concerts at the Warfield in San Francisco [in 1979] and sing hymns to an audience who wants to hear 'Like a Rolling Stone.' . . . Please tell me, who is he selling out to? I'm so full of admiration. I mean, one day he's a Christian, and then he's a Jew for Jesus. Who gives a f---? He can do what he wants. Especially since it's guaranteed in his Constitution. People have no right to slag him off."[12]

For the record, there was no shortage of interesting stage raps from Dylan in 1991, including this one in February in London, right after "Like a Rolling Stone": "On behalf of me and my band, may the good, old Daddy's face shine on you." (So much for the Aaronic benediction remaining the exclusive domain of "Forever Young.") In the same month, Dylan also informed his audience that "Gotta Serve Somebody" was one of his "early protest songs."

Following the string of London shows in February 1991, Dylan and his entourage flew back to the States. Shortly thereafter, on the evening of the twentieth, Dylan could be found at Radio City Music Hall in New York City. There he would receive a Lifetime Achievement Grammy at the thirty-third annual awards ceremony. After walking onstage during thunderous applause and an orchestra playing his 1966 composition, "I Want You," actor Jack Nicholson paid tribute to his friend:

> With the possible exception of Boston Celtic, Kevin McHale, he was the most famous person ever to leave Hibbing, Minnesota, and with the possible exception of Francis Bellamy, author of "Pledge of Allegiance," he was probably the best-ever poet to graduate from Hibbing High, Class of '59. On my way out here from L.A. as I was crossing the country, its . . . mountains, its rivers, its crimes, its lovers, that he's touched so deeply with his gifts, I was thinking what to say on this opportunity to honor . . . Uncle Bobby [laughs]. So I started leafing through the dictionary [laughs]. All the words seem to apply to him [laughs]. Under P, er, two words down from paradigm, which means model, was the word paradox, the fairest word for him, I think. It means a statement seemingly, self-contradictory, but in reality, possibly expressing a truth. He's been called everything from the voice of his generation to the conscience of the world. He rejects both titles and any others that try to categorize him or analyze him.
>
> He opened the doors of pop music wider than anybody else and yet returned time and again to the simplicity of basic chords and emotions to express himself. He's been, and still is, a disturber of the peace, his own as well as ours. When he talks about himself, it's often guarded and shrouded in mystery or humor, but every so often he allows a peek at the person behind the persona.[13]

Nicholson's comments were followed by a Dylan career retrospective via video clips and then the actor returned to continue his speech.

"When I was a kid growing up in Jersey, er, anybody who was a hoot or really funny or something, er, we'd call them a riot. Ladies and gents, this guy's a riot in more ways than one . . . Bob Dylan."

Then, in front of a worldwide television audience, Dylan launched into "Masters of War." Meanwhile, U.S. bombs were exploding in Iraq. The first Persian Gulf War was under way. A decade later, when asked about his song selection, he curiously told Edna Gundersen of

USA Today that "the song's got nothing to do with being anti-war. It has more to do with the military industrial complex that [President] Eisenhower was talking about."

Beyond the typical jokes about Dylan's singing voice, this particular performance of "Masters of War" in 1991 was especially difficult to decipher. It led a longtime friend to humorously reflect on the rendition given that night. "I don't know why he sang that song in Hebrew on the Grammy Awards," wondered Kinky Friedman. "I asked him about that [later] and he just smiled."[14]

"That song may be retired . . . the flu greeted me that morning in a big way," Dylan explained to Joe Queenan. "All my drainpipes were stopped up. Those kinds of things just happen to me, the night of . . . the night I'm going to be on a big TV show, and the inside of my head was feeling like the Grand Canyon or something. It was not a good night for me. But the song would have come off probably better if my head had been able to get more or less into it."[15]

After Dylan's performance of "Masters of War," Nicholson again joined Dylan onstage and concluded with this:

"Thank you for a constant restlessness that has enabled you to seek newer, better means of expressing the human condition with words and music, and for living your creative life fearlessly and without apology and leading the way no matter how the times changed. The National Academy of Recording Arts and Sciences joins a worldwide network of grateful fans in presenting you this Grammy Lifetime Achievement Award. Congratulations, Bob."[16]

As is (seemingly) always the case with Dylan, even the content of an obligatory acceptance speech wasn't immune from mystery. As millions around the world watched, a fidgety flu-ridden award-winner spoke these words while fiddling with his hat:

"Well, uh, all right . . . Yeah . . . Well, my daddy, he didn't leave me too much; you know, he was a very simple man, and he didn't leave me a lot. But what he told me was this: 'Son,' he said, um . . . [long pause] . . . He said so many things, you know. But he did say, he said,

'It's possible to become so defiled in this world that your own mother and father will abandon you. And if that happens, God will believe in your ability to mend your own ways' . . . Thank you."[17]

Joe Queenan of *Spy* magazine summed up the brief speech as "tantalizing," "inscrutable," and "nuts"[18] while biographer Heylin, tongue securely in cheek, thought Dylan delivered "a typically upbeat message about defilement."[19]

Dylan fan Ronnie Schreiber dug a bit deeper. He discovered some interesting information concerning the content of Dylan's speech:

> At the time of the acceptance speech, I turned to my wife and said that Dylan's comments were an allusion to Psalms 27:10: "When my father and mother abandon me, HaShem (God) will gather me up." . . . I went back to the sources and discovered that Dylan's remarks were almost a verbatim account of the commentary of Rabbi Shimshon Rafael Hirsch (the spiritual leader of traditional Jewry in Germany in the mid-nineteenth century) on that verse: "Even if I were so depraved that my own mother and father would abandon me to my own devices, God would still gather me up and believe in my ability to mend my ways."
>
> Now, I have no way of knowing if Abram Zimmerman really taught this to his son or if Bob simply picked it up from a commentary on the Jewish prayer book (Psalm 27 is recited at the morning and evening prayer services during the month before the Jewish New Year), but in any case, the wording is too similar to Hirsch's to ignore. . . . I didn't get the Hirsch citation from the original source, but rather from the commentary in the Metsudah Tehillim (Psalms) so I'm not sure if the language that Dylan almost quoted verbatim is Rabbi Davis' (who did the translation for Metsudah) or Hirsch's. Since the same comment can be found in the Metsudah *Daily Siddur* and the Metsudah Siddur has been popular with *ba'alei tshuvah*, my guess is that Dylan picked it up from the siddur.[20]

Although generally known for ferociously guarding his family's privacy, after tipping his hat to his dad during his acceptance speech, he showed up at the post-show Grammy party with a rather unusual (but honorable) date: his mom.

Years later, a journalist inquired about this very night at the 1991 Grammys, asking what was going through Dylan's mind as he delivered the speech. "I don't remember the time and place my father said that to me, and maybe he didn't say it to me in that exact way," Dylan told Mikal Gilmore of *Rolling Stone*: "I was probably paraphrasing the whole idea, really—I'm not even sure I paraphrased in the proper context. It might've been something that just sort of popped in my head at that time."

Although it may have simply been improvisation, Gilmore still wondered if the speech could be interpreted as a personal statement, or if it was just Dylan describing the world around him. "I was thinking more in terms of, like, we're living in a Machiavellian world, whether we like it or we don't. Any act that's immoral, as long as it succeeds, it's all right," Dylan dryly replied. "To apply that type of meaning to the way I was feeling that night probably has more to do with it than any kind of conscious effort to bring out some religiosity, or any kind of biblical saying about God, one way or another."[21]

Additionally, Dylan reminded readers how he was very sick with a high fever that night and also became disillusioned with the music industry because of how he was handled at the Grammys (excepting Jack Nicholson, whom he praised)—including how a number of unnamed artists were scheduled to show up, but ultimately backed out for various reasons. "I just lost all respect for them. There's a few that are decent and God-fearing and will stand up in a righteous way," Dylan observed, "but I wouldn't want to count on most of them."[22]

Not long after the Grammys, in March of 1991, *The Bootleg Series: Volumes 1-3* was released, a compilation of songs which showcased a number of Dylan's unreleased recordings from 1960 to 1989—and by its very title, paid homage to three decades of illegal bootlegs. Dylan's own publicist, Elliot Mintz, interviewed him about the release and here is how Dylan chroniclers Mike Wyvill and John Wraith highlighted the exchange:

> [Mintz made] a number of unsuccessful attempts to pin Dylan down on the circumstances behind the creation of some of his songs. Clearly, Bob was never going to warm readily to such interrogation. The mood of the interview can be captured by considering the last question. A struggling Mintz painstakingly, and at length, tries to elicit some message for the masses from Dylan. The reply? "Don't forget to look over their shoulder, something might be coming . . . like a train."[23]

Included in the first volume of *The Bootleg Series* were outtakes like "Ye Shall Be Changed" (a *Slow Train Coming* outtake), where Dylan gives a lyrical nod to the Jewish-born Apostle Paul's letter to the first-century church in Corinth, describing how believers will be transformed in "the twinkling of an eye, when the last trumpet blows."

In "You Changed My Life" (a *Shot of Love* outtake), Dylan sings about the God who mercifully invaded his personal life. He sarcastically refers to those who don't have time for things such as salvation; these same folks, when discussion of the topic is brought up, are prone to sudden fits of weariness and, of course, have a million other things to do. The song also describes the apparent wholeness of Dylan's salvation experience at the time, lyrically describing Jesus in a variety of ways: Lord, Savior, companion, friend, heart-fixer, mind-regulator, true, Creator, Comforter, and joy.

John Bauldie, who penned the album's liner notes, expressed these thoughts about the selection of "You Changed My Life": "Here's a powerful, compelling religious song, expressing heartfelt thanks to the Lord for having turned the singer's life around."[24]

Another inclusion on *The Bootleg Series* is "Lord Protect My Child," an outtake from Dylan's 1983 album, *Infidels*, which amounts to another heartfelt song/prayer. Whether written for one or all of his children, the sentiment remains the same: in a world filled with the tragic, depressing consequences of sin, an earnest plea is made to God for the protection of his child.

As for the lyrical smorgasbord of "Foot of Pride" (another outtake from *Infidels*), Edna Gundersen of *USA Today* wrote that it was "elliptical...brimming with biblical references" and "equals his best Christianity-themed songs."[25]

After hearing Dylan offer up "Gotta Serve Somebody" in Boston in May 1991, journalist Steve Morse of the *Boston Globe* wrote this: "during the funk-extended 'You Gotta Serve Somebody,' from his late '70s born-again Christian phase, he smiled again at the line 'You might be high' (an accurate assessment of some of the crowd)."[26]

Questions of audience sobriety aside, if Dylan's belief in Jesus was the ubiquitous "phase," then why even bother singing "Gotta Serve Somebody"? Dylan's faith in mere religion was never really the issue, as evidenced—at the same concert in Boston—by these comments before "In the Garden": "This is one of my anti-religion songs right here."

On May 24, 1991, Bob Dylan turned fifty, a fact that caused U2 lead singer Bono to submit a poem—"50 Reasons Why I Love Bob Dylan"—to *The Sunday Tribune*. The poem was published and here are eight of Bono's fifty reasons: "He's interested in names God gave animals. He is not pseudo-religious. He didn't die on a cross at thirty-three. T-Bone Burnett likes him. He's Jewish. He's a good story teller. He's singing better than ever. He is not dead."

Author and journalist Steve Turner asked Dylan friends and admirers what they might give him or wish for him on his birthday. Here are a handful of the responses:

> PETE SEEGER: A little peace and quiet and an invisible cloak that would enable him to go wherever he wanted without being hassled.
>
> JOHNNY CASH: Peace of mind.
>
> LITTLE RICHARD: Longevity both as a person and as an artist. I would also buy more paper for him to write more great poetry.
>
> MICK JAGGER: After seeing him on the Grammy Awards, I'd get him a new hat and a good song.

> ALLEN GINSBERG: I'd suggest that the major media commission lengthy essays that examine Dylan's works as a minstrel, sympathetically accounting the progression of his phases of interest, empathetically tracing his technical, ethical, religious, and political moves in a reasonable way, absent of smart-aleck cynicism, motivated by an admiration for his obvious intelligence, abundance, maintenance of dignified privacy and ability to manifest humane changes of spirit and thought—that he be accorded the same dignities as Yeats, Eliot, Stevens, Bunting, Pound and other twentieth-century poetic peers.[27]

Author Alan Jacobs noted Dylan's odd place in the rock 'n' roll pantheon when he wrote these words:

> In 1991, when *Rolling Stone* interviewed Dylan on the occasion of his fiftieth birthday, he gave a curious response when the interviewer asked him if he was happy. He fell silent for a few moments and stared at his hands. "You know," he said, "these are yuppie words, happiness and unhappiness. It's not happiness or unhappiness, it's either blessed or unblessed. As the Bible says, 'Blessed is the man who walketh not in the counsel of the ungodly.'" It is pleasurable to contemplate the reaction of the typical *Rolling Stone* subscriber to that comment. Here, at least, is a voice connected to something more than the speaker's conviction of his own virtue. For a long time now Dylan has reminded his generation, and anyone else who cares to listen, that the enormous self-confidence they had in the Sixties proved to be misplaced: the self that trusts in the righteousness of its own "indignant perception" must eventually discover that it does not inhabit a house of many mansions, but rather a place in which there's not room enough to be anywhere.[28]

Larry Yudelson, like Alan Jacobs, perceived Dylan to be an anomaly in the world of popular rock music. "The age of fifty, taught the sages of Mishna, is the age of counsel," Yudelson reminded. "Other rock stars of his generation may still be singing silly love songs, but Dylan seems, in his elusive way, to be counseling, even during the Grammy Awards where he preached, in the name of his father."[29]

On the very day of Dylan's fiftieth birthday, Senator Joe Lieberman of Massachusetts devoted several minutes on the Senate floor to a speech that expressed how much the singer and his work meant to him and America. "For me and so many others of my generation, Bob Dylan—together with John F. Kennedy—signaled a great change in our world, heralding a new frontier, while the old order is rapidly fadin'," said the forty-nine-year-old senator. "President Kennedy's death may have cut short our advance to that frontier, but Dylan played on as society erupted in great social ferment, matching the power of words with the power of music."

Less than a month after his 1991 birthday: Dylan informed an audience in Bad Mergentheim, Germany, prior to singing "Gotta Serve Somebody": "Now here's my anti-religion song. You know there's a new hit song out called 'Losing My Religion.' You can't lose what you never had. Well, this ["Gotta Serve Somebody"] is an anti-religion song."

Not unrelated were Dylan's onstage comments, on July 11, 1991, in Wantagh, New York, when he said this before "I Believe in You": "Alright, here's a song…everybody is looking for something to believe in. Some got this, some got that. Everybody's got something."

When it comes to embracing beliefs, some sit comfortably in the seat of scoffers. Take, for example, in September 1991, when journalist Greg Potter reviewed *The Worst Rock 'N' Roll Records of All Time* (a book by Jimmy Guterman and Owen O'Donnell). He informed readers of how the book succeeded in slaughtering various sacred cows. Potter writes of how "special chapters are set aside for subjects such as 'Twenty Ideas That Bob Dylan Should Have Thrown Into the Garbage.'" Besides the person of Joan Baez and the music video to the 1985 song, "Tight Connection to My Heart," Judaism and Christianity also make the garbage list. So much for tolerance.

On September 15, 1991, with guitar in hand, Dylan appeared for the third time on Chabad's annual telethon, this time alongside old friend Kinky Friedman for a performance of "Sold American." As they belted out Friedman's song, both donned their respective black cowboy hats. Prior to the song, Dylan spoke to the audience, encouraged people to contribute and thanked the rabbis who were present. He continued to have no problem embracing his Jewish heritage and a good cause.

Some might accuse Dylan of an aforementioned spiritual schizophrenia, considering that in the same year he appeared on the telethon, he was trotting out his Jesus-centered songs like "Gotta Serve Somebody" (ninety-one times), "I Believe in You" (twenty-nine times), and "In the Garden" (ten times). But an accusation like this is likely based on an ignorance of Dylan's history, the interviews he's given, and what it might mean for a Jewish person to believe in Jesus. It needs to be said that many of the songs Dylan sings in concert should not be construed as "religious" or "spiritual"—no problem there—but he has never neglected those songs which easily, and happily, can.

Toward the end of 1991, when Robert Hilburn of the *Los Angeles Times* asked about the puzzle of Dylan's cultural impact as an artist, the fifty-year-old singer shared these words: "There's no one to my knowledge that isn't surprised by their longevity, including myself, but it's very dangerous to plan [far ahead], because you are just dealing with your vanity. Tomorrow is hard enough. It's God who gives you the freedom, and the days you should be most concerned with are today and tomorrow."[30]

Dylan also addressed his perceived relationship with his audiences: "Older people—people my age—don't come out anymore. A lot of shows over the years were people coming out of curiosity and their curiosity wasn't fulfilled. They weren't transported back to the '60s. Lightning didn't strike. The shows didn't make sense for them, and they didn't make sense for me. That had to stop, and it took a long time to stop it. A lot of people in the past were coming out to see 'The Legend,' and I was trying to just get on stage and play music."

When the subject of "I Believe in You" came up, Dylan said this to Hilburn: "That song is just about overcoming hardship." Some of its lyrics certainly expressed the hardship Dylan faced after proclaiming his faith in Jesus some twelve years earlier.

Writer Martin Grossman has documented some of the pressures Dylan was contending with at the time:

"One Chabad rabbi from Toronto had written me earlier of his efforts to contact Bob through a letter hand-delivered to him by someone who knew them both. Elie Wiesel wrote to me [and said] he had considered Dylan's conversion a tragedy and hoped that efforts to reach him would succeed. . . . Evidently attempts to communicate with Dylan began to have an effect. Sara Dylan (the former Shirley Noznisky), who was divorced from him not long before his conversion, remarked to the press that Bob had tried hard to convert his family and friends at first, but had had a change of heart around that time [1983] that had been a relief to everyone."[31]

Contextually, this makes sense in light of Dylan's comments to Kurt Loder after the *Rolling Stone* reporter asked this question in 1984:

"When you meet up with Orthodox [Jewish] people, can you sit down with them and say, 'Well, you should really check out Christianity'?" "Well, yeah, if somebody asks me, I'll tell 'em," Dylan responded. "But, you know, I'm not gonna just offer my opinion. I'm more about playing music, you know."[32]

Dylan may have been the reluctant prophet, but the songs he chose to sing often seemed to express his allegiances, and did some of his talking for him. Take, for example, his summer 1992 recording sessions in Chicago with fellow Jew and longtime friend David Bromberg. Amid a number of songs from the folk and blues traditions (as well as some Bromberg compositions) Dylan included "Rise Again," a more contemporary song, which had debuted during the gospel tours. In fact, it was a Dallas Holm composition which was, in 1977, a top-charting hit in Christian music circles. In 1980–1981, the song featured an arrangement of Dylan on the piano, sharing vocals with Clydie King. For the 1992 studio version, a gospel choir from Chicago (more than twenty people) was brought in to augment the performance.

Clinton Heylin, in his book, *Bob Dylan: The Recording Sessions*, wrote this about its inclusion: "'Rise Again' certainly stands as an intriguing choice given the lack of ambiguity in the song's message. . . . Doubtless some half-wit will now claim that Dylan recorded this song in 1992 because he liked the melody, and not because he was unashamedly endorsing its sentiments!"[33]

What were the sentiments of "Rise Again"? Its first-person perspective revealed Jesus:

"Go ahead, drive the nails in My hands, laugh at me where you stand. . . . There's no power on earth can tie me down / Yes I'll rise again—death can't keep me in the ground / Go ahead and mock my name—my love for you is still the same. . . . 'Cause I'll come again—there's no power on earth can keep me back / Yes I'll come again—come to take My people back / Go ahead and say I'm dead and gone / But you will see that you were wrong."[34]

During this same year of 1992, Dylan sang "I Believe in You" on a few occasions, including one not long after the recording sessions with Bromberg. And like the maddening juxtaposition (for some) of "Go Down Moses" and "In the Garden" at his Tel Aviv concert some five years earlier, Dylan apparently didn't see any contradiction in his 1992 covering of "Little Moses" more than sixty times in concert alongside the latter-day compositions of "I Believe in You" and "Rise Again" (in concert, and in the studio, respectively).

"Little Moses," a traditional song sketching out the life story of God's chosen servant, may have received its stage debut in Adelaide, Australia, on March 21, 1992, but Dylan's history with the song went back much further. As we will soon see, he told one journalist that he used to play the song at the Gerde's club in Greenwich Village (1961–1962) and another report revealed him recording the song during a session for the much-maligned 1970 release, *Self Portrait*.[35]

Furthermore, in 1975, "Little Moses" was also included in a rehearsal for the Rolling Thunder tour, a recording that found its way into another maligned Dylan project—this time the 1978 film, *Renaldo and Clara*. Prior to its release, Dylan shared these thoughts about "Little

Moses" with Jonathan Cott of *Rolling Stone*:

> I used to play that song when I performed at Gerde's Folk City. It's an old Carter Family song, and it goes something like: 'Away by the waters so wide / The ladies were winding their way / When Pharaoh's little daughter / Stepped down in the water / To bathe in the cool of the day / And before it got dark / She opened the ark / And saw the sweet infant so gay.' Then Little Moses grows up, slays the Egyptian, leads the Jews—it's a great song. And I thought it fit pretty well into the movie [*Renaldo and Clara*]. Everybody's in the film: the Carter Family, Hank Williams, Woody Guthrie, Beethoven. Who is going to understand this film? Where are the people to understand this film—a film which needs no understanding.[36]

As the 1992 tour returned to the States, longtime friend T-Bone Burnett was an onstage guest at Dylan's concert in San Jose, California, on May 9, reportedly playing guitar on "Idiot Wind" and "The Times They Are A-Changin'." Around the same time period, Burnett granted an interview to Sharon Gallagher of *Radix* magazine, where there was this exchange:

> GALLAGHER: Whatever happened to Bob Dylan? There was a big brouhaha about his conversion, and all his secular fans were disappointed. Then they said, "Now he's Jewish again and everybody can relax."
>
> BURNETT: That whole thing from the beginning to the end was basically a media event. Someone gave me a tape of a show he did—I think in 1961 when he was nineteen or twenty years old—at Carnegie Recital Hall. One of the things he said on the tape was, "I believe in the Ten Commandments. The first commandment, I am the Lord thy God, is a great commandment. I believe that, as long as it's not the wrong people saying it," which, I think, is the same thing he was saying during the time when there was the big uproar about him. In other words, I'd say the whole story of Bob Dylan is one man's search

> for God. The turns and the steps he takes to find God are his business. I think he went to a study group at the Vineyard, and it created a lot of excitement. But he had written a song in the '60s called "Sign on the Cross": "I'm not going to get into an argument with anyone about the relative merits of Judaism and Christianity, and what it means for a Jewish kid to be a Christian—I'm just not interested in that argument. If it is true that we have a personal relationship with God, then that's enough for me."[37]

Looking back on 1992, civil rights activist, retired minister, Dylan fan, and author Bert Cartwright updated his 1985 book, *The Bible in the Lyrics of Bob Dylan*. In it, Cartwright made the case that you cannot fully appreciate Dylan's artistic career if you wholly ignore the influence of the Bible:

> Deep in his psyche remained the Jewish hope of history's fulfillment. First exploring the Bible's apocalyptic imagery from an artistic perspective of potent symbol, Dylan eventually adopted a quite literal understanding of the way God would get even with evil and, with His chosen few, prevail. Such an understanding of history wells up from the depths of a Jewish heritage that rehearsed each year within the family the liberating exodus of God's people from bondage. It is this understanding of history embedded deep in Dylan's Jewish heritage that haunts him with questions of justice in the face of a growing despair for the human transformation of the world.
>
> Ultimately there remains for Bob Dylan a tension between viewing the Bible as an artist and the Bible as a source of ultimate revelation. An artist tends to use the Bible freely for its rich imagery and insights, not worrying about literal teachings. The believer approaches the Bible as the ultimate revelation of God, which leads to the hope of salvation and a way of living. As a believing artist, Bob Dylan seeks to resolve the tension by expressing the human condition before God with artistic skill. He seeks to be in the world but not of the world. Whatever the verdict ultimately is as to Dylan's success in integrating

faith and art, a consideration of his use of the Bible cannot but be at the core of such evaluations.[38]

In June of 1993, Dylan revisited the Holy Land, performing before crowds in Tel Aviv, Beersheba, and Haifa. Included were biblically-inspired numbers like "I and I," "Little Moses," and "Cat's in the Well," the latter his then most-recent song, with a concluding line of "May the Lord have mercy on us all." His encores in Beersheba and Haifa had him slipping into reluctant prophet mode with his anthem "It Ain't Me, Babe." Mike Wyvill and John Wraith issued this report: "Prior to the first show, Dylan and the band visited the Wailing Wall in the early hours of the morning, accompanied by a sub-machine-wielding Israeli policeman."[39]

The album releases of *Good As I Been to You* (1992) and *World Gone Wrong* (1993) represented the first time in Dylan's career where consecutive albums consisted of non-original songs—not to mention an all-out return to the roots music he so enjoyed and absorbed as a young singer coming up in the coffeehouses of Minneapolis and Greenwich Village. If any fans felt cheated, Dylan made up for it with raw, out-and-out, heartfelt music (and some cryptic liner notes from the latter of the two albums). In covering Doc Watson's version of "Lone Pilgrim" on *World Gone Wrong*, Dylan explained why he liked the song:

> What attracts me to the song is how the lunacy of trying to fool the self is set aside at some given point. Salvation and the needs of mankind are prominent and hegemony takes a breathing spell. "My soul flew to mansions on high." Technology to wipe out truth is now available. Not everybody can afford it but it's available. When the price comes down, look out! There won't be songs like these anymore.[40]

"My soul flew to mansions on high," a lyric owing a debt to the words of Jesus, seemed connected to Dylan's lament about technology wiping out truth—an expression of the perceived reality that there were obstacles to salvation but that the old, tried-and-true American song could get someone headed in the right direction.

Additionally, in the liner notes to the traditional song "Delia," there is this theological diversion when Dylan speaks of a character he perceives in the song:

"He's not interested in mosques on the temple mount, Armageddon or World War III, doesn't put his face in his knees & weep & wears no dunce hat, makes no apology & is doomed to obscurity."[41]

The references to "mosques on the temple mount, Armageddon, and World War III" allude to the time-honored conflict in the Middle East and prophetic scenarios which some have interpreted from the Bible, a subject Dylan broached in lyrics and interviews, particularly between 1979 and 1981. Gary Hill, the only journalist to interview Dylan in 1993, perhaps captured some of the spiritual leanings of the fifty-two-year-old singer-songwriter when he wrote these words:

"Still a moral critic and crusader after all these years Dylan hopes his new album will nourish those who, like him, hear a lot of bad music and see a lot of bad values nowadays. He says *World Gone Wrong* offers the kind of truth-telling roots music young people are hungering for. 'It's underground,' he says. 'There are young people who are fed up with what they hear.' He says pop radio no longer plays music he cares about and country singers today are 'polluted and unclean' because they're too far from their 'hillbilly' roots. . . . Dylan who prefers not to pin down his personal brand of religion, is glad 'God was still in the schools' in his youth. 'A person without faith is like a walking corpse. And now people have to fight to get the faith back, especially in schools.' He says his religious education gave him a moral base. . . . But 'dues-paying religions,' he says, 'aren't really the essence of godly.'"[42]

Not long after Hill's article appeared, journalist Guy Garcia wrote a piece in *The New York Times* which focused on a common trend among younger artists and groups—a trend that reflected their spiritual longings in their songs. When Garcia solicited a comment from Dylan, he received this pithy remark: "People are lost because they can believe anything."[43]

Was there a narrow way that had been lost? Had too many choices confused matters? Was an ultimate truth attainable? Was it even a relevant thing to discuss? During a 1985 interview with Cameron Crowe, Dylan alluded to the words of Jesus—"Repent, the kingdom of God is at hand"—and observed how the sentiment didn't sit too well with many folks:

"They'd like to avoid that. Tell that to someone and you become their enemy. There does come a time, though, when you have to face facts and the truth is true whether you wanna believe it or not. It doesn't need you to make it true...that lie about everybody having their own truth inside of them has done a lot of damage."[44]

Garcia included in his article Dylan's quip that "a person without faith is like a walking corpse." This notion didn't exactly sit well with one Richard Harland Smith who vigorously responded in a letter to the *New York Times* that included these lines:

"Guy Garcia's article 'Rock Finds Religion Again' emphasizes the tragic rift separating the religious from the non-religious (or from the religions based in contradictory mythology). The remark by the former free-thinker and born-again curmudgeon Bob Dylan that 'people without faith are like walking corpses' chillingly illustrates the failure of the faithful to comprehend anything beyond their own persuasion."

Smith went on to cite no less than the Inquisition; the Crusades; the persecution of the Bahais in Iran; the Catholic-Protestant divide in Northern Ireland; the Jewish-Palestinian conflict in Israel; and singer Cat Stevens' support for the bounty put upon the head of author Salman Rushdie.

"For children of the '60s, this can be a difficult pill to swallow," concluded Smith, "but it serves us right for investing our trust in the malleable fancies of popular entertainers."[45]

In 1992–1993, Dylan may have extolled the virtues of others' songs and their ability to spiritually nourish, but he still couldn't escape the fact that many still looked to him for fulfillment. In 1994, Ellen Futterman broached the legend issue, asking, "Having had three decades to adjust, are you more comfortable being a living legend?" Dylan responded, "I try to be an illuminated person. Nobody should put anyone on a pedestal—it really can damage a person's mentality and lead to ignorance. At that point, a person ceases to be a person."[46]

Perhaps columnist Tony Norman captured the spirit of idolatry best when he attended a 1994 concert in Pittsburgh and recorded his thoughts: "Dylan performed his moving meditation on the passion of Jesus, 'In the Garden,' and turned what was already a fairly rowdy audience into an ecstatic mob at an open air revival meeting: 'Did they know He was the Son of God / Did they know He was Lord.' Maybe the sold-out audience didn't know that Jesus was the Lord, but they were pretty sure that Bob Dylan came close."[47]

Incidentally, this concert in Pittsburgh was only two months after Lubavitcher Rebbe Menachem Schneerson died at age ninety-two, leaving behind in his wake those who felt he was/is the Messiah—as well as devout followers who did not subscribe to this view. If anyone wondered whether Dylan, along the way, thought Schneerson was indeed the Messiah—because of Dylan's association with Chabad—Dylan's singing of "In the Garden" on numerous occasions into 1994 communicates *something*. For all of Dylan's delightfully ambiguous lyrics over the decades, the lyrics to "In The Garden" are unquestionably straightforward: Jesus is Lord. Dylan has never publicly spoken about Schneerson, but if he felt Schneerson was The Man, one would think he might go out of his way to inform the public of his convictions. He did so in 1979–1981. Why not in 1994?

Earlier in 1994, Dylan had prefaced "In the Garden" with these words (echoing what he repeatedly said onstage back in 1986, prior to the same song): "Everybody has a hero. Here's a song about my hero."[48]

Of course not everyone interpreted Dylan's words as an affirmation of a continuing faith in Jesus. Take, for example, Rabbi Laurence Schlesinger. In 1994, he viewed Dylan's prefacing "In the Garden" with the word "hero" as a far cry, theologically, from Dylan's descriptions of Jesus (in 1979–1981) as the "the solid rock made before the foundation of the world."[49] This seemed to argue that because Dylan had not sung "Solid Rock" since 1981, he was no longer tuned into its theology.

However, "Solid Rock" and "In the Garden" were off the same album (*Saved*) and certainly shared the same theology (for the record, years later, Dylan dusted off "Solid Rock" and brought it back to the concert stage).

During a touring hiatus in September 1994, Dylan penned the foreword to his book of drawings, *Drawn Blank*. Consisting mostly of pencil sketches, they were, according to Dylan, "done over a two or three year period from about 1989 to about 1991 or 1992 in various locations mainly to relax and refocus a restless mind."[50]

The Dylan fanzine *On the Tracks* noted that a cross appeared in the background of one of Dylan's sketches with "Jesus" inscribed on the horizontal beam and "Saves" on the vertical beam.[51] Perhaps a reminder of redemption served to relax and refocus a restless mind accustomed to landscapes from inside a tour bus or motel room.

In the fall of 1995, journalist John Dolen questioned Dylan specifically on a lyric from "Precious Angel," a lyric written in the same year he received Jesus.

> DOLEN: I remember the lines, "You were telling him about Buddha / You were telling him about Muhammad in one breath / But you never mentioned one time the man who came / and died a criminal's death." Those were fearless words. How do you feel about those words and the songs you wrote during that period now?
>
> DYLAN: Just writing a song like that probably emancipated me from other kinds of illusions. I can't say that I would disagree with that line. On its own level, it was some kind of turning point for me, writing that.

Dolen concluded his interview by asking Dylan if he still saw a slow train coming. "When I look ahead now it's picked up quite a bit of speed," said Dylan. "In fact, it's going like a freight train now."[52]

Here we have, in 1995, a familiar echo of a comment Dylan made before singing "Slow Train" at his final concert at the Warfield Theater in San Francisco in 1979: "This is called 'Slow Train Coming.' It's been coming for a long time and it's picking up speed."

Following his midnight telephone interview with Dylan in 1995,

John Dolen reflected on the experience and shared his perception of what went down:

> The quality of his voice surprised me; while not soft, it was not loud and not the slightest bit hoarse or raspy. Another thing that struck me later was somewhat of a revelation. Dylan is not an intellectual. He is wise, but he is more folksy than cerebral. In other words, he talks like a musician, which shouldn't be surprising because that's what he is. But being a little more on the bookish side myself, I was struck by this and realized I had put my own trappings on what he is, just as others have throughout the years. The final impression I have of him is that at times he spoke like a prophet, with that elliptical logic reminiscent of the biblical teachers, and that same sense of cutting to the core meaning of things. He did all this without pretense, without affectation, and with professional respect for where I was coming from.[53]

A week after his chat with John Dolen, Dylan reportedly rambled into a Yom Kippur service at the Temple Beth El synagogue in West Palm Beach, Florida. Journalist Scott Benarde picked up the story:

> You would have thought Elijah had come through the door as worshippers who recognized him did double takes. Say what you want about Bob 'Robert Zimmerman' Dylan's late-1970s experience as a born-again Christian, the enigmatic superstar's real roots were showing. Dylan's synagogue appearance made the local papers. It also made local Jews proud. It did not make national news, which is probably how Dylan, who likes maintaining an air of mystery, preferred it.[54]

Benarde's reference to Dylan's "real roots" pointed out the perceived incompatibility of Jewish roots and a belief in Jesus. "Interestingly, 'In the Garden' was featured on the October 6, 1995 set list [three days after the synagogue visit]—the second post-Yom Kippur concert," wrote Larry Yudelson, founder of the Tangled Up in Jews website. Yudelson maintained that this particular song from the *Saved* album "still stands as the strongest argument that Dylan has not decisively abandoned Christianity."[55]

A few weeks later, after taking in a Dylan concert in Houston, Texas, journalist Rick Mitchell was ultimately puzzled by a certain song choice:

"The most dated song in the whole two-hour set was 'In the Garden,' the sole surviving representative of Dylan's gospel period in the early '80s. While Dylan's apparent embrace of fundamentalist Christianity alienated many of his longtime fans, it briefly rejuvenated his song-writing with a dose of righteous anger. Unfortunately, 'In the Garden' is not one of his more memorable efforts from this period, and the band struggled with the awkward rhythm and chord structure. Dylan's continued fondness for the song was as puzzling as the omission of several of his longtime crowd-pleasers, from 'Like a Rolling Stone' to 'Knockin' on Heaven's Door.'"[56]

For the record, Mitchell is not accurate when he speaks of "In the Garden" as being the "sole surviving representative" of Dylan's gospel period; as concert-goers will attest, "Gotta Serve Somebody" and "I Believe in You" have also survived. To be fair, Mitchell was at least aware of "In the Garden." This probably cannot be said for the average reviewer who attends a Dylan concert. According to the singer, it is one of his favorite songs even though it is "lesser known," as he acknowledged from a stage in 1991.

In 1996, one journalist pondered the historically lethal combination of twenty-seven-year-olds who happen to be musical icons: Janis Joplin, Jimi Hendrix, Kurt Cobain, and others. Looking back in hypothetical retrospect, Michael Sweeney couldn't help but think of Dylan: "Advantages of dying at 27: Death after *Blonde on Blonde* [in 1966] leaves Dylan as a mysterious, cosmic figure; no 'born again' period."[57]

One man who appreciated Dylan's work long after the heyday of the mid-1960s—"Almost every record has some colossal classic"[58]—was Allen Ginsberg. On April 5, 1997, Dylan received news of his longtime friend's death. The legendary poet died in his apartment in New York's Greenwich Village at age seventy following a stroke and a long bout with liver cancer. Ginsberg's spiritual advisor, a Buddhist, was reportedly at his deathbed.

Fittingly, while onstage in Moncton, New Brunswick, on April 5, Dylan dedicated his 1965 epic, "Desolation Row," to his old friend and followed the song with these words: "A friend of mine passed away, I guess this morning. That was one of his favorite songs...poet Allen Ginsberg...Allen, that was for you."

On May 21, 1997, Dylan made an appearance at the Beverly Hilton Hotel in Los Angeles to participate in a charity benefit for the Wiesenthal Center. The center has a museum on its grounds and offers educational programs throughout the year that expose thousands of children and adults to the historical atrocities of the Holocaust. Some 1,100 guests arrived for the benefit and, before leaving, donated 1.6 million dollars to the cause.

According to Robert Eshman, the evening included dinner and entertainment and was a "deliriously effulgent affair" and symbolic of the diverse outreach of the Los Angeles Jewish community and the Wiesenthal Center. "In what other town," asked Eshman, "could you draw a lineup that included actor Michael Douglas, comedian Chris Rock, a packed crowd of top Hollywood executives, several heroes of the Holocaust, a reformed neo-Nazi skinhead, and Bob Dylan, who came out on stage to sing perfectly three perfect songs? . . . After Chris Rock came Dylan. Imagine that. He sang [those] three songs, beautifully, coherently, acoustically, ending with 'Forever Young.' Then he was gone, like a dream, leaving, by his decree, no pictures and no video."[59]

As for Dylan's three-song set, it consisted of his debut of an old country song "Stone Walls and Steel Bars," a Stanley Brothers staple that would soon be introduced in future tours; a classic 1962 Dylan original "Masters of War" (absent the verse—"Jesus would never forgive what you do"—ever since his experience of 1979); and, as Eshman noted, "Forever Young," a song reportedly penned for Dylan's youngest son, Jakob.

A mere four days after the Wiesenthal Center performance came Dylan's highly publicized hospitalization due to severe chest pains. The official medical diagnosis was pericarditis, brought on by histoplasmosis—a swelling of tissue around the heart. Doctors prescribed medication and rest. Meanwhile, wild rumors about the state of Dylan's health circulated, ranging from heart attack to even death. Although the illness was potentially fatal (in rare cases involving massive infection), Dylan's life was not in danger.

Following his release from the hospital, Dylan released a statement that included this eyebrow-raising sentence: "I really thought I'd be seeing Elvis soon."[60] Author Alan Jacobs observed that this was "a remark that in its substitution of Elvis for Jesus is both a witty reflection on American culture's uncertainty about the identity of the true King and a tantalizing comment on Dylan's own religious pilgrimage."[61]

The hospital visit even prompted a public statement from Columbia Records on June 2, 1997: "Bob Dylan was released from the hospital this weekend where he had been undergoing medical tests and subsequent treatment for pericarditis brought on by histoplasmosis. He was admitted on May 25. Doctors are continuing to treat him and are confident that Mr. Dylan will make a full recovery in four to six weeks."

The recovery period did require the cancellation of an already-planned summer tour in Europe with Van Morrison, but, after more than two months of rest, Dylan and his band were back at it again. "I was off my feet for six weeks," Dylan told Edna Gundersen of *USA Today*, "I'm still taking medication three times a day. I did get the doctors' okay to do this tour."[62]

Dylan would later explain to journalist Murray Engleheart what happened: "It was something called histoplasmosis that came from just accidentally inhaling a bunch of stuff that was out on one of the rivers by where I live. Maybe one month, or two to three days out of the year, the banks around the river get all mucky, and then the wind blows and a bunch of swirling mess is in the air. I happened to inhale a bunch of that. That's what made me sick. It went into my heart area, but it wasn't anything really attacking my heart."[63]

Within a few months of his release from the hospital, rumors abounded that Dylan would be singing before, of all people, the pope, and the rumor proved true as Dylan was one of the musical guests invited to a concert which capped off an annual weeklong event entitled the World Eucharistic Congress. Some three weeks before the event, Dylan managed this wry comment: "The Pope, huh? I guess if the Vatican is reporting it, it must be happening."[64]

On September 27, 1997, an estimated 200,000 to 400,000 people gathered for the concert in Bologna, Italy. An overactive imagination would seem to be required to believe that Dylan's appearance meant an "endorsement" of Catholicism or of the pope himself. However, the historical figure of Jesus and the symbolism of His body and blood that loomed behind this Eucharistic week were things familiar to Dylan, and, arguably, carried personal weight and meaning. Considering a chapter of the American Atheists took the trouble to picket Dylan's 1979 gospel gigs in Tucson, Arizona, one would think that someone would have alerted their Bologna comrades about this presumably equally dreadful day in 1997. But not a peep of protest was heard—at least from any atheist corner.

There was a humorous moment when *People Weekly* reported that "despite objections from Vatican critics, one of whom labeled Dylan a Communist, the Pope reportedly chose the aging rocker to perform."[65]

Unlike his appearance at the Simon Wiesenthal Center some four months earlier—an appearance more conducive to privacy, thus his reported decree of no pictures and no video seemed reasonable—there would be no escaping the camera's eye at this gargantuan outdoor event in Bologna, Italy. And there certainly would be no escaping the endless interpretations and commentary on why Dylan was there in the first place.

Besides the report that it was the pope himself who chose Dylan, event organizer Ernest Vecchi, a vicar in the Bologna Archdiocese, shed some light on the invitation: "We chose him as the representative of the best type of rock. He has a spiritual nature . . . his music is true and beautiful. The Church welcomes whatever is true and beautiful and good. Bob Dylan is one of the best representatives of a highly poetic and spiritual rock music."[66]

Queen Esther Marrow, a gospel singer who recorded and toured with Dylan from 1985 to 1987 and opened the Bologna concert, considered Dylan to be a "great writer" and valued the friendship of a man who "believes that there is a God and writes about this."[67]

After Marrow opened the concert with her performance, the Harlem Gospel Singers (a group Marrow founded in 1992) followed, along with Adriano Celentano, Barbara Colla, and Gianni. Catholic youth then recited Dylan's "Forever Young" in Italian, a performance that drew some papal applause. Then Lucio Dalto, Michael Petrucchaini and Andrea Bocelli all followed with their respective sets.[68] After the youth reappeared and recited the lyrical questions posed by Dylan's song "Blowin' in the Wind," the pope responded with a twenty-minute sermon that included this challenge:

"You've asked me, 'How many roads must a man walk down before he becomes a man?.' . . . I answer you, 'One!' There is only one road for a man, and it is Christ, who said, 'I am the Life.'"[69]

The pope's comments here were eerily reminiscent of an onstage rap that Dylan delivered in Albuquerque, New Mexico, on December 5, 1979:

"I told you 'The Times They Are A-Changin,' and they did. I said the answer was 'Blowin' in the Wind,' and it was. I'm telling you now Jesus is coming back, and he is. And there is no other way of salvation. I know around here you got a lot of people putting mess on you in all kinda ways, so you don't even know which way to believe. There's only one way to believe, there's only one Way, the Truth, and the Life. It took a long time to figure that out before it did come to me, and I hope it doesn't take you that long."[70]

As for the pope's comments, author James Carroll seemed to think they were not only irresponsible but deceptive: "As if justifying the presence of Bob Dylan and, not incidentally, defending Dylan's now renounced conversion, John Paul raised the epic question: 'How many roads must a man walk down / Before you call him a man?' And he answered it: 'One!' There is only one road for man, and it is Christ, who said, 'I Am the Life.' . . . Thus, at the Dylan concert, John Paul II was claiming for Jesus only what the earliest Church claimed for him—the claim which Jews dissent."[71]

If by "earliest Church" Carroll means the general body of believers in the first century, then it would be more accurate to say *most* Jews dissented; however, it is also true that many of the earliest followers of Jesus were, in fact, Jewish. Though it is still a belief from which the vast majority of Jews dissent, there are tens of thousands of contemporary Jews who do believe Jesus to be Messiah and God (one estimate has the figure at 150,000 to 200,000 worldwide[72]).

Contrary to what Carroll asserted, Dylan has never renounced his conversion, or, more accurately, never renounced his experience with Jesus. Ironically, by late 1983, the time period some attribute to this "renouncement," is when Dylan told Robert Hilburn of the *Los Angeles Times* that he did not "disavow any of that" (his gospel concerts) and he did not "particularly regret telling people how to get their souls saved."[73]

But why did Dylan accept this invitation to appear before the pope in 1997? Perhaps for the same reason he chose to appear at the Wiesenthal Center four months earlier: wherever he is welcome is where he will be. Maybe it has just come down to that.

Dylan's set in Bologna consisted of "Knockin' on Heaven's Door," "A Hard Rain's A-Gonna Fall," and "Forever Young." Following an electric version of "A Hard Rain's A-Gonna Fall"—the first since the final concert of the 1981 tour—the fifty-six-year-old singer greeted the pope, which was described in this way by one observer: "Dylan suddenly swept off his white cowboy hat and ascended the stairs of the dais. The people rose to meet him and, as Dylan bowed his head slightly, they clasped each others' hands."[74]

Dylan and the pope shaking hands?

Whatever they did, there were interpretations aplenty. According to Martin Grossman, Dylan friend Rabbi Manis Friedman had this to say: "When he greeted the Pope during his performance he didn't kiss his ring. There have been other Jews who didn't have the courage to refuse to kiss the Pope's ring, including statesman and other well-known personalities."[75]

This historic meeting didn't escape the notice of comedians. During his televised show, David Letterman delivered the following joke, based on a rather familiar premise: "What did the Pope say after hearing Bob Dylan?—'I speak twelve languages and I still couldn't understand him.'"[76]

When Dylan was asked about the concert, he simply said "Great show." But why was it a great show? Anyone awaiting a profound response would be disappointed. "It just was," he told a journalist from *Der Spiegel* magazine.[77]

Another journalist, Murray Engleheart, gave it a shot, wondering if it might have been a "tremendously moving" experience. "Well, it's all surreal, you know," said Dylan. "But yeah, it was moving. I mean, he's the Pope [laughs]. You know what I mean? There's only one Pope, right?" Given the context in Bologna, did Dylan sense any irony in playing "Knockin' on Heaven's Door"? "No," he said, "because that's the song they wanted to hear. It seemed to be a good correspondence to the situation."[78]

Although the publicity may have paled in comparison to the pope gig, on November 14, 1997, another historic concert took place. It all went down in San Jose, California, at the San Jose Arena. If, as Dylan has said, his material "isn't everybody's cup of tea," then surely his youngest son, Jakob, bridges the gap for some. As lead singer of the Wallflowers, he opened for his dad at this private concert sponsored by Applied Materials, an electronics firm.

Earlier in the year, in an interview with Gerri Hirshey of *Rolling Stone*, Jakob recalled the period when his father began to embrace Jesus: "During the conversion thing, I went where I was told. I was aware that it mattered to him. He's never done anything half-assed. If he does anything, he goes fully underwater."[79]

Some years before, Dylan had said as much: "When I get involved in something, I get totally involved. I don't just play around on the fringes."[80]

On December 6, 1997, less than three months after his appearance before the pope, Dylan would be, once again, rubbing shoulders with high society. U.S. President Bill Clinton was involved with the twentieth annual Kennedy Center Honors and held a reception in the East Room of the White House for the year's five honorees: actor Charlton Heston, actress Lauren Bacall, opera singer Jessye Norman, ballet dancer Edward Villella, and . . . rock singer Bob Dylan?

What did President Clinton have to say about Dylan being honored? "He probably had more impact on people of my generation than any other creative artist. His voice and lyrics haven't always been easy on the ear, but throughout his career Bob Dylan has never aimed to please," observed Clinton. "He's disturbed the peace and discomforted the powerful. . . . Like a rolling stone, Bob Dylan has kept moving forward, musically and spiritually, challenging all of us to move forward with him. Thank you, Bob Dylan, for a lifetime of stirring the conscience of a nation."[81]

Politically speaking, there is no doubt that Speaker of the House Newt Gingrich represented the polar opposite of Clinton, yet Dylan's bipartisan influence was evident: "The sheer magic, for I think everyone in my generation, is to finally have our nation recognize Bob Dylan," he said.[82]

The evening after the reception at the White House, the Kennedy Center Honors were held at the John F. Kennedy Center for the Performing Arts. Dylan was present, along with some family members, including his eighty-two-year-old mother and Ethel Crystal, his aunt—the woman who had introduced Beatty to Abraham Zimmerman at a New Year's party in Duluth, Minnesota, all those years ago. The honorees and their families were seated in the same balcony where, a few feet away, a couple of noted Washingtonians, Bill and Hillary Clinton, could be found.

Actor Gregory Peck narrated a bio of Dylan as a video montage of the singer's career played before the live audience. Then came country singer David Ball who paid tribute with a cover of "Don't Think Twice,

It's Alright." Bruce Springsteen followed with a gritty cover of "The Times They Are A-Changin.'" The third and final guest to honor Dylan was gospel legend Shirley Caesar, who brought down the roof with a powerful cover of "Gotta Serve Somebody," before which she said, "I just wanna say . . . to Bob, thank you so much for writing such a wonderful song." Caesar had covered the song on her 1980 album *Rejoice*, a move that prompted Dylan to tell Cameron Crowe in 1985 that he liked her version of "Gotta Serve Somebody" better than his.

On this December 1997 evening in the nation's capital, Caesar launched into her customized introduction to the song—"In the 24th chapter of Joshua, about the 15th verse, I heard Joshua say . . . "—and during the singing of the song added the gospel invitation: "Make up in your mind and come on the Lord's side." She also called forth Dylan's profession of faith, "I heard Bob Dylan say, 'It might be the Devil, let it be the Lord, you gotta serve somebody." Caesar, along with her backup singers, concluded "Gotta Serve Somebody" with this declaration—"Serve my Jesus . . . Jesus!"

Dylan could be spotted in the balcony applauding after he witnessed Caesar's stirring tribute. Did he know she would be appearing and singing this particular song from *Slow Train Coming*? "When I sang at the Kennedy Center Honors awards ceremony, it was Bob Dylan who suggested that I come," said Caesar. "In fact, he told me that he wasn't even gonna show up unless they had me [there] to sing in his honor. I praise God for that."[83]

Dylan's aunt, Ethel Crystal, who was in the balcony taking in the performance, later shared her thoughts on Dylan's experience of 1979 with biographer Howard Sounes: "I think it was for publicity, that's what I think. Because he is Jewish-minded, plenty Jewish-minded. He was brought up that way. He was bar mitzvahed."[84]

Most Jews naturally perceive an embrace of Jesus as being incompatible with being "Jewish-minded." Although this perspective could be interpreted as a misunderstanding, it is one that is understandable and based on a number of facts. The most significant fact of which is the violent, long history of anti-Semitism—a shameful history—that has been propagated in the name of Christianity. Author Ruth Rosen has put it this way:

"For the majority of Jews, the New Testament is a closed and unfamiliar book because it is identified with the age-long persecution of the Jewish people in the name of Christianity. Because most Jews believe that the New Testament promotes anti-Semitism, they think there could be nothing in it which would sustain Jewish life and values. Thus, the common Jewish assessment of the New Testament is formed by a preconditioned impression. In many ways, Jewish experience seems to support this assessment. However, the majority of Jewish people do not feel inclined to verify the assessment by an investigation of the New Testament itself . . . we have discovered that its authorship and cultural background are Jewish . . . the basic theme of the New Testament is uniquely a Jewish one: the fulfillment of the Messianic hope. This expectation was peculiarly the possession of Israel. An early passage in the Gospel of Matthew portrays Gentile wise men recognizing that the promised deliverer is to be 'King of the Jews.' In the early stages of the spread of the good news about the Messiah, it is only Jews and those Gentiles who are under the influence of Judaism who are prepared to receive and understand the message about the advent of the long-expected Redeemer. The primary centers for the initial preaching of the message are the synagogues in the communities of the Diaspora."[85]

Rosen concludes her minority perspective with this: "We see nothing in the New Testament that is non-Jewish or anti-Jewish. It is, to the contrary, woven with the warp and woof of Jewish hope and prophetic promise. If one can accept the revelation of Moses and the prophets with utter seriousness, there should be nothing really strange in the New Testament. The real challenge of the New Testament, as we see it, is not about Jewishness, but about faith. It is not a question of, 'Is it Jewish?' We believe that careful investigation will verify its Jewishness. The real question is, 'Is it true?' That, as we have stated, is really a question of faith and it holds a challenge for all people, Jew and

Gentile alike."[86]

Speaking of the New Testament, when discussing his songwriting endeavors with Jon Pareles of the *New York Times* in 1997, Dylan referred to a certain phrase that kept running through his head, a phrase that just wouldn't leave him alone.

"Environment affects me a great deal. . . . A lot of the songs [from *Time Out of Mind*, 1997] were written after the sun went down. And I like storms. I like to stay up during a storm. I get very meditative sometimes, and this one phrase was going through my head: 'Work while the day lasts, because the night of death cometh when no man can work.' I don't recall where I heard it. I like preaching, I hear a lot of preaching, and I probably just heard it somewhere.

Maybe it's in the Psalms, it beats me. But it wouldn't let me go. I was, like, what does that phrase mean? But it was at the forefront of my mind, for a long period of time, and I think a lot of that is instilled into this record."[87]

When assessing Dylan's mystery phrase, biographer Howard Sounes arrived at this conclusion: "He was sure it was from the Bible, but could not find the reference. Maybe he had invented it subconsciously."[88]

Not quite. The words at the "forefront" of Dylan's mind—"Work while the day lasts, because the night of death cometh when no man can work"—indeed had their origins in a biblical passage, one in which Jesus gives sight to a man who had been blind since birth. Here is the context of the story, taken from the gospel of John:

"And as Jesus passed by, he saw a man who was blind from his birth. And his disciples asked him, saying, 'Master, who did sin, this man, or his parents, that he was born blind?' Jesus answered, 'Neither hath this man sinned, nor his parents: but that the works of God should be made manifest in him. I must work the works of him who sent me, while it is day: the night cometh, when no man can work. As long as I am in the world, I am the light of the world.' When he had thus spoken, he spat on the ground, and made clay of the spittle, and he anointed the eyes of the blind man with the clay, and said unto him, 'Go, wash in the pool of Siloam (which is by interpretation, Sent). He went his way therefore, and washed, and came away seeing."[89]

Dylan's comments about *Time Out of Mind* were not the first instance where he alluded to the Scriptures in relation to songwriting. In 1985, he told Bill Flanagan about the influence of the Bible on his songwriting; his songs, he said, always came back to that.[90] In the same year, he told Cameron Crowe that he listened to preacher stations;[91] and in 1986, Mikal Gilmore heard Dylan's assertion that the Bible was the only thing that he knew that "stayed true."[92]

If Dylan couldn't rely on himself or others or religion to "stay true," then God, as revealed by a collection of sixty-six books, beginning with the book of Genesis and ending with the book of Revelation, was that ultimate truth. And that ultimate truth would sustain him in a world gone wrong. There is no doubt that much of the music in America's shadowy past—from the spirituals that slaves sang to the gospel songs of the rural countryside—is steeped in the Good Book.

And one could not just escape the God of time and space. Although at times He seemed absent, God was simply hidden in the shadows working out His will—or laying on the revelation and conviction so thick and heavy that folks either had to drop to bended knee or turn their hearts away.

In 1997 Dylan also shared this with Jon Pareles: "Those old songs are my lexicon and my prayer book. . . . All my beliefs come out of those old songs, literally, anything from 'Let Me Rest on A Peaceful Mountain' to 'Keep on the Sunny Side.' You can find all my philosophy in those old songs. I believe in a God of time and space, but if people ask me about that, my impulse is to point them back toward those songs. I believe in Hank Williams singing 'I Saw the Light.' I've seen the Light, too."[93]

Onstage during the days of 1979–1981 (and, on occasion, in an interview), Dylan would have effortlessly offered up the identity of "the Light" or revealed just exactly who this "God of time and space" was. But in 1997, readers of the *New York Times* would have to read between the lines: And discovering who the God and Savior of "I Saw the Light" was didn't seem like an exercise in ambiguity.

But what about the other songs Dylan alluded to in the same interview? If it is as he claims—his literal beliefs can be found in songs such as "Let Me Rest on A Peaceful Mountain" and "Keep on the Sunny Side"—then author Mark Joseph raises a legitimate question: when Dylan made these claims to both Jon Pareles of the *New York Times* and David Gates of *Newsweek* in 1997, then it "begged the question—which neither reporter attempted to answer—what was the theology in those songs?"[94]

As for "Let Me Rest on A Peaceful Mountain," this is an actual lyric from a Ralph Stanley song entitled "Hills of Home," written in honor of his late brother Carter, who died in 1966. Stanley's childlike faith is evident: "The Man who calls our number / Somehow, you fit into His plans / I never questioned His decision / For I'm only a human, just another man…rest in peace…For one day this earth I'll no longer roam / And once again we'll be together / Side by side / In the hills of home."[95] Themes of faith in God and longing for heaven aren't exactly foreign to Dylan's own work.

The other song, "Keep on the Sunny Side," is an A. P. Carter composition that includes these lyrics: "Let us greet with the song of hope each day / Though the moment be cloudy or fair / Let us trust in our Savior away / Who keepeth everyone in His care."[96] Considering the gospel foundation of American music, it doesn't take much research to determine the identity of A. P. Carter's Savior.

Also in 1997, Dylan told David Gates the following: "I don't adhere to rabbis, preachers, evangelists, all of that. I've learned more from the songs than I've learned from any of this kind of entity. The songs are my lexicon. I believe the songs."[97]

Yet just days earlier, Dylan had told Jon Pareles the following: "I like preaching, I hear a lot of preaching." So, is this a contradiction? Not necessarily. It's reasonable to assume that Dylan distances himself from following any single person and has revealed the fact that he is reminded of—and learns best from—the transcendent biblical truths that are found in certain songs. In 1980, he said a "real preacher" didn't require adherence: "The basic thing, I feel, is to get in touch with Christ yourself. He will lead you. Any preacher who is a real preacher will tell you that: 'Don't follow me, follow Christ.'"[98]

As fate would have it, *Time Out of Mind* became Dylan's highest charting album debut of his thirty-six-year recording career—No. 10 on the *Billboard* Top 200 chart.[99] Additionally (and perhaps ironically), it marked his first Top-10 album since 1979's *Slow Train Coming*.

Even a few years after its release, when asked about the essence of the album, Dylan still seemed miffed about the critics who prophesied with their distant pens: "People say the record deals with mortality—my mortality for some reason! [laughs] Well, it doesn't deal with my mortality. It maybe just deals with mortality in general. It's one thing that we all have in common, isn't it? But I didn't see any one critic say: 'It deals with my mortality'—you know, his own. As if he's immune in some kind of way—like whoever's writing about the record has got eternal life and the singer doesn't. I found this condescending attitude toward that record revealed in the press quite frequently, but, you know, nothing you can do about that."[100]

There were allusions to hope and faith that were generally overlooked by the press: the lyrics to *Time Out of Mind* were sprinkled with biblical allusions. Coupled with the assumption of human suffering and sorrow, there was a God who was the singer's "shield," a God who would not lead him "astray."

By January 1998, some eyebrows were likely raised, along with some scholarly head scratching, when Stanford University played host to the International Bob Dylan Conference. Mark Gonnerman, one of the speakers and a research fellow at Stanford's Center of Buddhist Studies, addressed Dylan's religious history during his cleverly entitled presentation, "The Sound of One Dog Barking: Bob Dylan and Religious Experience." Michael Ybarra was covering the conference and picked up the story: "'Song is the highest form of prayer,' Dylan once said [in 1976], and Gonnerman found a profound strain of invigorating religious skepticism, a probing and questioning faith, in the songwriter's earlier work. Paradoxically, Gonnerman said Dylan's least moving and least interesting treatment of religion came during his born-again phase, after he claimed to have seen Jesus in 1978. 'Who knows?' Gonnerman said, 'Maybe all his questions were answered.'"[101]

Perhaps. But even the first-century disciples of Jesus who regularly saw him did not exactly come down with severe cases of unwavering faith, according to the Scriptures. Furthermore, some of the people who were closest to Dylan in 1979 found him to be inquisitive and eager to learn. His mind was, arguably, open and not closed as so many assumed, and his personality was still intact.

Less than six months after the International Bob Dylan Conference at Stanford, a certain song was resurrected after a seven-year absence. The lyrics to "Gotta Serve Somebody" would likely disinterest most in the ivory towers of academia. If listeners did not like serving the Lord and making a joyful noise—or forsaking such apparent nonsense and dancing with the devil—they just could not find any middle ground in the spiritual realm. "Gotta Serve Somebody" remained a show opener for the balance of 1998, reminding the faithful few who were around in 1979–1981, of the song that kicked off all the furor in the first place.

While Dylan was busy making his usual tour rounds in Europe during the summertime, some interesting results could be found in the twentieth anniversary issue of *Contemporary Christian Music Magazine* (July 1998), as determined by a panel of its critics: *Slow Train Coming* was voted No. 7 in their Top-100 Albums, and checking in at No. 6 in their Top-10 Songs from the past two decades was none other than "Gotta Serve Somebody." What is intriguing about these results is that for many listeners of the contemporary Christian genre, Dylan remains a relatively unknown figure. The older folks, the critics, were well aware of Dylan's encounter with Jesus and his subsequent art reflecting the experience, but many younger listeners, ironically, remember him only in connection with the 1960s.

Alex Ross, who attended Dylan's concert in Concord, California, on September 25, 1998, wrote down these reflections: "The crowd is dominated by ex and neo-hippies from Berkeley, twenty miles to the west. Dylan threatens to dampen the enthusiasm by opening with 'Gotta Serve Somebody,' the snarling gospel single with which he had horrified the counterculture in 1979. But he works his way back to the sing-along anthem 'Blowin' in the Wind.' I was sitting near a teenage girl who had first heard Dylan in a class on the '60s and was there with her teacher."[102]

Ross, on assignment for *The New Yorker*, and only a Dylan fan himself for several years, sensed some of his colleagues' apprehension (some were bemused at his assignment; others did not know Dylan still played); he humorously recounted how he once perceived Dylan:

> I had mentally shelved him as the archetypal radical leftover, reeking of politics and marijuana. I'd read a story that went something like this: He was born in Minnesota. He went to Greenwich Village. He wrote protest songs. He stopped writing protest songs. He took drugs, 'went electric.' He was booed. He fell off his motorcycle. He disappeared into a basement. He reappeared and sang country. He got divorced. He converted to Christianity. He converted back to something else. He croaked somewhere behind Stevie Wonder in 'We Are the World.' And so on. If you're not in the right age group, the collected bulletins of Dylan's progress read like alumni notes from a school you didn't attend.[103]

Another stop on Dylan's 1998 tour was the city of his birth, Duluth, Minnesota, and oddly enough, it marked his first-ever concert there. "Welcome Home" signs adorned some downtown business windows. The local newspaper, the *News-Tribune*, ran a front-page story for two days. As for the concert itself, the fifty-seven-year-old singer/songwriter opened with "Gotta Serve Somebody" and closed his encore with "Forever Young." So from "it may be the Devil or it may be the Lord" to "may the Lord bless and keep you," the native son was willing to let the echo decide who was right or wrong.

Certainly some audiences in early 1999 were pleasantly surprised by stage debuts for Jimmie Rodgers' "My Blue-Eyed Jane," Lefty Frizzell's "You're Too Late," Hank Williams' "Honky Tonk Blues," and an ever-present encore inclusion of Buddy Holly's "Not Fade Away." This was likely a tribute to the twenty-two-year-old singer whom Dylan had seen in concert forty years earlier, at age seventeen, in his hometown of Duluth, just days before Holly's death.

But a crowd in Pensacola, Florida, on February 2, 1999, may have been downright mystified: Dylan gave an onstage debut to a Christian hymn—more than two centuries removed no less: Augustus Toplady's composition from 1776, "Rock of Ages."

Considering that eight concerts earlier, a crowd in Rochester, New York, heard both "Gotta Serve Somebody" and "I Believe in You," it does not seem unreasonable to conclude that Dylan was expressing the faith he expressed back in 1979, in new and different ways. In fact, songs with overt lyrics about Jesus began to appear more often in 1999. Prophetic now, it seems, are Dylan's comments to Jon Pareles in 1997: about his lexicon, about his beliefs being rooted in those old songs, songs that pointed back toward "a God of time and space."

What nudged Dylan to sing "Rock of Ages" is anyone's guess, but a prompting from on high coupled with a Stanley Brothers recording does not seem too preposterous a notion. Whatever the case, the folks in Pensacola witnessed an interesting selection as Dylan returned to that same Rock he had sung about twenty years before. The "Solid Rock" of 1979-1981 carried the great urgency of newborn zeal; the "Rock of Ages" in 1999 sounded, and felt, much different. Although it was given a mellow, country treatment—as opposed to the fiery, bristling delivery of an up-tempo "Solid Rock"—the references to Jesus as Savior were apparent.

If Dylan's belief that the highest form of song is prayer remained intact, then "Rock of Ages" amounted to a humble prayer offered up to the Most High. By 1999, it was no secret to those who had followed Dylan's career, that the tour years that followed the so-called gospel tours (1984, 1986–1998) were not void of the songs from 1979 to 1981. But by 1999, songs about Jesus began to appear more often as cover songs.

A few weeks after Pensacola, in Buffalo, New York, Dylan brought another hymn to the stage. This time it was "Pass Me Not, O Gentle Savior," a composition originally penned by the noted nineteenth-century hymn writer Frances "Fanny" Crosby, but most likely heard by Dylan through the Stanley Brothers. Dylan had the opportunity to record a song with Ralph Stanley in late 1997, a moment he later said was the "highlight of his career."

"Two different hymns within the space of one month," observed concert attendee Martin Abela, "Our man must be having those old-time religious feelings again."[104]

The next evening in Amherst, Massachusetts, Dylan sang "Pass Me Not, O Gentle Savior" again. Gil Walker was an eyewitness and thought the hymn to be a "letter-perfect rendition," but noted that "at least around me, most of the audience received it with a chilly indifference, perhaps even a bit of resentment."[105]

Award-winning author Alan Jacobs had this to say about the 1999 gospel offerings: "The one that really surprises me is 'Pass Me Not, O Gentle Savior,' which is an old Fanny Crosby song, and absolutely reeks with evangelical spirituality: 'When on others thou art calling / Do not pass me by.' And the lyrics of the verses are based on the man who said to Jesus, 'Lord, I believe, help thou my unbelief.'"[106]

When it was announced that Dylan would be joining fellow Jewish singer Paul Simon for a summer tour of 1999, *Time* magazine listed some "pros" and "cons" of their impending collaboration. Under the "pros," the two could bond over "failed projects"—Simon's *The Capeman* and Dylan's Christianity.[107]

Four shows into the tour, Dylan debuted the traditional song, "Hallelujah, I'm Ready to Go," which became somewhat of a tour staple, and included these lyrics: "Sinner don't wait / Before it's too late / He's a wonderful Savior to know / I fell on my knees / He answered my pleas / Hallelujah, I'm ready to go." It was in the same theological vein as "Rock of Ages" and "Pass Me Not, O Gentle Savior." The failed project of Dylan's Christianity showed no signs of abating.

On June 14, 1999, Dylan played a solo gig in Eugene, Oregon, and debuted "Down Along the Cove," a song off 1967's *John Wesley Harding*, which did not exactly jibe with the countercultural rumblings of its time. After this live debut—some thirty-two years after it was recorded—with a good sense of history and humor, Dylan had these words for his crowd in Eugene: "I wanna say hello to all the ex-hippies tonight. I've never been a hippie myself, but...I'm an honorary hippie!"[108]

Less than a month later, Dylan found himself in Maryland Heights, Missouri, introducing "Somebody Touched Me" to the stage. This marked another traditional song he opened a show with and like its predecessor, "Hallelujah, I'm Ready to Go," it received a number of outings during the tour. Its lyrics repeatedly spoke about "the hand of the Lord." Some nineteen years earlier, Dylan the interviewee spoke about his then-recent experience. "Jesus put his hand on me. It was a physical thing. I felt it. I felt it all over me," he told journalist Karen Hughes. "I felt my whole body tremble. The glory of the Lord knocked me down and picked me up."[109]

"Somebody Touched Me," sung by Dylan in 1999, included these lyrics: "Glory, glory, glory, somebody touched me / Must have been the hand of the Lord . . . while I was praying somebody touched me."

The crowd who heard the song's debut in Maryland Heights also heard an increasingly jokey Dylan (one-liners between songs had emerged during the summer tour with Paul Simon) when he referred to his lead guitarist Larry Campbell: "Larry almost wrote a song today. He wrote a song about his bed, but it hasn't been made up yet."

Although it was now summer, Dylan's comedic efforts were on display back in February when, before singing "Silvio" to an crowd in Normal, Illinois, he had this to say: "People told me I'd never get close to normal. But they were wrong." Many fans may have felt that, two decades earlier, his onstage comments during the gospel tours of 1979–1980 were too serious, quite able to evoke collective groans, but during many a show in 1999 there were groans as well; instead of salvation, though, the subject matter concerned, of all things, Dylan's new foray into cornball comedy.

How refreshing for an artist to feel free enough to sing songs about salvation *and* tell corny jokes. Might this have been evidence of a joyful heart? "A joyful heart is good medicine," observed one of the writers of Proverbs, "but a crushed spirit dries up the bones."[110]

Apparently unaware of Dylan's recent comedic efforts, *Rolling Stone*'s Mark Jacobson issued this commentary: "Whatever his current theology, I, for one, would like to know what ever happened to the Jewish jokes in Bob Dylan. . . . Maybe being born-again beat the stand-up out of him, or maybe it was just the sheer weight of being Bob Dylan for so many years."[111]

Jacobson noted that it wasn't "completely clear if Dylan was still a Christian" and quoted two prolific Dylan authors: "Clinton Heylin says yes—'Listen to the songs.' Paul Williams says Dylan's current Christianity or Jewishness is secondary to his 'overriding fundamentalism. . . . He is someone who believes in the literalness of the Word. He will be a fundamentalist in whatever he believes.'"[112]

During a month-long touring hiatus in August 1999, Dylan helped realize the dream of Curtis Hanson, the award-winning film director (*L.A. Confidential*). A longtime Dylan fan, Hanson wanted to enlist the singer's help ever since the 1973 film, *Pat Garrett and Billy the Kid* (Dylan's last substantial soundtrack contribution). Fast-forward to August 1999: Dylan pops into the editing room, checks out footage for Hanson's film project, *Wonder Boys*, and subsequently pens "Things Have Changed," a song especially for the film. One of its lyrics speaks of "walking forty miles of bad road" and "if the Bible is right, the world will explode."

This was hardly a shocking line considering Dylan's history. There was the final line of "See That My Grave Is Kept Clean," the last song on his debut album of 1962: "now I believe what the Bible told." There was the apocalyptic "Rainbow Sign," the song his female singers belted out during the gospel tour of 1979–1980; it warned there would be "no more water but fire next time." There was Dylan's 1990 composition

"God Knows" that borrowed these exact words from "Rainbow Sign." For Dylan, it was old hat to pen a single line in a song that attributed the end of the world being nigh to the Bible.

Not long after recording "Things Have Changed," Dylan hit the road again. On September 4, 1999, in Atlanta, Georgia, he opened his concert with another debut. This time it was "I Am The Man, Thomas" (a song credited to Ralph Stanley and Larry Sparks), which tells the story of the crucifixion and resurrection of Jesus. Considering its lyrical thrust and first-person perspective (Jesus addressing his doubting disciple), it echoed Dallas Holm's "Rise Again"—the song Dylan performed in 1980 and recorded in 1992. "I Am the Man, Thomas" also became a tour staple with Dylan, opening a number of his concerts.

In October 1999, on National Poetry Day in the United Kingdom, Andrew Motion, the reigning Poet Laureate, had this to say when asked what it was he especially liked about Dylan as an artist: "The concentration and surprise of his lyrics, the beauty of his melodies and the rasp of his anger; the dramatic sympathy between the words and the music; the range of devotions; the power of self-renewal; his wit; his surrealism; the truth to his experience."[113] As for Motion's favorite song lyric ever written by Dylan—the 1966 masterpiece, "Visions of Johanna."

During the same month back in the States, Dylan appeared with old friend T-Bone Burnett in an episode of the situation comedy *Dharma and Greg*, an episode ("Play Lady Play") in which Dharma found herself auditioning for a band and engaged in some down-to-earth banter with Dylan.

From being praised by a poet laureate on foreign shores to opening shows with songs about Jesus and telling jokes onstage to being seen on a television comedy show in his home country, Dylan seemed to be comfortable in his own skin.

On November 9, 1999, Dylan surprised the faithful in Philadelphia by playing the one song from his *Saved* album—"A Satisfied Mind"—that had never been aired before a live audience. It was the only non-Dylan composition from the album, a Red Hayes/Jack Rhodes song with which Porter Wagoner had a country hit.

The songs about Jesus that Dylan introduced to audiences in 1999—"Rock of Ages," "Pass Me Not, O Gentle Savior," "Hallelujah, I'm Ready to Go," "Somebody Touched Me," and "I Am the Man, Thomas"—all contained lyrics as overt as anything he penned for *Slow Train Coming* (1979), *Saved* (1980), and *Shot of Love* (1981). This caused one fan, Ken Wilson, to ponder the meaning of it all:

"Here's my two cents' worth. If I'd had a dramatic conversion to any religion and written songs espousing it, and preached about it in concert, and then later came to think of it as bunk, I'd have to swallow awfully hard before singing any of those songs again! And I sure wouldn't be covering—much less opening concerts with—other songs espousing that same delusive faith."[114]

On November 19, Dylan played two shows in Atlantic City, New Jersey, at the 750-seat Sands Casino Copa Room. During the second show, the late-night crowd was in for a surprise. Near the stroke of midnight, sandwiched between "Visions of Johanna" and "A Hard Rain's A-Gonna Fall" was the gentle gamble of the aforementioned "Rock of Ages," a sweet song of salvation seemingly calling out to some of the bleary-eyed bunch in the Copa Room not too far from the jingle-jangle morning of the new day. Singer/songwriter, music writer, and Dylan aficionado Peter Stone Brown heard the song as a "nice surprise, the hymn done more or less in a haunting bluegrass version that was truly beautiful."

Following the twin bill in Atlantic City, Dylan concluded 1999 (and his performances in the twentieth century) in Newark, Delaware, on November 20, where he opened with "I Am the Man, Thomas." Before the night was out, the crowd heard the debut of "This World Can't Stand Long." Akin to a lyric from his newly written "Things Have Changed"—"If the Bible is right, the world will explode"—the song spoke of a life somewhere beyond that arena in Newark, Delaware. It also seemed to call up Sister Rosetta Tharpe's comment that, "There's something in the gospel blues that's so deep the world can't stand it."

"This World Can't Stand Long" was an intriguing inclusion for

Dylan's final concert of the twentieth century. Its lyrical impetus easily parallels the between-song bantering of a Bob Dylan back in 1979-1980. It has been clear for some time now that the singer is quite content to have some of his songs do the talking for him.

However, a gentle reminder may have been issued to Dylan fans when authors Davin Seay and Mary Neely wrote these words:

> Jesus, it seems, does not need Dylan's astonishing gifts to complete His work, and if Dylan needs Jesus to be complete himself, he has set down the path of the humble and contrite. . . . Dylan himself ran and ran hard, but for every stride he slipped two steps back toward the altar of Yahweh. . . . Everywhere he turned, and everywhere his followers turned with him, Dylan confronted the Most High. And what he might choose to deny was writ large in the body of his work.
>
> Ask Stephen Pickering, a.k.a. Choftez Chaim Ben-Avra-ham, Jewish mystic and author of numerous tracts relating to the ancient Hebrew prophetic tradition. In *Bob Dylan Approximately: A Portrait of the Jewish Poet in Search of God*, Pickering declares, "Bob Dylan's poetry centers upon God, upon Heaven (paths to the Gates of Eden, where man will knock on Heaven's door), upon the extant Jewish-messianic tradition. His sense of impending apocalypse (the dialectical struggle between darkness and light) burns into the Jewish heart. In his moral anger, his ethical monotheism, Bob Dylan is a Jewish voice aware of the struggles that can tear apart the heart: what one ought to do as opposed to what one wants to do. Dylan has, in his 'Wedding Song,' admitted that it was never his 'intention to sound the battle charge.' However, the fire is in him like Jeremiah: he cannot be silent."[115]

Seay and Neely continued: "Avowing elsewhere in his midrash that 'Poetry/prayer is the language of Bob Dylan's soul,' Pickering made his impassioned interpretation of Dylan's music before the artist became a born-again Christian. But if there is, as Christians, at least, insist, an unbroken linkage between the Old and New Testaments, between the hope of the Jews and the work of Christ, then Dylan has only strengthened Pickering's argument. Here is a man squarely in the Davidic tradition: poet, leader, man after God's own heart, and archetype."[116]

Author Larry Yudelson, after reading Dylan's mother's interview of the late 1990s, noted this: "In her interview Beattie mentioned that their family regularly gathered for Christmas." Yudelson viewed this disclosure as "significant" and observed that "Dylan grew up in a family that knew it was Jewish, but without much religion. That goes a long way to explain the early rootlessness of Dylan who has always in his lyrics had a very strong religious sense, from the early 'With God on Our Side' to 'All Along the Watchtower,' with its imagery from the Book of Isaiah."[117]

"He's very Jewish. He's very connected to his Jewishness," said Chabad rabbi and longtime Dylan friend Manis Friedman, when speaking to writer Martin Grossman. "He thinks like a Jew. He tries to act like a Jew. That's about as much as I can say."[118]

It would be, no doubt, a difficult task to divorce Dylan's essence as an artist from the biblical tradition. His composition "Things Have Changed" was, according to *Rolling Stone*, "one of those grim, intense Book of Deuteronomy howls he comes up with whenever he's in the mood to make all other rock and roll singers sound like scared kittens."[119]

That's the thing with Bob Dylan. How many rock n' rollers are doing what he's doing? Who else is raising support for an Orthodox Jewish ministry, or singing about Jesus, or continually mining the depths of American roots music, or performing within the confines of a county fairground, or before the pope, or in a casino in Atlantic City, or is the subject of endless academic theses?

Speaking of which, in November 1999, a few days after Dylan had performed in Chicago—and opened his show with "I Am the Man, Thomas," another song about that "God of time and space"—the National Communication Association held their annual convention. A panel of four, on behalf of the Religious Communication Association, presented their respective papers on Dylan: "Street-Legal: Dylan's

Pre-Christian Period" (Jeff Shires); "Slow Train Coming: A Metaphorical Analysis" (Joseph Blaney); "A Simple Twist of Faith: Spiritual Ambiguity and Rhetorical Perspectivisim in Bob Dylan's *Infidels*" (Brett Miller); and "Jokerman: Bob Dylan's Metaphors of Space, Time and Eternity" (Joe Munshaw). If academia had a tendency to ignore the spiritual dimension of Bob Dylan's work, some were now making up for lost time.

Also at the tail end of 1999, Michael Gray's book *Song & Dance Man III: The Art of Bob Dylan* was released. In his preface, he looked back at the period when his second volume left off in 1981, observing that "Dylan's latest album was *Saved* and he was touring with ugly musicians around stadiums of the resentful damned. He was about as hip as General Franco."

But Gray also reflected on the more recent Dylan tours in the 1990s where the singer has arguably become, once again, hip: "The presence of the young in the audiences at his concerts proves that many newcomers are drawn to him, in wave after generational wave, in spite of everything. Such people have in front of them the enviable pleasures of getting to know his vast back catalogue."[120]

Someone who got to know the vast back catalogue quite well was Bucky Baxter, a member of Dylan's band for over 700 concerts, spanning 1992–1999:

"I like playing all the songs just fine. Bob's a great songwriter. I never really remember any songs that I didn't like. Sure, I got sick of playing 'All Along the Watchtower.' But, on the other hand, there are songs like 'Tangled Up in Blue' that we played seven nights a week and I never got sick of it."[121]

As for touring, Dylan was showing no signs of slowing down at the end of the century: In 1999, he played to 121 audiences, the most ever in his career. Before the year concluded, Peter Garrett of ABC-TV (Australia) took the trouble to address the subject of Dylan's faith:

> It was the singer/poet Bob Dylan who at one of his most outwardly religious stages, a stage of his career many people deplored, as I recall, wrote, "You've got to serve somebody." And this was a very succinct

> statement of a central biblical theme. But I think he was also pointing something else out at the same time, and that is, he was implying that you cannot live fully if the only thing that you're living for is yourself. And later on, in a reflective voice, he re-surveyed the moral landscape in later albums, like *Oh Mercy* [1989] where he wrote a song where the line was, "There's a disease of conceit," and the disease of conceit is also a familiar notion from the biblical tradition. It goes along with its partner disease of hubris and idolatry and faithlessness.[122]

Some observers, though, weren't as studious as Garrett. Take, for example, a writer at PBS who, after referring to when Dylan became a born-again Christian, casually asserted that "This phase, too, passed, and the end of the century found Dylan still touring, creating new songs for new generations."[123] Touring and creating new songs is all well and good (and true), but the writer's lack of awareness was evident. The slow train had not been abandoned.

6

2000–2009: NO NEED TO CONFESS AGAIN

His songs made him a rich man, made him very popular among the people, and I thought it was nice for him to think about the Lord—that he had a soul to save, like everybody else.

—CLARENCE FOUNTAIN OF THE BLIND BOYS OF ALABAMA, 1999

Pop [Staples] used to say, "I don't know where this boy comes from, don't know where he gets these great songs." One time Pops told him, "Bob, I think this is God's gift to you. His gift is that these words come into your head."

—MAVIS STAPLES, 2004

ON JANUARY 25, 2000, BOB DYLAN suffered the loss of his mother, Beatrice Rutman, who died at the age of eighty-four in St. Paul, Minnesota. A private funeral service was held the next day in Duluth, the city where Robert Allen Zimmerman was born some fifty-eight years earlier. Rutman's appearance at the Kennedy Center Honors, as her son's guest, in December 1997 and an interview she granted to *Moment* magazine in 1999 marked two of the occasional moments when she stepped into the glare of her son's public spotlight.

"She was a tremendously vivacious and warm woman," said Rabbi Jonathan Ginsburg of the Temple of Aaron in St. Paul, where Rutman worshipped. "She would pass the time of day with anybody," added Noel Pearman, who lived across the street from her. "She was very gracious to kids, and she was just an all-around very good neighbor."[1]

"I'm forty miles from the mill / I'm droppin' it into overdrive / Settin' my dial on the radio / I wish my mother was alive," Dylan wrote not long afterwards in "Lonesome Day Blues." It would be one of Dylan's most heated affairs with the blues, and a song he would eventually perform live at the Grammys.

Less than two weeks into the first leg of his 2000 tour, Dylan included the five gospel songs he had introduced to crowds the previous year: "Rock of Ages," "Pass Me Not, O Gentle Savior," "Hallelujah, I'm Ready to Go," "Somebody Touched Me," and "I Am the Man, Thomas."

As this same tour got under way, journalist Roy Rivenburg humorously broached the perceived mystery of Dylan's religious stance. "Is he Christian, Jewish, Hare Krishna, or what?" asked Rivenburg, in a piece that appeared in the *Los Angeles Times*. "The debate started in 1979, when Dylan released *Slow Train Coming*, and distressed rock critics did back flips trying to explain how songs about Jesus were actually parables about social injustice and/or former baseball player Jesus Alou."[2]

A few months after Rivenburg's piece appeared, a Jewish-run website in the United Kingdom bestowed an informal accolade upon the fifty-nine-year-old singer. Dylan (just) made their list of the "Kosher Top 10 Pop and Rock Stars." David Lee Roth of Van Halen topped the list, while Dylan came in at No. 10. "[Dylan] should be higher up because he made such classics as 'Like a Rolling Stone' and 'Blowin' in the Wind,'" acknowledged one critic, "but as a dabbler in Christianity he slides down the list."[3]

On June 26, 2000, 16 million American viewers stumbled upon a bit of Dylan's dabbling when they tuned into Peter Jennings' two-hour documentary, *Search for Jesus*. A clip from Dylan's 1979 song

"When You Gonna Wake Up?" played in the background while John the Baptist's ministry of repentance was being described ("Do you ever wonder what God requires?" snarled Dylan). The night before the ABC broadcast, Dylan could be found on a stage in Reno, Nevada, gambling with gospel songs like "Somebody Touched Me" and "Gotta Serve Somebody."

The next month Ronnie Keohane would publish her *Dylan & The Frucht: The Two Wits*, a book that connects Dylan with theologian Arnold Fruchtenbaum. In her foreword, Keohane writes that these are "two Jewish men, who I believe are faithful watchmen, in the fact that what God has revealed to them, they have boldly proclaimed throughout the world." To point out her revelations, Keohane meticulously documented the words of Fruchtenbaum and Dylan in light of biblical passages.

The market for writing about Dylan—which was nicely captured by the 1991 title *Oh No! Not Another Bob Dylan Book*—was further evidenced in the twenty-first century by the October 2000 issue of *Q*, a music magazine published in England. Wholly devoted to Dylan, its foreword included these words from U2's lead singer: "In your '20s you're more interested in 'The Times They Are A-Changin'," wrote Bono. "But Bob Dylan's got you from the cradle to the grave. For instance, I loved *Slow Train Coming*. I even loved *Saved*. People thought *Saved* was his bumper-sticker-Christianity album, but for me it sounds like a real cry for help."[4]

Along these lines, on November 11, 2000, a crowd in Lowell, Massachusetts, heard Dylan's lyrical variation to his 1990 song, "God Knows": "God sees every circumstance / Is there no reason / If you only give Him half a chance."

Some four months later, Dylan was on the receiving end of his first Oscar, an Academy Award win for his song "Things Have Changed" (penned for the aforementioned *Wonder Boys* film). His acceptance speech, via satellite from Sydney, Australia, where he was on tour: "I want to thank the Academy who were bold enough to give me this award for this song which obviously...is a song which doesn't pussyfoot around or turn a blind eye to human nature. And God bless you all with peace, tranquility, and goodwill. Thanks."

Considering Dylan's history, it seems reasonable to conclude that "turning a blind eye to human nature" is code for eschewing the premise of original sin. Dylan's gratitude to the Academy for rewarding honesty in a song was evident; what was less evident was whether anyone in the history of Oscar acceptance speeches had employed the words "pussy-foot" and "tranquility."

Also in March 2001, Dylan's longtime label released a live album. The Japanese import, *Bob Dylan Live: 1961–2000*, began with the traditional gospel song "Somebody Touched Me" and was followed by a forty-year-old recording of Dylan singing another traditional song, "Wade in the Water." The lyrics spoke of the Almighty troubling the waters that the children of Israel, led by Moses, would be passing through.

As Dylan's sixtieth birthday loomed on the horizon, there was no shortage of articles summing up his forty years as an artist. Not a few writers referred to his "Christian period" as a passing phase, something akin to a hangover that was given a good riddance. Curiously, a press release was issued a week before his birthday indicating that Dylan would participate on a track for a forthcoming album that would pay homage to the songs of *Slow Train Coming* and *Saved.* If Dylan no longer believed Jesus to be God and the Messiah, then perhaps only the Almighty knew why he would get anywhere near—much less affirm—a tribute album that celebrated overt sentiments about Jesus, judgment, and redemption.

When asked by *Rolling Stone* magazine to pay tribute to Dylan on his sixtieth birthday, author Camille Paglia observed that the essence of Dylan's roots was a "total product of the Jewish culture, where the word is sacred."

Green Day's Billie Joe Armstrong wasn't unaware of Dylan's song output of 1979–1980. "Even as a Jesus freak, he was trying to challenge himself and go with his instincts," Armstrong told Edna Gundersen of *USA Today*. "It's so human. He's seen as such a legend that people forget his human qualities."[5]

"Jews still wince at the memory of his forays into gospel music," wrote David Vest. "As for Christian fans, they still scramble for the merest hint that Dylan might actually share their dogma."[6]

But as J. J. Goldberg of *Forward* has noted, some Jewish fans have done their share of scrambling: "Over the years, a cottage industry grew up to ferret out Judaic content—some genuine, some merely imagined—in his lyrics. Fans stalked him on his spiritual journeys the way other performers might be staked out during restaurant outings. Jewish Dylanophiles raged when he publicly dabbled in Christianity around 1980, then exulted when he flirted with Lubavitch chasidism a few years later. Throughout, Dylan seemed to become more and more desperate to preserve his privacy."[7]

The Jewish Journal of Los Angeles also reflected on the birthday boy at sixty: "His religious identity has always been a source of mystery (and obsession) to Jewish fans. He flirted with Christian messianism, sent his children to a Beverly Hills Hebrew school, nearly joined a kibbutz, and danced with the Lubavitchers. A generation that looked to Dylan for The Way seemed forever disappointed that he was often lost himself."

Infamous Dylanologist A. J. Weberman once wrote that he worshipped Dylan, and that he saw his own role as "similar to that of the ancient Talmudic scholar or Cabalist attempting to decipher God-given truth from what appeared to most as an arbitrary arrangement of words."

At a press conference in Rome in the summer of 2001, an unidentified journalist asked Dylan if he thought there was a "religious feeling" amongst his "hardcore fans."

"And then what religion are they?" quipped Dylan, without skipping a beat. "I mean, what sacrifices do they make? . . . and to whom do they sacrifice, these hardcore fans? If they do sacrifice, then, okay, we've got hardcore religious fans. And I'd like to know when and where they make their sacrifices, because I'd like to be there."[8] Dylan's knack for the witty and the profound remained intact.

On September 11, 2001, Dylan's album "*Love and Theft*" was released. On the heels of the epic tragedies in New York City, Washington, D.C., and Shanksville, Pennsylvania, Richard Gehr of the *Village Voice* saw the album as "riddled with images of hopelessness, futility, apocalypse and revelation."

In an article that appeared in *USA Today* on September 10, Edna Gundersen observed how "Tweedle Dee and Tweedle Dum" (the album's opening track) conveyed the "nature of wickedness in modern times."

"That evil might not be coming your way as a monstrous brute or the gun-toting devilish ghetto gangster," offered Dylan. "It's the bookish-looking guy in wire-rimmed glasses who might not be entirely harmless."[9]

Robert Hilburn sat down with the singer just days after the horror of September 11 ("How Does It Feel?: Don't Ask," *Los Angeles Times*, September 16, 2001). Hilburn asked for an example of a song that has been widely misinterpreted. "Take 'Masters of War.' Every time I sing it, someone writes that it's an anti-war song. But there's no anti-war sentiment in that song," Dylan insisted. "I'm not a pacifist. I don't think I've ever been one. If you look closely at the song, it's about what Eisenhower was saying about the dangers of the military-industrial complex in this country. I believe strongly in everyone's right to defend themselves by every means necessary."

As for Dylan's perceptions of himself as an artist, there was an intriguing exchange where Hilburn asked what it was like to be both adored and booed at different times, citing the *Slow Train Coming* gospel tours of 1979. Dylan reminded him that boos came at Newport (1965) and that you can't worry about it, citing Igor Stravinsky, Hank Williams, and Miles Davis, saying "You're nobody if you don't get booed sometime."

Hilburn wondered if it affected Dylan as an artist and how he tended to respond. Dylan submitted a scenario with three types of artists: superficial artists have nothing to say and shouldn't be onstage to begin with; natural artists are up there with their talent, doing the best they can; and supernatural artists are the ones who go deep—"and the deeper you go, the more buried gods they'll find."

When Hilburn asked Dylan how he'd describe himself, Dylan laughed and dodged the question by saying that he should apply this framework to others, not himself, that he wasn't certain where he fit, and that he could be called any one of the three types of artists. However, Dylan followed what appeared to be a dodge with this: "But I always felt that if I'm going to do anything in life, I want to go as deep as I can."

This 2001 exchange with Hilburn is revealing. Dylan's reference to the "supernatural artist" might at first glance appear a self-righteous sneer (an artist who has God on his side?), but a corrective is right around the corner: The supernatural artist will find "buried gods" in his/her quest, an acknowledgment that an ever-increasing spiritual journey involves the discovering/uncovering of one's own idols.

On September 25, Dylan sat down with Mikal Gilmore of *Rolling Stone* for his final interview in support of "*Love and Theft*."[10] According to Dylan, the album dealt with "power, wealth, knowledge, and salvation," great themes he hoped would speak across the ages. At this point in his career, he didn't simply want to make another record:

"Career, by the way, isn't how I look at what I do," Dylan remarked. "*Career* is a French word. It means 'carrier.' It's something that takes you from one place to the other. I don't feel like what I do qualifies to be called a career. It's more of a calling."

"The call of my master compelled me from home / No kindred or relative nigh / I met the contagion and sank to the tomb / My soul flew to mansions on high," Dylan sang on "Lone Pilgrim"—with unmistakable pathos—on his 1993 album *World Gone Wrong*.

Whether it was the songs of others that Dylan covered or his own songs, it was a calling or destiny he had embraced. At the time, he was working on *Chronicles*, the first installment of his memoirs. He also spoke about destiny in 2001, when he told Christopher John Farley of *Time* that he had "a God-given sense of destiny"; he similarly told Edna Gundersen of *USA Today* that from the start he had "an extreme sense of destiny."

Dylan's unique way with words does not exclusively reside in the realm of the lyric page. His interviews can be jarring affairs that provoke contemplation, bewilderment, or bemusement.

Not long after Dylan's round of interviews in 2001, he was, according to Merav Tassa of *The Jewish Journal of Los Angeles*, in a synagogue for the holiday: "Keeping a low profile this year over Yom Kippur, musician Bob Dylan attended services at Chabad of Encino. He received an aliyah during the morning service, attended Yizkor, and didn't leave until the end of Neila, when the holiday had ended."

In October 2001, as Dylan passed through Chicago for a concert, he spent time with journalist Dave Hoekstra who was working on a television documentary on the Staple Singers. Hoekstra recounted the following anecdote:

"WTTW [a Chicago television station] rented a suite in the North Side Hotel where Dylan was staying. We invited Mavis and her sister Yvonne to watch the interview; they had not seen Dylan since Mavis sang background on Dylan's 'Like a Rolling Stone' for David Letterman's tenth anniversary show in 1992. Dylan arrived on time and alone. He wore a black riverboat gambler outfit, framed by a black cowboy hat and black gypsy boots. Like a schoolboy, Dylan tiptoed into the room with a shy stride. He carried a single red rose for Mavis. They embraced. Mavis also had a gift for Dylan. It was a Beanie Baby bear. The bear was praying with its hands raised upward. As Mavis handed the yellow and tan bear to Dylan, she said, 'This is called 'Hope!' Dylan cradled the Beanie Baby, smiled and said, 'Of course.' He was touched."[11]

Just over four months after their meeting, Dylan and Staples would collaborate on a song from *Slow Train Coming*. The general public was unaware, but a heartfelt tribute for Dylan's songs from *Slow Train Coming* and *Saved* was being prepared.

According to the Mishna (a collection of oral laws compiled about AD 200 and forming the basic part of the Talmud), at age sixty, elder status is conferred. In early 2002, the elder Dylan opened up a number of his concerts with "I Am the Man, Thomas," the cover song that covered the doubting Thomas of history and the resurrected Jesus. Had Dylan's recent penchant for this song reflected accurately on the long-awaited Messiah? In the song, Jesus is repeatedly letting his Jewish disciple Thomas know that He is the Man.

The gospel accounts (75 percent of which were written by Jews) tell the story of a Thomas who refused to believe in the rumor of a resurrected Jesus unless he could see him and his nail-scarred hands—and put his fingers where the nails once were. According to the New Testament, a week after his request, Jesus granted a startled Thomas his wish and then uttered these words, which are still with us twenty centuries later: "Because you have seen me, you have believed; blessed are those who have not seen and yet have believed."[12]

It is worth mentioning that Dylan's contemporary brethren do not necessarily recognize his history with and affinity for Jesus. Take, for example, the March 2, 2002 issue of *World*, a newsmagazine edited by Marvin Olasky, an author, university professor, and Jewish believer in Jesus. Although Dylan didn't make the magazine's timeline of "notable Jewish Christians" of the past five centuries, he did manage to make the magazine's short list of those who "almost crossed over." According to *World*, Dylan's Jewish Christian status was nullified in the 1980s when he "apparently reaffirmed his Judaism."[13]

Ironically, just two days after the publish date of the magazine, Dylan entered a studio with a rewritten version of one of his songs from *Slow Train Coming*. On this day, March 4, 2002, he and Mavis Staples collaborated on "Gonna Change My Way of Thinking," which now included this theological declaration: "Jesus is calling / He's coming back to gather up his jewels."[14]

Although the song's gospel sentiments are apparent in the lyrics, its sound unites the blues and rock. Additionally, the recorded version features an introduction where a lighthearted, quirky moment is captured via some dialogue between Dylan and Staples.

But the rewritten "Gonna Change My Way of Thinking" was merely a part of a larger mosaic, one that wound up being the Jeff

Gaskill-produced project, *Gotta Serve Somebody: The Gospel Songs of Bob Dylan* (Columbia, 2003). Besides Dylan's contribution, the recording mainly consisted of traditional gospel singers and groups covering Dylan's material from *Slow Train Coming* and *Saved.*

If Bob Dylan, aka Robert Zimmerman, had indeed renounced Jesus somewhere along the line, or currently wanted to distance himself from his experience and his very public proclamations of 1979-1980, then some clever and creative explanations were needed to explain his participation in this project.

"Look up, look up / Seek your Maker / Before Gabriel blows his horn," Dylan sings in "Sugar Baby," the final song from 2001's *"Love and Theft"* album. Here, a pretty rudimentary sentiment is being expressed—all wrapped up in the blues, no doubt—and that sentiment has its biblical roots. A quick check of the Good Book reveals that the angel Gabriel makes four appearances: twice in the Hebrew Scriptures (in the book of Daniel) where details of no less than the end of time are revealed to the Jewish prophet through a vision. Gabriel also appears twice in the book of Luke in the New Testament. The occasion is when two pregnant Jewish women receive an angelic visit and information concerning just whom they are carrying to term—the two whom history knows as John the Baptist and Jesus.

In the latter days of March 2002, just weeks after Dylan and Mavis Staples left that studio, longtime Dylan friend Kinky Friedman penned an introduction to a friend's book. Friedman was adding fresh blood to Larry "Ratso" Sloman's 1978 classic, *On the Road with Bob Dylan*, a chronicling of the Rolling Thunder tours of 1975-1976.

Friedman noted how more than a dozen people from the tours "have now been bugled to Jesus" and how many others, himself included, wished they were dead. For that fate—considering what Sloman would likely pay Friedman for this writing assignment—is preferable. In his inimitable style, Friedman included this in his introduction:

"The one person we know that hasn't gone to Jesus yet is Bob Dylan. Bob may stay on the road forever. He may never be bugled to Jesus.

Maybe Bob is Jesus. They're both skinny little boogers. And they're both Jeeeews. Today, of course, we like to refer to them as fellow Red Sea pedestrians."[15]

One week after Friedman penned these words, Dylan opened his spring 2002 tour in Europe with "Solid Rock," the uncompromising song about Jesus from the much-maligned *Saved* album of 1980. He had not played the tune since 1981. Its lyrics could not qualify as covert in nature: "For me He was chastised / For me He was hated / For me He was rejected / By a world that He created."[16] Are these the expressions of a man who has forsaken belief in Jesus?

As David Dawes wrote in 2001, "Surely, we can assume that Bob Dylan has enough money that he can afford not to sing things he doesn't believe in."[17]

During 2002, Dylan sang "Solid Rock" a number of times. Some of these occasions included a guest appearance where old friend and drummer Jim Keltner joined in (Keltner drummed for Dylan during the gospel tours of 1979-1981). Not long before Dylan and Keltner's stage reunion in 2002, Clinton Heylin's updated biography from 2000—*Bob Dylan: Behind the Shades Revisited*—had the following quote from Keltner:

"I think that it's a pity those songs [from *Saved*] were recorded in the studio, instead of live. There was a show in Seattle [in November 1980] when we got a standing ovation after 'Solid Rock' for almost five minutes. It was so extraordinarily powerful, and the people just flipped out and I'd never seen that before—ever."[18]

Speaking of people flipping out, Dylan's concert of August 15, 2002, in Hamburg, New York, certainly fit the bill. Regular concertgoers were accustomed to the following routine words which preceded Dylan's taking the stage:

"Good evening, ladies and gentlemen, would you please welcome Columbia recording artist—Bob Dylan!" However, on this summer evening in upstate New York, Dylan's longtime stage manager, Al Santos, uttered these words instead:

"Good evening, ladies and gentlemen, please welcome the poet laureate of rock 'n' roll, the voice of the promise of the '60s counterculture, the guy who forced folk into bed with rock, who donned makeup in the '70s and disappeared into a haze of substance abuse, who emerged to find Jesus, who was written off as a has-been by the end of the '80s, and who suddenly shifted gears and released some of the strongest music of his career beginning in the late '90s, Columbia recording artist—Bob Dylan!"

And then—as if a wordy official introduction wasn't startling enough— Dylan launched into a song no audience in forty years had ever heard him sing before. He trotted out "A Voice on High," a bluegrass gospel tune penned by the legendary Bill Monroe and Bessie Lee Mauldin. Like Dylan's other recent cover song choices, the lyrics pointed to an unmistakable figure: "The Savior has paid a great price for me / He gave his life on Calvary / So follow his footsteps up the narrow way / And be ready to meet him when he calls on that day."

Perhaps Dylan's new concert introduction, with its reference to the singer emerging to "find Jesus," may not have been the silly joke some thought it was in 2002. (It served as the introduction to every Dylan concert for the next decade!) The unlikely backstory is that the exact words for the introduction were lifted from a piece written by Jeff Miers in advance of Dylan's concert in Hamburg. Miers was astounded as he sat at the show as a journalist and fan and heard his own words in the new introduction.

On October 25, 2002, in Bernalillo, New Mexico, Dylan reintroduced his 1981 composition "In the Summertime." With Dylan now positioned at the keyboard for concerts, it seemed songs like this one from *Shot of Love* were begging for rediscovery. For those concertgoers in 1999–2002 who scratched their heads at the Jesus cover songs (and the reintroduction of original material from Dylan's so-called Christian phase), the tours in 2003 would further confuse matters.

On February 6, 2003, in Canberra, Australia, "Saving Grace" was unearthed after a twenty-two-year absence. This original Dylan composition from *Saved*, with its lyrical assertion that "there's only one road and it leads to Calvary" was, no doubt, a spiritual bedfellow to his recent penchant for gospel covers.

As if to tempt superstition itself, April 1, 2003, brought the release of *Gotta Serve Somebody: The Gospel Songs of Bob Dylan.* Was the rumor true? Did Dylan participate? The CD was issued through his longtime label Columbia Records. This was no April Fool's joke. Dylan was on board.

Mavis Staples, who sang with Dylan (per his request) on "Gonna Change My Way of Thinking," spoke to journalist Masato Kato about the events surrounding Dylan's compositions of 1979–1980:

> I thought they were great. He took a lot of static from other singers. They didn't like it, but I thought that it was a great thing that he did, 'cause he found the Lord, so he felt like he wanted to sing some gospel songs; so what was wrong with that? I didn't see nothing wrong with that, but it was just like when he began playing the electric guitar! People gotta do what they think they should do and people shouldn't say, "Oh you should do that and you shouldn't do that.' Who are they to judge someone else?"[19]

By spring of 2003—nearly a quarter of a century after *Slow Train Coming* hit the record bins—the negative criticism was largely absent for this *Gotta Serve Somebody* tribute CD. Though the critically positive judgments in publications such as *Christianity Today*, *Charisma*, *Sojourners*, *Gospel Flava*, and *CCM* were not necessarily surprising, the CD garnered positive support from big city newspapers like the *Dallas Morning News*, *St. Petersburg Times*, *Boston Herald*, *Detroit Free Press*, *Philadelphia Inquirer*, *St. Louis Post-Dispatch*, *New York Post*, and the *Chicago Sun-Times*, as well as publications as diverse as *Sing Out!*, *Rolling Stone*, *Billboard*, and *Country Music Today*.

Dylan's participation in the project, a signpost of sorts for his spiritual journey, received scant media attention. Of all the Dylan tribute albums created in the studio across the decades, the man behind the songs had never directly participated in one. *Not a single one.* But this time, he did participate. The type of people that were honoring his songs from *Slow Train Coming* and *Saved* honored him. (And singing with Mavis Staples probably didn't hurt either.)

A few lyrics from the song he contributed, in his own pen, referred to no less than the Second Coming, an admonition for daily prayer, and an acknowledgment from the singer that there isn't any friend like the Lord. Back in 1979–1981, these kinds of Dylan utterances would have received a healthy dose of scorn. By 2003, for whatever reason, attention was being paid elsewhere.

The song eventually wound up in the Dylan canon through an updated version of the singer's *Lyrics* book (2004). It is now known as the alternate version of "Gonna Change My Way of Thinking."[20] The CD from which it came received a Grammy nomination for Best Traditional Soul Gospel Album.

Just months after *Gotta Serve Somebody: The Gospel Songs of Bob Dylan* was released, Dylan's film *Masked and Anonymous* gradually hit theaters as it crisscrossed America. Between cryptic and slapstick scenes, with dialogue written by Dylan and comedy writer Larry Charles, fans also received some musical performances from Dylan, er, Jack Fate (the main character, played by Dylan).

If Dylan's God-given destiny was to write songs and perform, as the singer had recently told several sources in the press, then, in Jack Fate, viewers could discern a reluctant missionary amid the circus-like (yea, apocalyptic) atmosphere of *Masked and Anonymous.*

In other words, just like many of Dylan's songs, the film was not without its biblical allusions. In the opening scene, we hear a radio broadcast of a preacher thundering about the nature of God and challenging his listeners:

"Will man destroy the earth to move on? Is that his destiny? Ask yourselves a question, people: 'Are you humble before God?'" At the conclusion of this broadcast snippet, we hear these words from the preacher:

"Would you swear on the Bible? I'd swear on the Bible. A book of treachery and murder and genocide. Of course, I'd swear on that. And

I'll tell you why. The false Christianity you subscribe to is nothing more than the cult of the Virgin. People, it's time to evaluate every threat on your lives! God has turned his back on his nation, think about it! What did Martin Luther King get out of the whole thing?! A broad?"

Later in the movie, we hear another radio broadcast. This time, an anxious Nina Veronica (Jessica Lange) is listening to a news announcement about some entity that has been digging the world's deepest hole; the thirty-mile mark has been reached:

"Scientists have measured the temperatures down there up to 3,000 degrees," the voice intoned, "They have lowered microphones into the pit and heard the sounds of millions of suffering souls." Here, the late Allen Ginsberg's comments to Dylan after hearing a tape of *Empire Burlesque,* come to mind: "I see you still have the judgment of Jehovah hanging over our heads!"

At another point in Dylan's *Masked and Anonymous,* Veronica is pondering with concert promoter Uncle Sweetheart (John Goodman) why the television network wants Jack Fate to sing "Jailhouse Rock" for the benefit concert:

> VERONICA: They want to plant the seeds of hope.
>
> SWEETHEART: A lot of people try to plant the seeds of hope.
>
> VERONICA: Yeah, but the seeds won't grow if you plant them on the carpet. Or the hardwood floor. You gotta put them in the earth.

For those familiar with the biblical parables—parables Dylan said he was familiar with as early as 1968—the parable of the seed found in the gospel of Luke is the source for Veronica's line.

The words of Jesus were alluded to when Oscar Vogel (Ed Harris in blackface) appears on the scene in the shadows, and delivers his cryptic message, which includes the line, "It's not what goes in the mouth, it is what comes out that counts." Vogel referred to his speaking out when everybody else was "scared." Vogel appears to have made his stand for moral reasons.

At another point in the movie, promoter Uncle Sweetheart declares, "Does Jesus have to walk twice on water to make a point?" When Sweetheart is asked by Jack Fate about his girth, he replies that it's due to his "eating from the tree of knowledge of good and evil," a not-so-subtle nod to the first book of the Hebrew Bible (Genesis). Character Pagan Lace's (Penelope Cruz) "333" tattoo represents another example of a biblical allusion, this time a divisive nod to the "666" spoken about in the final book of the New Testament (Revelation).

Oddly enough, Larry Charles, Dylan's screenwriting partner of comedic fame, acknowledged that the God of the Bible was one of the main characters in the film. Charles also shared his perceptions of Dylan's 1979 experience:

"I think when Dylan was 'born again,' he was just expanding his feeling about religion and God. In his mind—this is my interpretation—I don't think he saw such a disconnect between his Judaism and his Christianity. I think he sees it all as streams running from the same source."[21]

Lest one think the main man behind *Masked and Anonymous* has it all theologically figured out, the closing scene has a bemused Jack Fate rolling along in a bus, being returned to prison (from which he was sprung at the film's start) with "Blowin' in the Wind" playing in the background. These words, uttered by Fate, serve as reflection:

"I was always a singer, and maybe no more than that. Sometimes it's not enough to know the meaning of things. Sometimes we have to know what things don't mean as well. Like what does it mean to not know what the person you love is capable of. Things fall apart, especially all the neat order of rules and laws. The way we look at the world is the way we really are. See it from a fair garden, everything looks cheerful. Climb up to a higher plateau and you'll see plunder and murder. Truth and beauty are in the eye of the beholder. I stopped trying to figure everything out a long time ago."

As *Masked and Anonymous* snaked its way through theaters across America in the summer of 2003, garnering countless negative reviews, "Saving Grace" happened to be one of the many songs Dylan offered his concert audiences. The song from his album *Saved* was also, back in the day, a part of a largely unwelcome greeting via the press reviews.

In 2003, a long-awaited Dylan tome by an academic heavyweight saw the light of day when Christopher Ricks published his *Dylan's Visions of Sin*. Ricks was criticized by some for its organizing principle: Songs received critical treatment in light of the seven deadly sins, the four cardinal virtues, and the three heavenly graces. Ricks' background was well known in certain literary circles, having published books on Samuel Beckett, T.S. Eliot, John Keats, John Milton, and Alfred Lord Tennyson. Perhaps what was not as well known was that Ricks, a long-time Dylan fan who happens to be an atheist, had consistently given Dylan a fair shake as a person and artist when it came to the singer's theological expressions. This, it seems, is no small thing—inside or outside of the Academy.

Speaking of the Academy, in the summer of 2004, a sixty-three-year-old Dylan actually appeared and accepted an honorary doctorate degree from the University of Scotland (that nation's oldest university). Incidentally, at age twenty-nine, back in 1971, Dylan had accepted his first honorary degree, also a Doctor of Music, from Princeton University in Princeton, New Jersey. This time around, coinciding with his summer 2004 tour of the U.K., Dylan attended the ceremony as the laureation was delivered up by Neil Corcoran of the School of English. It included these lines:

"There are so many other songs and other kinds of song [in his songbook]: devotional songs like 'Precious Angel' and 'I Believe in You,' and poignant songs of older age such as 'Not Dark Yet,' songs of resilience, songs of what it means to have come through. Truly, there is God's plenty in Bob Dylan's work; and something Franz Kafka said about Charles Dickens seems to apply to him too—'his vast, instinctive prodigality': a kind of volatile super plus of creative energy and momentum. Bob Dylan's work has been one of the places where the English language has extended itself in our time."[22]

When Dylan was being publicly honored in Scotland, he was also being privately courted for a not-so-small film project. As news was fast being made about Mel Gibson's 2004 blockbuster, *The Passion of the Christ*, Bob Dylan's work lurked behind a soundtrack or two that were devoted to the controversial film. *The Passion of the Christ: Songs Inspired By* (Universal South) was compiled by Lian Lunson with Gibson consulting.[23] The CD concluded with the undeniable blues of Dylan's "Not Dark Yet," the foreboding song off his 1997 Grammy winning album *Time Out of Mind.*

Other tracks included Leonard Cohen's "By the Rivers Dark," Ricky Skaggs' "Are You Afraid to Die?" (featuring an introduction by the Rev. Billy Graham), the Blind Boys of Alabama covering "Precious Lord," Elvis Presley's "Where No One Stands Alone," and Holly Williams covering her grandfather (the late Hank Williams) via "How Can You Refuse Him Now?" On Amazon.com, part of the product description of the CD reads:

"Gibson felt that the songs should complement the message in the film and inspire spiritual reflection, but not in an obvious way. The CD takes the listener on a journey, often a dark and reflective one."

The other CD connected to the movie, *The Passion of the Christ: Songs* (Lost Keyword/Wind Up), included no Dylan songs but an intriguing backstory of what might have been. The CD's producer, Mark Joseph, approached Dylan's camp for an original song and to attend a screening. Dylan agreed and was set to attend a private screening at Gibson's office at 6:00 p.m. At 3:00 his representative called to inquire who was attending; at 4:00 to ask if it would be okay if Dylan didn't speak with anybody; and again at 5:30 to say he wouldn't be coming after all.

Nevertheless, Dylan was still willing to participate, and Joseph suggested two possibilities: "Rock of Ages" and "Rise Again," both of which Dylan had performed live or previously recorded. Dylan's representative said no to "Rise Again," but yes to "Rock of Ages." Excited to have Dylan on board, Joseph was turned down by officials at the record label who wanted the soundtrack to be youth-oriented. He then had the difficult task of telling Dylan's representative thanks but no thanks.

The other performers on the CD were a generation removed from Dylan: Mark Hoppus of Blink 182, Yolanda Adams, Steven Curtis Chapman, Sara Evans, Kirk Franklin, Lauryn Hill, MercyMe, MxPx, P.O.D., Brad Paisley, Scott Stapp of Creed, Third Day, Angie Stone, Dan Lavery, Big Dismal, Charlotte Church, and BeBe Winans.

Critics and observers have been questioning Dylan's words and deeds for decades now, so an autobiography or memoir from the man himself could potentially clear things up. Enter Dylan's *Chronicles* (2004), his first serious book which seemed like a genuine attempt to share his thoughts, feelings, and memories with his public. "I'm used to writing songs, and songs—I can fill 'em up with symbolism and metaphors," he told David Gates of *Newsweek*, "but when you write a book like this, you gotta tell the truth, and it can't be misinterpreted."[24]

When asked about the biblical title of the book that David Rosenthal (Simon & Schuster's publisher) had suggested, Dylan had this response: "*Chronicles* just means—I'm not sure what it means [laughs], but it would seem to be some kind of thing where you can make right use of the past."

As to the style and some of the content, there was no shortage of intrigue. Although the first installment of these memoirs did not cover the so-called religious period of 1979-1981, Dylan couldn't help but catch the biblical echoes that have bounced around his lyrics and interviews for decades.

For Dylan, his favorite city, New York, was a "modern-day Gomorrah" and when he arrived in Manhattan, at age nineteen, he was exposed to "protest songs," including Woody Guthrie's "Jesus Christ." But when Dylan shed his skin as a student and interpreter of various forms of music (folk, gospel, blues, country) to become an original songwriter, his "little shack in the universe was about to expand into some glorious cathedral."

During this significant transition in the early 1960s, Dylan informed his readers that he visited the public library in New York City to scour the archives from a century before his time—the Civil War era. "Back there, America was put on the cross, died, and was resurrected," Dylan unabashedly wrote. "There was nothing synthetic about it. The godawful truth of that would be the all-encompassing template behind everything that I would write."[25]

We also learn that Dylan was singing the Woodstock blues in a big way, circa the late 1960s, when the fan[atic] factor was overwhelming. "Eventually different anachronisms were thrust upon me—anachronisms of lesser dilemma—though they might seem bigger. Legend, Icon, Enigma (Buddha in European Clothes was my favorite)—stuff like that, but that was all right," wrote Dylan. "These titles were placid and harmless, threadbare, easy to get around with them. Prophet, Messiah, Savior—those are tough ones."

Fast-forward to the late 1980s and Dylan finds himself in a New Orleans store talking to a character named Sun Pie who asks him if he is a "prayin' man." And if the Sun Pie anecdote in *Chronicles* isn't amusing enough for readers, then Dylan also issues what appears to be a somewhat sympathetic editorial on the fallen televangelist Jimmy Swaggart.

As for the critical response to *Chronicles*, it could not have been much better. If the critically panned *Masked and Anonymous* from the previous year was too cryptic and obscure for the tastes of the general public, then *Chronicles* was downright accessible. The reviews were largely positive, even gushing, and the book was nominated for the National Book Critics Circle Award in the biography/autobiography category. Jay Michaelson, writing for *Forward*, included these lines in his review:

"Dylan's 'religious phase' might have taken some people by surprise, just as U2's recent hymn, 'Yahweh,' has, but anyone who's followed either artist knows that images of God—whether as 'Father of Night' or 'Solid Rock'—always have been at the center of Dylan's work."[26]

Journalist Alan Light pitched in his commentary through Beliefnet.com and concluded the following: "Dylan's new memoir traces his spiritual and musical journey through modern America."[27]

Toward the end of his review of *Chronicles*, John Tintera of

Explorefaith.org had this to say: "If the vocation of the prophet is to look behind the veil and to boldly state what he sees, then Dylan in his golden years is doing that as well as any person alive today. . . . For those looking for spiritual insights, Dylan's current work, both the new book and the recent CDs, carve out a sacred space amongst the reckless materialism of our age. That space is filled with suffering, but it's a suffering that points the way to redemption."[28]

The month after the publication of *Chronicles*, in November of 2004, Dylan was winding up yet another year of touring and stopped off at Messiah College in Grantham, Pennsylvania. In one of the few outings of the year for his then twenty-five-year-old composition, "In the Garden," Dylan gave the crowd at this Christian liberal arts college a musical reflection of the Messiah's identity.

Less than two weeks later, Dylan was in Bethlehem, Pennsylvania, playing at Lehigh University. Before the concert, an article was published in the town's local newspaper and quoted some eager fans anticipating Dylan's arrival. Staff writer Geoff Gehman informed readers that concert attendee Kathy Marsters "will hope against hope to give her hero an illustrated edition of the Psalms by King David, one of the musician's heroes." "I just feel like Dylan nails the truth on the head; it's just truth for me," Marsters said. Her sixteen-year-old son, Noah, had his take on Dylan too:

> It's not incredible music, but the words Dylan writes can be incredible. I think he's more of a poet than a musician. It's not just a bunch of crap he's writing. He's standing up for black people and other stuff. He's probably the first person to have a punk attitude. I'd call him the first punk, really.[29]

The day after the Bethlehem gig, online readers of *Rolling Stone* found a Q&A session with Dylan that included this exchange:

> Q: What's the last song you'd like to hear before you die?
>
> A: How 'bout "Rock of Ages"?[30]

Before 2004 concluded, Dylan was featured on CBS's *60 Minutes* as Ed Bradley conducted the first television interview with the singer/songwriter in nearly two decades. (Might any other pop culture icon avoid television interviews as diligently?) If one still doubted Dylan's recent commentary about his "calling" and "destiny," then he reiterated it in charming fashion for the viewers of *60 Minutes*:

BRADLEY: Why do you still do it? Why are you still out there (touring)?

DYLAN: Well, it goes back to that destiny thing. I mean, I made a bargain with it, you know, long time ago. And I'm holding up my end.

BRADLEY: What was your bargain?

DYLAN: To get where, er, I am now.

BRADLEY: Should I ask who you made the bargain with?

DYLAN: [laughs] With, with, with...you know, with the Chief, with the Chief Commander.

BRADLEY: On this earth?

DYLAN: [laughing] On this earth and in the world we can't see.

And with that, the interview piece ended. By the time CBS viewers had witnessed a low-key, almost melancholic Dylan conclude his first television interview since the mid-1980s, the singer had finished his tours of 2004.

In 2005, *Moment* magazine treated fans to a cover story entitled "Bob Dylan: The Unauthorized Spiritual Biography,"[31] a lengthy account which included this quote from Hibbing resident Cantor Schwartz regarding Dylan's coming to Jesus: "[It] certainly was a topic of discussion in whatever Jewish community I was a member of, but those of us that came from the hinterlands like he did predicted that it wasn't going to last, and we were right."

Moment writers Nadine Epstein and Rebecca Frankel let readers know that Dylan began to "distance himself from Christianity" and suggested that "perhaps the time has come for his Jewish fans to forgive Robert Zimmerman for his brief sojourn away from the faith" and added that "many ardent Jewish Dylan admirers believe that he had to leave Judaism in order to return more fully."

What Epstein and Frankel conveniently left out of their story are the innumerable instances where Dylan continues to sing about Jesus, whether through the same songs he wrote during his experience of 1979 or the cover songs in recent years—not to mention the interview snippets along the way that shed further light.

With that said, they should be commended for tackling a subject that is too often neglected in the traditional biographical sketch of Dylan. (Clinton Heylin is a notable exception.) The man sings and speaks about spiritual things. To ignore or underestimate this aspect of his life and art is to miss a large part of what, arguably, makes him tick.

Another interesting Dylan-related story of 2005 was the fact that the popular band Switchfoot took their inspiration for their song "Happy is a Yuppie Word" from nothing less than a Bob Dylan interview! No typo here: the inspiration did not come through a Dylan song, but an *interview* from 1991 when *Rolling Stone* asked the singer if he was happy. Dylan, dismissive of the words *happiness* and *unhappiness* (attributing them to yuppies), preferred instead the biblical notion of either being blessed or unblessed.

In the fall of 2005, as the holidays approached, it was reported that Dylan had, yet again, found his way to a synagogue. Faithful chronicler Larry Yudelson typed these words into his blog: "Bob Dylan made it *shul* again this Yom Kippur, in the town known as Oyster Bay, Long Island [New York] . . . well, actually, in the town of Woodbury, Long Island, in the Chabad of Oyster Bay. My non-rabbinical source for this cites as eyewitnesses his father's friend, and his accountant. What's not to believe?"[32]

In December of 2005, an announcement came forth that was, arguably, as mind-blowing and unbelievable as the singer appearing before the pope or in a Victoria's Secret television ad: a new deejay gracing the airwaves of XM satellite radio in 2006 would be none other than Bob Dylan.

It did make sense in a way, considering that Dylan's formative musical influences were drawn, in no small measure, from the radio stations he was picking up in Minnesota as a young man. Back in 1985, when interviewed by Cameron Crowe for the *Biograph* release, Dylan had this to say about radio: "Pop music on the radio? I don't know. I listen mostly to preacher stations and the country music stations and maybe the oldies stations." In 1993, Dylan granted an interview to Reuters where he took a jab or two at the state of pop radio and contemporary country singers.[33]

In February 2006, the documentary DVD *Gotta Serve Somebody: The Gospel Songs of Bob Dylan* was released, an historical document tracing the artists who contributed to the 2003 CD of the same name. Throughout the beginning of the video, we see a new tape of snippets (its producers had access to the Dylan vaults) of Dylan singing "When He Returns" from a widely bootlegged concert in Toronto, Canada, in April 1980.

Viewers are also treated to interviews with author Paul Williams who wrote the seminal book, *Dylan—What Happened?* (1979), and producer Jerry Wexler, who provided disarming wit and gave Dylan kudos on what he achieved during the *Slow Train* era.

The documentary also includes interviews with the artists who recorded and toured with Dylan during the controversial 1979–81 era (guitarist Fred Tackett, drummer Jim Keltner, singer Regina McCrary, and others). Additionally, viewers get to see the artists who covered Dylan's songs of faith for this project (since they were videotaped in the studio). This unique combination of the CD (2003) and DVD (2006) was ultimately inspired by Jeff Gaskill, an eyewitness to one of Dylan's gospel gigs in 1980. He had always wanted to have gospel artists interpret these Dylan compositions.

Arguably, the ultimate seal of approval for Gaskill's project came when Dylan himself, in 2000, agreed to participate. What began as an agreement for a supportive role (harmonica or guitar on a track) turned into, by 2002, the previously mentioned rewritten version of "Gonna Change My Way of Thinking" that Dylan sang. He was not contractually obligated to do what he did—but he did it.

On May 3, 2006, Dylan's deejay debut (with the theme of weather) included songs from as diverse quarters as Muddy Waters, Dean Martin, Jimi Hendrix, Judy Garland, Fats Domino, Stevie Wonder, and Frank Sinatra. It also included gospel numbers by The Consolers, Sister Rosetta Tharpe, the Staple Singers, and the Carter Family. Tharpe's song "Didn't It Rain?" was not unfamiliar territory for Dylan: "Well, it rained forty days and forty nights without stopping / Noah was glad when the water stopped dropping / When I get to heaven, sitting right down / Asking Jesus for my starry crown."

The second show, in which the theme was mothers (in honor of Mother's Day), had Dylan spinning the records of everyone from Randy Newman and the Rolling Stones to Merle Haggard and LL Cool J. Also included was Dylan issuing this introduction to Buck Owens' "I'll Go To The Church Again With Momma": "Here's Buck singing about hymns that warm your heart in the sweet by-and-by, that chapel in the sky." Dylan's choice was likely owed to Owens' recent death. Here is an excerpt from the song: "Now momma's gone to heaven to meet Jesus there / And I know she's happy there, Lord / And I know someday I'll meet her up there / And we'll sing and praise the Lord."

Another early show tackled the theme of cars and featured artists such as Bruce Springsteen, Joni Mitchell, Prince, and Chuck Berry. A song by the gospel group the Dixie Hummingbirds, "Christian Automobile," included these lyrics: "Well, you know every child of God / Is running for Jesus . . . Faith is your steering wheel . . . When you get on your road to glory, Satan's gonna try to flag you down." The Dixie Hummingbirds recorded Dylan's 1980 gospel song "City of Gold" for their widely acclaimed 2003 album, *Diamond Jubilation: 75th Anniversary.* This same track appeared on the soundtrack to Dylan's 2003 film, *Masked and Anonymous.*

Dylan's affinity for gospel shouldn't exactly be news, but more newsworthy is how at least one gospel legend became aware of the Minnesota songwriter:

"I wasn't too familiar [with Dylan] until he wrote 'Gotta Serve Somebody,'" recalled Clarence Fountain of the Blind Boys of Alabama. "That song gave me the idea that we could take one or two of his gospel songs and fit 'em into our repertoire."

What did Fountain think when he heard Dylan singing about Jesus?

"I thought that, well, that he has a soul to save, just like I do. And I think it was a nice gesture that he could take . . . you know he doesn't sing that well, you know that already, but he could write so good that it makes up for all of the singing—and I thought that was a nice gesture, in him coming to God. That's what we all should do, is turn to the Lord. His songs made him a rich man, made him very popular among the people, and I thought it was nice for him to think about the Lord—that he had a soul to save, like everybody else."[34]

On August 29, 2006, *Modern Times* (Dylan's thirty-second album) saw its release as the sixty-five-year-old singer proved yet again that he wasn't finished singing about the blues and spirituality. Listeners would be hard pressed to find a song on the album that didn't contain some kind of biblical allusion.

In "Thunder on the Mountain," the rollicking song that kicks off the album, there is a bold reference to a whole-hearted confession; the singer concludes that he does not need to confess again.

Apocalyptic blues seems to be in order when experiencing "Rollin' and Tumblin'," a song that includes a plea for mutual forgiveness. Forgiveness is also a part of the plan described in the resigned yet confident "When the Deal Goes Down." Images of invisible prayers compared to clouds in the air and midnight rain following the train—all look and sound like the lyrics of Robert Allen Zimmerman.

Dylan is feeding his soul with thought in the touching "Workingman's Blues #2" and spiritual allusions are scattered all over the place in "Beyond the Horizon": wretched hearts; an angel's kiss; someone praying for someone's soul; the singer's plain repentance;

countries, kingdoms, and temples of stone; and a life being spared.

Although the pathos-filled "Nettie Moore" wins the mournful award with its pile of sins to pay for, it is not without humor: Dylan links the world of research with going berserk—due to too much paperwork. Additionally, two characters from the opening song of Dylan's 1992 album *Good As I Been to You* make an appearance: Frankie & Albert are in the graveyard raising hell, and are causing the singer to "believe what the Scriptures tell." The singer is later standing in faith and raising a voice of praise; yet it is draining to stand in that light and he is wishing to God it were night.

Only the Lord could make a day or season like the one described in "The Levee's Gonna Break." The singer is not ready to stop his journey because riches and salvation could be behind the next bend in the road. Who is the "I" who is picking someone up from the gutter and not getting adequate thanks—and is not done, quite yet, with the former gutter-bound person? The singer is looking into this entity's eyes and sees nobody other than himself—and is thinking of all he is, and all he hopes to be. According to the song, there are still a few more years of hard work but then there will be a thousand years of happiness.

"Ain't Talkin'," the concluding song of *Modern Times*, is chock full of bluesy sentiment: a weary world of woe; talk of prayer being an antidote for an evil spirit in possession of a heart; attempts to love one's neighbor but things not going well; slaughtering sleeping opponents where they lie. The singer is practicing a faith long abandoned—and this long and lonesome road has no altars to speak of. Heavenly aid is apparently available, though. Dylan ends *Modern Times* with an allusion to walking with a toothache in his heel; an absent gardener; and being in the last outback, at the end of the world.

Jonathan Lethem, a forty-two-year-old moonlighting novelist, took on interviewing duties for *Rolling Stone* in the wake of Dylan's latest release. Lethem's history with Dylan dated back to a certain album from the late 1970s: "The first Dylan record I was able to respond to as new—to witness its arrival in stores and reception in magazines, and therefore make my own—was 1979's *Slow Train Coming*."

As an interviewee, sitting in a hotel in Santa Monica, California, Dylan's opening line is priceless: "I don't really have a herd of astrologers telling me what's going to happen. I just make one move after the other, this leads to that." As for the songs that comprised *Modern Times*, they were "just in my genes and I couldn't stop them comin' out."

Dylan's touring band, which backed him on the recording, was "the best band I've ever been in, I've ever had, man for man." Lethem and readers of *Rolling Stone* also heard Dylan's take on his general approach to concerts and his perceptions of the role of an artist:

> They say, 'Dylan never talks.' What the hell is there to say? That's not the reason an artist is in front of people. An artist has come for a different purpose. Maybe a self-help group—maybe a Dr. Phil—would say, 'How you doin'?' I don't want to get harsh and say I don't care. You do care, you care in a big way, otherwise you wouldn't be there. But it's a different kind of connection. It's not a light thing. It's alive every night, or it feels alive every night. It becomes risky. I mean, you risk your life to play music, if you're doing it in the right way.[35]

Less than a year later, in spring of 2007, Dylan would chat again with *Rolling Stone*. The magazine's founder Jann Wenner was celebrating the fortieth anniversary of his publication. The same man who wrote a glowing review of Dylan's *Slow Train Coming* (one of the very few in the press to do so) was still curious about the religion question.

He asked if Dylan found himself being a more religious person these days. After saying religion has "supposedly" been a force for positive good, Dylan directed two questions back to his interviewer: Where in our world can we see religion's positive effect, and where has humanity been uplifted by a connection to a godly power?

Did Dylan mean organized religion, Wenner wondered. Corporations are religions and anything can be made into a religion, Dylan responded. Wenner then narrowed down his questioning to Dylan's personal history:

WENNER: At one point, you took on Christianity in a very serious way, and then Judaism. Where are you now with all that?

DYLAN: Religion is something that is mostly outward appearance. Faith is a different thing. How many religions are there in the world? Quite a few, actually.

WENNER: What is your faith these days?

DYLAN: Faith doesn't have a name. It doesn't have a category. It's oblique. It's unspeakable. We degrade faith by talking about religion.

Author and blogger Douglas LeBlanc of GetReligion.org summed up the exchange: "God bless Jann Wenner for trying so hard to coax Bob Dylan out of his fiercely guarded privacy on spiritual matters."[36]

Back in the late 1960s, even an emerging figure like Jann Wenner had to scratch and claw to land his first Dylan interview.[37] He wrote Dylan letters until a response came—some six months later. Two months on, they met in late 1968 to discuss the mere prospect of an interview. Finally, in June 1969, the interview took place in Wenner's New York hotel. The twenty-three-year-old magazine founder pointed out how writers, college students, and college writers were incredibly affected by Dylan's music. The audience had a feeling, an expectation that Dylan had "the answer." "What answer?" Dylan asked. The founder of *Rolling Stone* referenced the film *Dont Look Back* and how people were "tremendously hung up on you and what you write and what you say." Wenner wondered if Dylan responded to this, and if he felt responsible to said audience. If he could ease someone's mind, lighten every load, and straighten out every burden, said Dylan, he'd be the first one to do it. "I don't want anybody to be hung up . . . [laughs] especially over *me*, or anything I do. That's not the point at all."

Wenner's inquiry about Dylan's religious views in 2007 seemed more of a follow-up curiosity, but in 1969 he further pressed Dylan on whether he was a great "youth leader" since he was an extremely important musical figure and "in the experience of growing up."

Dylan's response was telling: "If I thought I was that person, wouldn't I be out there doing it? Wouldn't I be, if I thought I was meant to do that, wouldn't I be doing it? I don't have to hold back. This Maharishi [Mahesh Yogi], he thinks that—right? He's out there doing it. Don't you agree, right? So obviously, I don't think *that*."

It could be said that by 1979 Dylan thought he was meant to be out there doing it a la his experience reflected through *Slow Train Coming* and *Saved*. Dylan wasn't the guru to guide your every move, but he had the gall to point to the Answer. For his part, Wenner closed his gushing review of the 1979 album by citing "When He Returns" and remarked how Dylan's voice had "the sound of the soul itself."[38] Though Dylan originally intended to have his singers sing the song, producer Jerry Wexler remembered his own suggestion for "When He Returns": "Let's put it this way; when I heard it, I said, 'Bob, you should do this,'" said Wexler. "He started to sing it and wasn't really doing it, you know, up to snuff, so Barry Beckett made a piano demo of it. And Dylan went home that night and worked with it and came back the next day and recorded it beautifully."[39]

On August 15, 2008, Jerry Wexler died at age ninety-one in his home in Sarasota, Florida. On tour, Dylan presumably heard news of Wexler's early morning passing and included the *Slow Train Coming* track "I Believe in You" in his set list that evening in Mashantucket, Connecticut.

The song for which Dylan received his first-ever Grammy—"Gotta Serve Somebody"—was also the song he opened with in New York City for his final gig of 2008. This was the same song for which Dylan thanked the Lord and Jerry Wexler during a brief Grammy acceptance speech in 1980. Worthy to note here that when many in the fan base thought Dylan was at his most closed-minded, he managed to publicly thank both his Creator and a fellow Jew, an atheist, in the same breath.

By late 2008, fans tracking Dylan's recorded output had another album to add to the pile—the eighth installment in *The Bootleg Series: Tell Tale Signs: Rare and Unreleased: 1989-2006*.

Within the "Red River Shore," an outtake from *Time Out of Mind*, Dylan includes an unmistakable line about hearing of the resurrection power of Jesus, as he longs for that girl from the Red River shore.

"Marchin' to the City" opens with the singer sitting in church in an old wooden chair, knowing nobody would look for him there (a simple, humorous, and telling line). "Lord have mercy" is heard in the song and with Dylan one tends to doubt it is a throwaway line: nothing can heal him but someone's touch; he's thinking and wondering about paradise—and that train keeps rolling all night long.

In the first stanza of "Cross the Green Mountain," a song from the *Gods and Generals* soundtrack, heaven is blazing in the singer's head. There is an image that alludes to the Book of Revelation: the singer is looking into the eyes of a merciful friend; pondering the souls in heaven; yet there is a declaration that all must yield to "the avenging God"; blasphemy is on tongues; and an admonishment to serve God and be cheerful while you're at it.

Another outtake from *Time Out of Mind*, "Dreamin' of You," has Dylan hiding his faith in the rain; church bells are ringing as he's wondering who they're ringing for. "Can't Escape From You," an unreleased song dated December 2005, has Dylan plowing the fields of heaven; hoping he can be forgiven, and singing the blues about a woman he can't get away from.

Jon Pareles, writing in *The New York Times* about the album, concluded that "It's Mr. Dylan in his wandering, God-haunted, apocalyptic philosopher mode, a man utterly alone with his only firm footing in the blues."[40]

By April 2009, Dylan was in Amsterdam on Easter weekend being interviewed by Rice University history professor, Dr. Douglas Brinkley. The occasion was a cover story for *Rolling Stone*.[41] Brinkley decided, after the concert at the Heineken Music Hall, to push Dylan on the significance of Christian Scripture in his life. "Well, sure, that and those other first books I read were really biblical stuff. *Uncle Tom's Cabin* and *Ben-Hur*," said Dylan. "Those were the books that I remembered reading and finding religion in."

Interestingly, here with the historian and professor, Dylan doesn't seem bothered by the connotation of the word "religion," unlike the norm and unlike two years earlier when the founder of *Rolling Stone* received more resistance during his line of questioning.

That Easter 2009 weekend, on April 12, the historian and other attendees at the Amsterdam concert witnessed Dylan reflecting his faith through the show-opening "Gotta Serve Somebody."

Dylan's thirty-third album, *Together Through Life*—released some two weeks after the interview with Brinkley—will not go down in history as a document of Dylan's faith. But sprinkled throughout the musical backdrop of the blues and Tex-Mex sound were lyrical allusions to a spiritual landscape.

The narrator of "If You Ever Go to Houston," counsels sister Betty to "pray the sinner's prayer," a staple in evangelical Christian circles. In "Forgetful Heart," a companion was an answer to his prayers, yet there is the tension of a door closing forevermore—and even a question as to whether or not the door existed. Opportunities, passages, and experiences seem long gone when the singer has got the blues of a forgetful heart.

An admonition to raise your voice and pray is issued in "Shake Shake Mama." In "I Feel a Change Comin' On," besides the juxtaposition of listening to singer Billy Joe Shaver and reading literary giant James Joyce, there is the image of someone's baby walking with the village priest. Although the singer sings of people informing him that he's got "the blood of the land" in his voice, it just as easily could be "the blood of the Lamb." Either way, the landscape of America and the figure of Jesus are bound to Dylan's voice and experience. In *Chronicles*, Dylan wrote of how the Civil War was a template for his work. As previously mentioned, he unabashedly employed the metaphor of the cross of Jesus—his crucifixion, death, and resurrection—to describe what happened to the country and his art that followed.

Together Through Life concludes with "It's All Good", a wry allusion to a popular phrase in the Twenty-first century. But all is not well as we are marched through the song's targets, which include: gossip; politicians' lies; wives leaving their husbands; people tearing people down; sick people who can barely stand; the widow's cry and the orphan's plea; a killer stalking the town; and crumbling buildings in the neighborhood. Bob Dylan believes in a fallen world, no doubt, but as the album's title *Together Through Life* suggests, there is the reality of fellowship that makes life's journey more bearable.

By October 2009, comedian David Letterman's longtime sidekick Paul Shaffer published his memoir *We'll Be Here for the Rest of Our Lives*. Readers soon discovered its opening chapter title to be no less than "Dylan and Me." By 1979, when Shaffer was employed at *Saturday Night Live*, he certainly wasn't oblivious to the spiritual underpinnings of the Dylan story:

"Then came the rumors that our man Zimmy had ventured beyond the Old Testament into the New. I didn't want to believe it," wrote Shaffer. "I clung to the notion that once they cut the tip, you're always hip. Yet there he was, onstage in Studio 8H at 30 Rock in the middle of New York City, singing 'You Gotta Serve Somebody.' And I knew damn well that 'somebody' sure wasn't Moses. I was bothered and bewildered. Dylan was bewitched."[42]

Shaffer recalled an exchange between himself and the *Slow Train Coming* co-producer: "'Can we lose the cross, Jerry?' I whispered in Wexler's hairy ear. 'Oh, I wouldn't say anything,' he said in a panic. 'Bob takes this s--- seriously.' 'I'm kidding,' I said. But I wasn't."

Shaffer acknowledged that he lost track of Dylan's spiritual journey over the years but hastened to add: "I myself have remained consistent. I'm Jewish, I'm happy. I love the tradition."

Not many days after the publication of Shaffer's book, a very public movement in Dylan's spiritual journey manifested itself: Dylan's thirty-fourth album, an unexpected holiday affair, *Christmas in the Heart*, saw release on October 13, 2009. It came nearly thirty years to the day since Dylan debuted his Jesus-centered songs in front of a stunned Paul Shaffer, *Saturday Night Live* studio crowd, and national television audience.

If some contemporary Christians have lamented that Jesus is often left out of an increasingly commercialized Christmas, Dylan's 2009 album title suggested where Christmas belonged. Traditional songs about Santa and the winter season were not neglected ("Here Comes Santa" and "Winter Wonderland"); but solemn and celebratory songs about the Savior being born were present too: "Do You Hear What I Hear?" "Hark the Herald Angels Sing," "Little Drummer Boy," "O Come All Ye Faithful," and "O Little Town of Bethlehem." In the months leading up to Dylan's Christmas album, more than a few souls wondered—and posted online—that this *had* to be some kind of joke. In 1979, likewise, long before the advent of the Internet, not a few fans presumed Dylan's reported coming to Jesus *had* to be a joke.

But by late 2009, when it came to discerning the motives of a sixty-eight-year-old Bob Dylan, there were no doubting Thomas tendencies from historian Sean Wilentz. He took stock of Dylan's Christmas album and posted these words for the *Daily Beast* website at 12:28 a.m., the very day of its release:

> In fact, making this record is a generous act that is fully in keeping with Dylan's past and with his ever-developing art. The crass reason for artists to release special albums of Christmas songs had always been to cash in on the lucrative Christmas sales market. Dylan understands as much—but in the Christian spirit of *caritas*, he has donated all of his royalties from the album ahead of time, and in perpetuity, to buy meals for millions of needy persons through the organizations Feeding America, Crisis (in Great Britain), and the United Nations' World Food Program.[43]

The Princeton professor of history was well aware of the doubters of Dylan's latest studio effort. "But the album contains not a single ironic or parodic note," wrote Wilentz. "It is a sincere, raspy-voiced homage to a particular vintage of popular American Christmas music, as well as testimony to Dylan's abiding spiritual faith; hence, its title."

Bill Flanagan interviewed Dylan some five weeks after the album's release.[44] The journalist who had first interviewed Dylan back in 1985 was struck by one song in particular:

FLANAGAN: You really give a heroic performance of "O Little Town of Bethlehem." The way you do it reminds me a little of an Irish rebel song. There's something almost defiant in the way you sing, "The hopes and fears of all the years are met in Thee tonight." I don't want to put you on the spot, but you sure deliver that song like a true believer.

DYLAN: Well, I am a true believer.

For those with ears to hear, that simple six-word response from Dylan could not have been clearer. The interview, conducted on behalf of the North American Street Newspaper Association, made the rounds online, and also included this intriguing exchange:

FLANAGAN: You know, some people will think that Bob Dylan doing a Christmas album is meant to be ironic or a put-on. This sounds to me like one of the most sincere records you've ever made. Did anybody at your record company or management resist the idea?

DYLAN: No, it was my record company who compelled me to do it.

FLANAGAN: Why now?

DYLAN: Well, it just came my way now, at this time. Actually, I don't think I would have been experienced enough earlier anyway.

Flanagan even brought up one review of the album that concluded the effort fell short:

FLANAGAN: The *Chicago Tribune* felt this record needed more irreverence. Doesn't that miss the point?

DYLAN: Well, sure it does; that's an irresponsible statement anyway. Isn't there enough irreverence in the world? Who would need more? Especially at Christmas time.

Dylan's response here is reminiscent of his saying that the "Is God Dead?" *Time* magazine headline of 1966 was irresponsible (that headline coincided with the Easter season).

If there is a song that Dylan wrote that nicely captures an abiding faith that Sean Wilentz wrote about, it is the alternate version of "Gonna Change My Way of Thinking" from *Gotta Serve Somebody: The Gospel Songs of Bob Dylan.* The song received its live debut in Seattle, Washington, on October 4, 2009—just before the release of *Christmas in the Heart.*

Meanwhile, on the culture war front, conservative radio host Laura Ingraham played a clip from Dylan's "Precious Angel" (from *Slow Train Coming*) in the background on her radio show while introducing her guests Christopher Hitchens and Doug Wilson. On October 25, 2009, the two men were on her show to promote *Collision: Is Christianity Good for the World?* a DVD that was the result of a rhetorical collaboration, and to argue their respective points (Hitchens, a prolific author and notable atheist, and Wilson, an author and Christian pastor). After Ingraham made some introductory comments, Hitchens had an interesting response at the top of the show:

> INGRAHAM: I don't think any other host in the United States would set up this debate with Dylan's studio gospel CD, which is one of my favorites, okay, because this is Bob Dylan embracing, as he embraced all different genres of music, gospel.
>
> HITCHENS: It's funny though; I have to say it: He never seems more beautiful than in this phase of his life.

Hitchens' comment about Dylan's disposition was delightfully unorthodox, but his use of the word "phase" was orthodox: all phases must end. However, Christmas was still, apparently, in the heart for Dylan and being manifested in public ways.

Before 2009 concluded, Dylan chose to perform "Gonna Change My Way of Thinking" as his opening song at ten concerts, including the evening of November 15 at the Wang Theater in Boston, Massachusetts.

A photograph taken from that day, featuring Dylan, Betsy Siggins, and Maria Muldaur, is now a part of the New England Folk Music Archives. Siggins, the founder of the archives (and former college roommate of Joan Baez), was a fixture of Boston's Club 47 in the 1960s. Though some old friends from their folkie days were captured by a photographer in this late 2009 photograph, Muldaur also has a deep connection with Dylan from the gospel concerts of 1979–1980. She too had an experience of her own with Jesus around the same time as Dylan. Muldaur vividly remembers 1979 as her daughter Jenni escaped a near-death automobile accident that year—and Dylan's album *Slow Train Coming* played no small part in a transformative personal experience. She had no reservations about Bob Dylan's spirituality:

"He was anointed before he even knew what the word meant. He was anointed; his songs are totally anointed songs. It was coming through him. It's just like when God chose Moses; it wasn't that he was so perfect or learned. A lot of guys that God chose to work through were not the most learned rabbis. They were people that would open up to hear the Word from the Spirit. Moses came to being a prophet kicking and screaming all the way. Even Jesus said, 'Why me, Lord?' and 'Do I really have to, Father?' I think Bob was really chosen. A lot of his most incredible songs have come from the Lord, from before he even knew it."

Muldaur has known Dylan since the folkie days of the early 1960s and admired his songs then. As in 2009, their paths occasionally crossed. For example, in 1979–1980, she linked up with Dylan during the tours in San Francisco. When reflecting on an interview she granted for Martin Scorcese's 2005 Dylan documentary, *No Direction Home*, she couldn't shake from her mind Dylan's song "In The Garden" from the *Saved* album:

> That's an incredible song. I remember telling Dylan that I thought that there was such a sense of ascension in that song, the way he built that song. He's deceptively simple but each verse went up just like somebody rising. I want to read you what I felt like I had wanted to say when these people were recently interviewing me for a Dylan

> special. I just looked up in the dictionary a couple of words: *prophet*: "a person who speaks by divine inspiration, or as the interpreter whom through divinity expressed His will or message to the people; the chief spokesman of a movement or cause; one who speaks beforehand, a proclaimer." In that sense, for sure, he is. And then there's the verb *prophesy*: "to reveal by divine inspiration; to predict, prefigure, foreshow; to reveal the will and message of God." So there's no doubt in my mind that that's what he was doing before he even knew what he was doing. I was talking in the interview about the early 1960s; that's what they were asking me about.[45]

Thirty years after *Slow Train Coming*'s release, in a theater in Boston, it seemed appropriate that Muldaur and Dylan would share some fellowship together and she would get to witness Dylan's rewritten "Gonna Change My Way of Thinking" as the show opener. Dylan had plugged in. Electric. Gospel. All of the above. The slow train was still chugging along.

7

2010-2016: STAND BY ME

Saint Paul said we see through the glass darkly. There's plenty of mystery in nature and contemporary life. For some people, it's too harsh to deal with. But I don't see it that way.

—BOB DYLAN, 2011

I've always been drawn to spiritual songs. In "Amazing Grace" that line—"that saved a wretch like me"—isn't that something we could all say if we were honest enough?

—BOB DYLAN, 2014

FORMER U.S. PRESIDENT JIMMY CARTER wanted Bob Dylan to perform at the White House on the heels of the release of *Slow Train Coming* in 1979. That didn't materialize, but some thirty years later, on February 9, 2010, Dylan finally did make it to the White House—and performed before an audience that included President Barack Obama and First Lady Michelle Obama. Dylan's performance marked one of many for an event entitled "The White House Celebration of Music from the Civil Rights Movement."

Later in the year, *Rolling Stone* published an interview with President Obama. Not surprisingly, Jann Wenner asked Obama about the Dylan appearance; he received this response from the United States' commander in chief:

"Here's what I love about Dylan: He was exactly as you'd expect he would be. He wouldn't come to the rehearsal; usually, all these guys are practicing before the set in the evening. He didn't want to take a picture with me; usually all the talent is dying to take a picture with me and Michelle before the show, but he didn't show up to that. He came in and played 'The Times They Are A-Changin'. A beautiful rendition. The guy is so steeped in this stuff that he can just come up with some new arrangement, and the song sounds completely different. Finishes the song, steps off the stage—I'm sitting right in the front row—comes up, shakes my hand, sort of tips his head, gives me just a little grin, and then leaves. And that was it—then he left. That was our only interaction with him. And I thought: That's how you want Bob Dylan, right? You don't want him to be all cheesin' and grinnin' with you. You want him to be a little skeptical about the whole enterprise. So that was a real treat."[1]

In previous interviews, Obama revealed that some of Dylan's songs reside in his iPod. At the time of Obama's birth, a twenty-year-old Dylan was finding his way around New York City, ultimately creating what would become his debut album. Dylan's cross-generational appeal can now be seen in U.S. presidents.

Former UPI reporter Wesley Pippert reminded us that it was Dylan's song "Man Gave Names to All the Animals" that President Carter's grandkids loved when *Slow Train Coming* was playing on a record player in the White House back in November of 1979.[2] It is doubtful that Obama's iPod includes this relatively obscure Dylan tune, but it is nonetheless interesting to note that the song some criticized as a throwaway ultimately has endured. Around the same time the *Rolling Stone* interview with Obama was published, an illustrated book entitled *Man Gave Names to All the Animals* was one of the latest Dylan-related books to emerge. Dylan granted permission for his lyrics to be used as illustrator Jim Arnosky created a beautiful children's book.[3] However, this is not the first illustrated book of the same title that connects up with the same Dylan song; back in 1999, illustrator Scott Menchin was there first.[4]

How "Man Gave Names to All the Animals" even made the cut in the first place for the *Slow Train Coming* album makes for an interesting story. Regina McCrary, one of Dylan's singers at the time, remembered a particular studio session:

> I remember being in Muscle Shoals, Alabama, and Bob Dylan and Jerry Wexler weren't sure if they were even going to put that song on the record. I remember Bob coming in and letting us hear the cut of "Man Gave Names to All the Animals." At that time, my son Tony was three years old, and he was with me. When Bob played the song and it started talking about "Ooh, I think I'll call it a cow," my son was falling over on the floor, laughing. Then he heard "Ooh, I think I'll call it a pig," and my son was just cracking up! Dylan looked over and saw how my son was laughing, and he said, "I'm going to put that on the record." And so that song was particularly my favorite because of my son.[5]

Also seeing the light of day in 2010 was the U.K.-based CD, *How Many Roads: Black America Sings Bob Dylan*. Its product description, via Amazon.com, reads as follows: "Bob Dylan's songs impacted on 1960s black American singers in a way that few (if any) of his peers were able to. It was through Dylan's important protest songs that artists such as Sam Cooke found their way to articulate dissatisfaction at being regarded as second-class citizens. Some of the best recordings of Bob's later love songs have been covered by artists from the worlds of Soul, Jazz, and Blues."

The CD contains twenty songs spanning four decades and includes artists such as Solomon Burke; the Staple Singers; Gary U.S. Bonds; the Persuasions; Patti LaBelle; Bobby Womack; the Neville Brothers; Nina Simone; the O'Jays; and the Isley Brothers.

Dylan's impact as an artist, though, should not simply be seen through one president or one generation or one skin hue. This author took the pulse of a Bob Dylan concert in October 2010 in Clemson, South Carolina.[6]

When it came to Dylan's religion or spirituality, what were some of these concertgoers aware of? Or not aware of? Here are a few snapshots in time, some anecdotal evidence:

Gene Green, sixty, a retired member of the U.S. military, has known Dylan's music since he was stationed in Duluth, Minnesota, the city of Dylan's birth. "I followed him since the '60s, but only musically," he said. According to Green, from the songs you can tell Dylan is a religious guy; however, he is not clear on Dylan's specific beliefs.

Isabella Cuesta, twenty-two, a student from nearby Converse College, chose a Dylan book for a philosophy class project. "I know he was kinda like an agnostic, skeptical of religion, but then he became immersed in Christianity," she said.

Clemson University student Evan Tripp attended this Dylan concert for no less than extra credit for his History of Rock & Roll class. "I know that Dylan got in a motorcycle accident and shortly afterward found Christ and made one or two gospel records," said the twenty-one-year-old Tripp.

Steve Van Zandt, fifty-four, an account manager for a transportation company, knew from what he had read in *Rolling Stone* and other music trade magazines that Dylan's *Slow Train Coming* marked his departure from secularism. "Who knows what he is now?" said Van Zandt.

"He found Jesus after his bike wreck," chuckled Catherine Sandifer, twenty-one, a student from Greenville Tech. "Hasn't he gone back to Judaism?" asked her forty-seven-year-old father, Billy Sandifer.

Robert Booker, sixty-six, a retired radiologic x-ray tech, has been a Dylan fan since the early 1960s. Booker, a Christian himself, was thrilled when Dylan entered the fold in the late 1970s, but has heard since that Dylan is now not a Christian; he doesn't know if what he's heard is true or not.

Perhaps the most visible Dylan fans at the Clemson University gig this October 2010 evening were the members of the Steele family. Thirty-eight-year-old Joshua and his wife Lindsay brought along their sons, Isaiah, twelve, and Ira, nine. Everyone sported a homemade Dylan -related t-shirt: Joshua ("Ain't Talkin'"); Lindsay ("Hey, Bob, give me a shot of love"); Isaiah ("Born in Time"); and Ira ("That's my favorite Dylan song" read the front of the T-shirt—the back countered with "Until the next one I hear").

Joshua Steele, the family patriarch, offered up that his other son, seven-year-old Jude, was not in attendance because of a last minute decision to hang out at home with his granddad instead (for the record, Jude's t-shirt read "Property of Jesus"). This proud thirty-eight-year-old father became a Christian and came to Dylan's music "kinda late" (in his mid-twenties). He was very familiar with *Slow Train Coming*. "What I do know comes from his lyrics and there was a point where I thought he had given up his faith but I eventually realized it never stopped," said Steele. "There are tons of songs with biblical references and he's obviously got a grasp on the whole Bible."

A month to the day after this Clemson concert, an audience in Binghamton, New York, heard Dylan open with "Gonna Change My Way of Thinking," the song that left little doubt that Dylan was ready to rock and roll and sing the blues—and was still singing about Jesus. Like 2009, the final concerts of 2010 saw Dylan employ the same opener that had its roots in *Slow Train Coming*.

Whether for regular concertgoers or someone as well known as Sinead O'Connor, questions about Dylan's faith still linger. "People say—and I hope it's not true—that Dylan doesn't stand by that record," O'Connor remarked about *Slow Train Coming*. "It's a staggering album for anyone to make, but especially him."[7]

On February 13, 2011, Dylan performed his song "Maggie's Farm" at the Grammys. But why was he there in the first place? It's not as if Dylan were a regular at the annual gala. Was the invite a tip of the hat to his fifty years in the music industry? Considering Dylan's performance of "Maggie's Farm" was backed by The Avett Brothers and Mumford & Sons, something else might have been going on. This unexpected lineup suggests Dylan was not only familiar with but approved of their music and graciously shared the stage with these up-and-coming bands. Both bands sure looked to be having the musical time of their lives as Dylan growled out the song he had penned in 1965 as a twenty-three-year-old young man.

Singer Bette Midler delivered a tweet following Dylan's Grammy performance: "Did Bob Dylan forget the sound check? Did the engineer drown him out on purpose? A word to the wise: Quit smoking, babe."

Dylan's voice is certainly not what it used to be, but "what used to be" isn't exactly what many critics and contemporaries were writing (or tweeting) home about anyway.

But the twenty-four-year-old lead singer of Mumford and Sons, Marcus Mumford, wasn't critiquing the performance. He was just thrilled to share the moment with one of his musical mentors. Mumford told *Rolling Stone* that he was ecstatic to discover through his manager, just days before the Grammys, that they would actually be *playing* with Dylan:

"I got out of bed and ran outside and jumped around like a madman!" he said. "You can imagine the reaction of someone who probably wouldn't be playing music at all if it wasn't for Bob Dylan." Just days earlier he had been visiting a friend in California and staying up until the wee hours of the morning listening to Dylan's music.

Mumford first heard Dylan through his mother's vinyl copy of *Slow Train Coming*. "It's pretty much the first vinyl I ever listened to," he recalled.[8] Mumford's parents, John and Eleanor, were married in 1978 and have been involved for years with the Vineyard Church. They first connected with the California church decades ago (like Dylan). Ultimately, they moved to London where they served in a church from 1987 to 2008, a church that had its beginnings in their home. (They also served as national directors of the Vineyard in the U.K. for nearly two decades until 2015.)

By late March 2011, the U.K. tabloid the *Daily Mail* had published an exclusive about a Dylan sighting at a Los Angeles synagogue.[9] How the writer, Hugo Daniel, connected this visit to the recent death of Dylan's former girlfriend from the early 1960s, Suze Rotolo, was unclear. However, the online article was accompanied by a handful of photographs of a hooded Dylan presumably making his way into the house of worship.

Daniel informed his readers that it is unclear how often Dylan visits the synagogue but "until now his chosen religion has been a long-standing mystery." Without providing any specifics, he also made this bizarre claim: "These exclusive pictures are the first conclusive pieces of evidence that the folk music icon has come back to Judaism after the loss of his beloved ex-girlfriend."

Additionally, Daniel let readers know that Dylan "has been exceptionally undecided about religion during his life and on the rare occasion that he has spoken about his faith he has been quite cryptic." At the end of the article, we are told that Dylan was due back on tour on April 3, 2011, in Taipei, Taiwan.

Without any fanfare, Dylan stepped onstage in Taiwan for the first time and opened with "Gotta Serve Somebody." Daniel Hugo and the *Daily Mail* took no exclusive pictures and offered no explanation. It is hard to get around the fact that Dylan still visits synagogues *and* still sings his songs about Jesus. It is more tidy to report one and not the other.

Meanwhile, Dylan hit the road for the remainder of his Asian tour. Religion would not be the subject of most of the discussion in the press. Instead, Dylan the political figure—or not—would largely form the narrative angle. Tour stops in China, Vietnam, Hong Kong, and Singapore were met with no less than an international media blitz when it was suggested that Dylan had bowed down to communist censors in China (when it came to his concert set lists).

New York Times columnist Maureen Dowd scolded the sixty-nine-year-old poet as a sellout extraordinaire; her opinion piece set off emotional reactions in the blogosphere as well as more traditional media outlets. But just what constituted a sellout?

For his part, Dylan sang most of his compositions from decades *other than* the 1960s. He sang the *Slow Train Coming* number "Gonna Change My Way of Thinking." He did not sing "Blowin' in the Wind" or "The Times They Are A-Changin'" but he did sing other gems from the '60s that could easily be interpreted as "subversive." He gave no interviews before, during, or immediately after his Asian itinerary, which was, perhaps, his most subversive act of all.

The coverage of Dylan in China was downright remarkable. Reuters and the Associated Press picked up the story. Prominent, trendy websites such as *Daily Beast*, *Huffington Post*, and *Gawker* weighed in. The Center for American Progress and MarketWatch deemed the Dylan story was worthy. A diverse and impressive array of magazines thought the same, including *Time*, *Billboard*, *Mother Jones*, *New Republic*, *Hollywood Reporter*, *The New Yorker*, *Reason*, *Nation*, and *Atlantic*.

Daily newspapers in the U.S. such as *Washington Post*, *Knoxville News Sentinel*, *Minneapolis Star Tribune*, *Pittsburgh Post-Gazette*, *Des Moines Register*, and *Toledo Blade* covered and pondered the Dylan story. Traditional television outlets like CBS, NBC, CNN, and MSNBC also tossed their hats into the ring. The long-running VOA (Voice of America) carried the story over the radio airwaves.

The fact that the man could still cause such turbulence amounted to an amusing spectacle. As another chapter was written in the Dylan story to grapple with, the subject headed to Australia for more concerts in 2011. Nothing too extraordinary, really. But then, out of nowhere, the singer who is certainly more of a Luddite than a technophile, took time to peck out a message for his fans; it was posted on his official website, bobdylan.com. This was, arguably, bizarre. Dylan delivering an official online message?! On the eve of his seventieth birthday, one sure thing remained: Dylan was not oblivious to his press. Dated May 12, 2011, with a headline "To my fans and followers," there was a four hundred-word note on his website clarifying the so-called China controversy, including these lines:

"As far as the censorship goes, the Chinese government had asked for the names of the songs that I would be playing. There's no logical answer to that, so we sent them the set lists from the previous three months," noted Dylan. "If there were any songs, verses or lines censored, nobody ever told me about it and we played all the songs that we intended to play."

So much for the China controversy.

In the summer of 2011, Dylan played in Israel for only the third time in his fifty-year career. During his 1987 debut in the Holy Land, a forty-six-year-old Dylan, who supposedly had gotten over his Jesus hangover, managed to perform songs from *Slow Train Coming*. In 2011, he opened his Tel Aviv concert with "Gonna Change My Way of Thinking." On this warm June evening at the Ramat Gan Stadium, Dylan was unabashedly singing about Jesus. Many other songs, of course, were performed too. Nothing new was under the sun.

On January 12, 2012, Dylan appeared with his band at the Hollywood Palladium for the Critics' Choice Movie Awards where Martin Scorcese was the recipient of the Music and Film Award. Probably few in Las Vegas would've placed bets on a Dylan appearance via live television and hosted by VH1, but there Dylan was, on stage, with no keyboard or guitar. Gripping the microphone with one hand and holding a harmonica in the other, the seventy-year-old sang an outtake from his 1983 album, *Infidels*—the stupendous "Blind Willie McTell":

"This land is condemned / All the way from New Orleans to New Jerusalem," croaked Dylan before an audience that included the likes of Steven Spielberg, Brad Pitt, Meryl Streep, George Clooney, Leonardo DiCaprio, Charlize Theron, and Owen Wilson. "God is in Heaven / And we all want what's His / But power and greed and corruptible seed seems to be all there really is."

Less than a minute later, the song was over and a robust and rather lengthy standing ovation ensued. Who knows how many in the crowd that night in Hollywood or how many looking on from their television screens (or how many later perusing the performance through the Internet) were aware of the rootsy down-and-out gospel blues they had just heard. A land being condemned? By whom? New Jerusalem? Where? Corruptible seed? What?

Two weeks after the Critics' Choice Awards, a four-CD compilation began its effort of raising funds and awareness for a certain human rights organization. The project, *Chimes of Freedom: The Songs of Bob Dylan Honoring 50 Years of Amnesty International*, pulled off a rather amazing feat: all the artists, producers, and engineers of this seventy-six-track compilation donated their time and efforts (for his part, Dylan also donated his publishing royalties).[10] The many dozens of artists who contributed ranged from Miley Cyrus to Elvis Costello to My Morning Jacket to Pete Townshend to The Chocolate Drops.

It isn't too overwhelming that a scant few of the song selections were chosen from the trilogy of *Slow Train Coming*, *Saved*, and *Shot of Love*. Eric Burdon, though, did take on "Gotta Serve Somebody" while Blake Mills and Sinead O'Connor plucked two songs from *Shot of Love*: "Heart of Mine" and "Property of Jesus," respectively. O'Connor may well have chosen, in "Property of Jesus," the least-covered Dylan song of all time.

How O'Connor's contribution to the Amnesty project was received is an adequate metaphor for Dylan's religious bent: it either works for you or it doesn't. Jim Farber, writing for the *New York Daily News*, nominated the song as one of the best of the compilation: "Sinead re-channels her too-rarely used shout to turn this righteous ode from *Shot of Love* into a riveting declaration."[11] On the other hand, Chris Willman of Reuters wasn't moved: "Some numbers that sound promising on paper fizzle, like Sinead O'Connor's 'Property of Jesus.' If it seems like having pop's most defensive singer cover Dylan's most defensive song is a natural, that's before you hear the bleating tone she adopts for the whole thing."[12]

On this mammoth compilation for Amnesty in 2012, not a single soul chose to cover a song from Dylan's 1980 album, *Saved*. What this fact communicates is up for grabs but Dylan himself, back in 1988, went *way* out of his way to nominate his song "In the Garden" (from *Saved*) to the powers that be at Amnesty International. He wanted it to be showcased in the Amnesty tour and said as much on several occasions from the concert stage. There wasn't any press coverage about it at the time and maybe Dylan didn't think his onstage pleas would be taken seriously; in 2012, royalties were simply raised. Dylan's public gospel donation remains his 2002 rewrite of "Gonna Change My Way of Thinking" for Jeff Gaskill's tribute *Gotta Serve Somebody: The Gospel Songs of Bob Dylan.*

On April 26, 2012, a White House press release revealed that President Barack Obama had chosen the annual recipients of the Presidential Medal of Freedom, the country's highest civilian honor. The award was instituted in 1963 through an executive order by the late President John F. Kennedy.

Bob Dylan found himself among an eclectic list of people (abbreviated bios courtesy of C-SPAN's website):

MADELEINE ALBRIGHT: 64th U.S. secretary of state, the first woman to hold that position

JOHN DOAR: Former Justice Department official that led federal efforts to protect and enforce civil rights during the 1960s

WILLIAM FOEGE: Physician and epidemiologist that led the successful campaign to eradicate smallpox in the 1970s

JOHN GLENN: Former United States Marine Corps pilot, astronaut, and United States senator

GORDON HIRABAYASHI: Openly defied the forced relocation and internment of Japanese Americans during World War II

DOLORES HUERTA: Notable human rights activist and co-founded the National Farmworkers Association in 1962

JAN KARSKI: Officer in the Polish Underground during World War II who carried some of the first eyewitness accounts of the Holocaust to the world

JULIETTE GORDON LOW: Founded the Girl Scouts in 1912

TONI MORRISON: Celebrated American novelist

SHIMON PERES: Advocate for Israel's security and for peace

JOHN PAUL STEVENS: Associate justice of the U.S. Supreme Court from 1975 to 2010

PAT SUMMITT: All-time winningest coach in NCAA basketball history

When the White House's Office of the Press Secretary issued its press release, Dylan's bio read as follows:

"One of the most influential American musicians of the 20th century, Dylan released his first album in 1962. Known for his rich and poetic lyrics, his work had considerable influence on the civil rights movement of the 1960s and has had significant impact on American culture over the past five decades. He has won 11 Grammys, including a lifetime achievement award. He was named a Commandeur dans l'Ordre des Art et des Lettres and has received a Pulitzer Prize Special Citation. Dylan was awarded the 2009 National Medal of Arts. He has written more than 600 songs, and his songs have been recorded more than 3,000 times by other artists. He continues recording and touring around the world today."

By May, a Tuesday date of the twenty-ninth was set. The thirteen honorees (and for those deceased, their descendants) were invited to the White House for a ceremony in the East Room. Would the seventy-one-year-old Dylan show up? A betting crowd might hedge their bets since it would mark his second appearance at the White House in two years. Prior to 2010, Dylan had never even been in the house where the U.S. president resides.

But sure enough, though, there he was—captured by C-SPAN television cameras—on a Tuesday afternoon entering the East Room of the White House. Donning no less than a suit, Bolero tie, and black shades (yes, black sunglasses), he took his assigned seat next to the most winningest college basketball coach and a retired U.S. Supreme Court justice. Most observers likely missed the alphabetical nature of the proceeding: the list maker considered the final recipient a Zimmerman.

Then, arguably the most powerful man on the planet entered the room and took his place behind a podium with the presidential seal. In the background, viewers could see adorned gold curtains, ornate candelabras, and a prominent American flag. After a round of hearty applause, Obama referenced the packed house and how the capacity audience was a testament to how "cool" the honorees were. According to Obama, what set these people apart wasn't merely their talent and drive: "What sets these men and women apart is the incredible impact they have had on so many people, not in short, blinding bursts, but steadily, over the course of a lifetime."

When it was Dylan's turn to be introduced, the forty-fourth president of the United States expended one minute with these words:

"Bob Dylan started out singing other people's songs but as he says, there came a point where I had to write what I wanted to say because what I wanted to say nobody else was writing. Born in Hibbing, Minnesota, a town he says where you couldn't be a rebel; it was too cold [laughs]. Bob moved to New York at age nineteen. By the time he was twenty-three, Bob's voice, with its weight, its unique gravelly power, was redefining not just what music sounded like, but the message it carried and how it made people feel. Today, everyone from Bruce Springsteen to U2 owes Bob a debt of gratitude. There is not a bigger giant in the history of American music. All these years later, he's still chasing that sound, still searching for a little bit of truth, and I have to say that I'm a really big fan."

Obama may well be a big fan, but more than a few fans noticed he got Dylan's birthplace wrong. Dylan was born in Duluth, not Hibbing.

Fast-forward twenty-five minutes into the ceremony and Dylan patiently sat waiting for his name to be called. Hands clasped, some finger twiddling, and black shades effectively protecting against any official or unofficial photographers and onlookers—be they in person, watching on television, or Internet archive diggers from now until Armageddon.

The moment was broken up by the president vocalizing a good-natured "C'mon, Bob" with a hand gesture. Dylan stood up and walked the short distance, slipped between the president and the podium, and went to the spot where Obama had directed him. The president flashed a big grin but then composed himself, almost as if to say, "I know you can't be loving this Bob, but here you are and I'm thrilled."

Obama recalled listening to Dylan in college. He didn't make reference, but his college days were when Dylan's then-current album output consisted of *Slow Train Coming*, *Saved*, *Shot of Love*, and *Infidels*. If the commander in chief as a young man was giving Dylan's gospel treatment a fair shake, he was presumably also taking in healthy doses of Dylan's more popular creations from the 1960s. As the two stood together for this brief moment in 2012, a White House narrator uttered the following:

"A modern-day troubadour, Bob Dylan established himself as one of the most influential musicians of the twentieth century. The rich poetry of his lyrics opened up new possibilities for popular songs and inspired generations. His melodies have brought ancient traditions into the modern age. More than fifty years after his career began, Bob Dylan remains an eminent voice in our national conversation and around the world."

With that, President Obama fastened the medal around Dylan's neck. The two shook hands and briefly embraced: Dylan patted Obama on his shoulder, nodded, and the president responded in kind.

By fall of 2012, the flurry of words devoted to Dylan's latest album, *Tempest,* shouldn't be surprising considering: the artist at hand, a fifty-year anniversary hook since his debut album, and an ever-increasing Internet age that seems to bring out critics from every nook and cranny. Most lavished praise, but a few faithful dissenters managed to call the artist's thirty-fifth album mediocre or lackluster.

Tempest included ten compositions, clocked in at sixty-eight minutes, and was recorded at Groove Masters, Jackson Browne's studio in Santa Monica, California.

Over the decades, Dylan's stomping grounds have certainly included

Santa Monica: His concert there in 1965 at the Civic Auditorium occurred just days after the release of *Bringing It All Back Home*, an album that kicked off an incredible run. What used to be a factory in a rough part of Santa Monica became his Rundown Studios, significant geographical terrain for the transitional era that was *Street-Legal/Slow Train Coming*, 1978–1979. The city has also been home to some properties Dylan owned, including a business complex bought in the 1990s that featured a coffeehouse which housed an antique jukebox filled with old vinyl. Additionally, the Santa Monica complex had a private gymnasium (equipped with a boxing ring) and rental space with offices and a synagogue.[13]

A Santa Monica restaurant was the site of a mind-bending Dylan interview in 2012, where Dylan responded to a fair number of religiously oriented questions from a *Rolling Stone* reporter. Santa Monica was also the location of four of Dylan's exclusively gospel gigs in November 1979. Longtime *Los Angeles Times* music critic Robert Hilburn was present for opening night, and his report included this:

"The only movement in the audience was toward the front of the stage when hundreds of fans wanted to be as close to the action. Among those pressed against the stage at the end was Andrew Finkelstein, whose yarmulke indicated he was supporting Dylan's music, not his religious sentiments. 'Yes,' said Finkelstein, twenty-two. 'I can separate the two. I can see that he's singing music that's important to him and that he's sincere about it. That's OK with me.' Cookie Lennartson, thirty, of Santa Monica, said she did feel a 'sense of loss' when Dylan's fundamentalist views surfaced in the recent *Slow Train Coming* album and that she still felt uncertain about his new direction. But, like Finkelstein, she tried to separate the religious and musical issues. 'If he's happy now, that's good,' she said after the show. 'He has always seemed to feel persecuted. When the album came out, I was very upset, but he has made people happy for so long, I feel he has a right to be happy himself.'"[14]

With *Tempest* in 2012, would some fans have to separate anything after digesting the latest Dylan effort? Too much violence and death? Too much darkness in general? What about Dylan's purported spirituality? Can darkness and light coexist? Do they? Didn't Johnny Cash musically pursue a similar trail back in the day, including a time or two in the twilight of his earthly days? Don't songs about tragedy and death have a place in the American songbook? Is Dylan happy himself?

Back in 2011, the Chief Curator Emeritus of Painting and Sculpture at the Museum of Modern Art in New York was asking questions of Dylan. One question concerned how some of Dylan's recently exhibited paintings were very enigmatic and some were also very straightforward. "So did you want a mixture of the more direct and the more mysterious (again, like putting together a great album)?" asked John Elderfield.

"Saint Paul said we see through the glass darkly," Dylan responded. "There's plenty of mystery in nature and contemporary life. For some people, it's too harsh to deal with. But I don't see it that way." Dylan went on to reflect about the chaos and mysteries of life.[15]

A few weeks before *Tempest* made its way into the public square, *Rolling Stone* procured these tantalizing Dylan quotes: "I wanted to make something more religious. I just didn't have enough. Intentionally, specifically religious songs is what I wanted to do. That takes a lot more concentration—to pull that off ten times with the same thread—than it does with a record like I ended up with."[16]

After the release of *Tempest*, these quotes did not escape the notice of some religious folks who happened to be Dylan fans. Take, for example, writer Darren Hirst:

"Many of Dylan's albums recently have had the theme of God's judgement and the apocalypse and the possibility of salvation (including *Time Out of Mind*, *Modern Times* and many of the out-takes on *Tell Tale Signs*). Dylan has jibed at us for being surprised about this: 'I was sitting in church / on an old wooden chair / I know nobody would look for me there' ('Marchin' to the City', *Tell Tale Signs*). But he is preoccupied with the apocalypse, religion and God, no matter how we might see the world. *Tempest* is another testimony to this even if ultimately it is an uneven album. But in 2012 when Dylan is good, he is very good—and the end of the age he sees coming should scare us indeed.

Even for those who seek God it is one that holds little comfort and no escape from trouble until the salvation is finally realized."[17]

A.T. Bradford, who penned the 2011 book *Out of the Dark Woods: Dylan, Depression and Faith*, wasn't subtle about his interpretations when surveying "Pay in Blood." It was the *Tempest* song "Described by secular reviewers as malevolent and murderous," wrote Bradford. "But the blood that Dylan is singing of as 'paying for him', is surely not the blood of any mortal man, but of Christ. 'You know that you were not redeemed with corruptible things, as silver and gold, from your vain conversation received by tradition from your fathers; but with the precious blood of Christ, as of a lamb without blemish and without spot' (1 Peter 1:18–19). Dylan's line, 'Nothing more wretched than what I must endure' echoes the Apostle Paul's struggle with sin—'wretched man that I am! Who shall deliver me from the body of this death?' (Romans 7:24)."[18]

It wasn't just websites of the faithful dissecting Dylan's history and current leanings via *Tempest*. David Yaffe, a columnist for thedaily-beast.com, saw the context of a spiritual journey and Dylan's general disposition:

"When Dylan found Jesus for three albums, then subsequently discovered his Jewishness on another, his religiosity gave him another pulpit for his rage. His targets were no longer the Military Industrial Complex, racist crackers, or a lover who's just gone out the door, but Judas, the Devil, even Yasir Arafat. Eventually, the years piled up, and Dylan became more cryptic. He kept his second marriage and divorce secret for years, and no one has been able to pin him down on his personal life, his politics, or his religion. All we have are the songs and the performances, which is how he wants it, and which is just as well."[19]

Neil McCormick, writing for the *Telegraph* in the UK, picked up on things old and new in *Tempest* and happily pinned Dylan down to the old-time religion:

"Dylan establishes themes [in the confluence of religious faith and apocalyptic portent] on one of his darkest, bloodiest and most foreboding collection of songs, set in a barren landscape of Godless self-interest, moral equivocation and random violence. The perspective of Dylan's narrator constantly blurs and shifts, moving from world-weary cynicism to sorrowful compassion to the morbid glee of a fire-and-brimstone preacher perversely satisfied that, as predicted, the worst has come to pass. As the firebrand of social protest in the Sixties, Dylan was sometimes hailed as a lyrical prophet leading the young generation to a better future. In his seventy-first year, he seems more like an Old Testament figure, proclaiming the end is nigh. The times they have a-changed indeed."[20]

Yet it can be easily argued that Dylan cut an Old Testament-like figure on albums long ago, from *John Wesley Harding* (1967) to *Slow Train Coming* (1979) to *Oh Mercy* (1989).

"Certainly Dylan's beliefs, occasionally leavened by his offbeat humour, are a key thread running through the bulk of these ten compelling tracks [from *Tempest*]," wrote Joe Breen of the *Irish Times*. "But the spectre of death is here, too, and the reflection afforded by age. Frequently he wraps all three into the dark and complex texts."[21]

Simon Cosyns of *The Sun* singled out track No. 4 on *Tempest* for praise, linking it with a composition created way back in the Summer of Love:

"One of the most affecting songs is the gospel-tinged, half spoken 'Long and Wasted Years' with Dylan's wistful drawl calling to mind some Southern preacher man and bearing a similar vibe to an old unreleased *Basement Tapes* song of his called 'Sign on the Cross' [1967]."[22]

The gospel-tinged and half-spoken aspects of "Long and Wasted Years" also called up "Brownsville Girl" (1986), an eleven-minute doozy of a song from probably one of Dylan's most least-listened to albums, *Knocked Out Loaded*.

When Allan Jones, a reviewer for *Uncut*, referenced Dylan's interview comments about the original intent for *Tempest*—the explicitly religious one—he summed it up this way: "There are inklings, though, of the album Dylan originally envisioned on, for instance, 'Duquesne Whistle', where a voice the singer hears 'must be the mother of our

Lord,' and even more apparently on the devotionally-inclined 'Long and Wasted Years' and the gospel-influenced 'Pay in Blood', which follows. The testing of belief in extreme circumstances is a recurring theme."[23]

Certainly a mixed bag can be found in *Tempest* in that the God of the Scriptures is present but the free will of man is seemingly giving the Creator a run for His money. Ambiguity, mystery, and uncertainty aren't shied away from.

Although the apostle Paul wrote of the mystery of faith in what we now know as the New Testament, some Dylan fans assumed the Dylan of 1979-1981 had all the mysteries solved. But this seems a shallow reading because it doesn't allow for the newborn angle of his journey; Dylan is a more mature man of faith now. Of course, a jaded view might argue that he hasn't grown at all—and is still an infant in the faith (or a man of no faith at all)—but if lyrics, interviews, and actions count for anything, a different portrait emerges.

Dylan himself, in the 2009 interview with Bill Flanagan, alluded to how he wouldn't have been "experienced enough" to pull off his Christmas album in an earlier day. This is the same interview where Flanagan didn't want to put Dylan on the spot but let his interviewee know that he sounded like a "true believer" in the song "O, Little Town of Bethlehem." As mentioned before, Dylan's response was straightforward: "Well, I am a true believer."

In 1967, Noel Paul Stookey took some advice from a post-motorcycle accident laid up Bob Dylan in Woodstock, New York. It concerned how he should check into both the Bible and the stomping grounds where he grew up. Dylan has also visited the stomping grounds of friends and peers like John Lennon, Bruce Springsteen, and Neil Young. So maybe it shouldn't be too surprising that Lennon received an excruciatingly tender tribute via "Roll On John"—the closing song on *Tempest*.

Back in 1998, the same year Dylan was playing "Gotta Serve Somebody" in many of his concerts, the general public became aware of "Serve Yourself" through *The John Lennon Anthology*. The song was

Lennon's send-up of "Gotta Serve Somebody" after taking in Dylan's live debut of the song on the *Saturday Night Live* television broadcast on October 20, 1979.

Lennon was the man who penned "God" (1970), a song that included declarations that the narrator didn't believe in the Beatles, Zimmerman, or Jesus, also penned "Imagine" (1971), a song that famously asked listeners to imagine there was no heaven.

By 2012, some reviewers of *Tempest*, reflecting on one of the songs, "Roll on John," suggested that Dylan and Lennon were in some great conflict back in 1979-1980. "Lennon was at odds with Dylan in the year before his death," writes Darren Hirst. "Perhaps that row has stayed with Dylan all these years and he felt a need to honour and respect Lennon and put that uneasy time to rest."[24]

"Having initially been on good terms, Dylan's conversion to Christianity provoked a furious backlash from Lennon, most notably in a song recorded shortly before his death," wrote A.T. Bradford.[25]

Hirst and Bradford are imagining something that is likely not there.

As for Lennon's song "Serve Yourself," a more accurate assessment can be found in the product description of *The John Lennon Anthology* via Amazon.com. The song was simply "a snipe." Lennon may have been annoyed in private and dashed off a song that made its way into the public years after his death, but in an interview for *Playboy* conducted in September 1980, Lennon told David Scheff the following:

"I was surprised that old Bobby boy did go that way but if he needs it, let him do it. . . . But I understand it. I understand him completely, how he got in there, because I've been frightened enough myself to want to latch onto something. . . . I don't like to comment on it. For whatever reason he's doing it, it is personal for him and he needs to do it. But the whole religious business suffers from the 'Onward, Christian Soldiers' bit. There's too much talk about soldiers and marching and converting. I'm not pushing Buddhism because I'm no more a Buddhist than I am a Christian, but there's one thing I admire about the religion: There's no proselytizing."[26]

After witnessing Dylan singing "Gotta Serve Somebody," "I Believe in You," and "When You Gonna Wake Up?" in 1979 on live television right down the road from his New York City home, Lennon wrote the aforementioned "Serve Yourself." The song included the line, "Christ, you gotta serve yourself." Yoko Ono, for her part, remembered the song and how her husband was "kind of upset and it was a dialogue. He showed his anger but also . . . his sense of humour."[27]

Was Lennon antagonistic toward Jesus? Who can forget his infamous comments in a 1966 interview where he claimed the Beatles were more popular than the Man from Galilee. That whole brouhaha was generally misunderstood (primarily by Christians): Lennon wasn't the force some made him out to be, staunchly opposed to the figure of Jesus.

In the *Playboy* interview from 1980, he addressed the issue: "People always got the image I was an anti-Christ or anti-religion. I'm not. I'm a most religious fellow. I was brought up a Christian and I only now understand some of the things that Christ was saying in those parables. Because people got hooked on the teacher and missed the message."[28]

Dylan acknowledged that some of the songs on *Tempest* had been in the pipeline for a while. Some reviewers wondered why "Roll On John" came in 2012, over three decades after Lennon's death. One clue can certainly be found in a 2009 article in a Liverpool newspaper.[29] Dylan visited Lennon's childhood home on a bus tour by himself. At the time, he was on tour, and performed the Beatles' "Something" at his Liverpool concert.

Many *Tempest* reviewers pegged "Roll On John" as either pedestrian or a simple, heartfelt tribute. Among the song's touching biographical details of Lennon's life, profoundly sad metaphors, and no small amount of religious references, it amounts to a fitting homage to an old friend, someone who shared all the pitfalls, horrors, and blues of idol status.

Idols tend to be followed and those who follow Dylan to any degree will likely acknowledge how his interviews can occasionally be events unto themselves. Dylan's interview with *Rolling Stone* contributor Mikal Gilmore in 2012 may well be matchless.[30] In some ways, it serves as an anti-idol affair with Dylan fiercely protecting his humanity.

When the interview hit the shelves and cyberspace, there would be news made from more than one excerpt, and not just within Dylan fan circles. The interview was wild and woolly, an incredible moment documenting Dylan scaling the heights of rage, revelation, wit, frankness, ribald language, and myth. Two commonly used words to describe Dylan over the decades come to mind: inscrutability and irascibility. Here's how Gilmore himself described the experience which began as a sit-down interview at a restaurant in Santa Monica, California:

"At moments, I pushed in on some questions, and Dylan pushed back. We continued the conversation over the next many days, on the phone and by way of some written responses. Dylan didn't hedge or attempt to guard himself as we went along. Just the opposite: He opened up unflinchingly, with no apologies. This is Bob Dylan as you've never known him before."

Some observers labor under the impression that Dylan rarely gives interviews. "As rare as hen's teeth" is how one reviewer put it during the aftermath of *Tempest*. But way back in 1991, Dylan biographer Clinton Heylin issued the reminder that his research included poring over Dylan's words from over 200 interviews![31]

Dylan, in 2012, wasn't happy about those who dared called him a Judas way back in the mid-1960s. But not everyone bought the literal words issued by Dylan and printed in the aging rock journal that is *Rolling Stone*. Enter Harold Lepidus, a writer for examiner.com, who took it upon himself to track everything remotely Dylan related on a daily basis (this is no part-time job). His report was instructive. He suggested that we do not know whether Dylan was being serious, cranky, or playful. We also don't know his tone or mood. It is, after all, on the printed (or electronic) page. Lepidus acknowledged his own speculation, but felt Dylan was putting his audience on again. A brilliant public relations move is how Lepidus characterizes the sizzle of the interview. Because of Dylan's provocative words, potential buyers of *Tempest* might be prompted into becoming active buyers.

"Sorry, but the idea that Dylan is even the slightest bit concerned with that moment [1965's Newport Folk Festival] from nearly a half century ago does not ring true," Lepidus writes. "The expletive at the end, so out of character for a wordsmith like Dylan, just emphasizes that it is an attempt to attract attention."[32]

For the record, after calling his detractors from yesteryear a name that cannot be repeated here, Dylan let those "Judas!" folks know that he wished them eternal strife. This is putting it mildly.

When it comes to slights from years gone by, perhaps Dylan has more of a memory than Lepidus (and others) gives him credit for. Granted, forty-seven years ago is an extreme case but this is the same man that has memorized the lyrics to "Desolation Row" and, if *Chronicles* is to be believed (yes, there's debate), Dylan's gift of memory is downright exquisite.

When chatting with Cameron Crowe in 1985 for *Biograph*, Dylan singled out that rude reception he received at a concert some six years earlier, in Tempe, Arizona. In 2001, when Gilmore interviewed him for *Rolling Stone*, Dylan addressed his agitation with critics who reviewed *Time Out of Mind*, an album from four years earlier—and even went back an entire decade to grumble about the Grammys when some artists pulled a no-show for his Lifetime Achievement Award.

In the 2012 interview with Gilmore, Dylan isn't surprised that some listeners might still interpret "Rainy Day Women # 12 & 35" as code for getting high. But those folks "aren't familiar with the Book of Acts," Dylan quipped. Gilmore didn't follow up to see what in the world the song's sentiments might have to do with a book of the New Testament.

As for touring, Gilmore wondered if it was a fulfilling way of life. Dylan insisted that performing in itself can't make one happy but touring is rather something you learn how to do, improve, and keep at it. "Is it a fulfilling way of life? Well, what kind of way of life is fulfilling? No kind of life is fulfilling if your soul hasn't been redeemed," Dylan said.

This is vintage Dylan. Follow a question with a question and then deliver a proclamation about redemption. "Everybody has a calling, don't they?" asked Dylan of Gilmore. "Some have a high calling, some have a low calling. Everybody is called but few are chosen. There's a lot of distraction for people, so you might not never find the real you. A lot of people don't."

How has Dylan dealt with the distraction of people obsessively following his career, say, in the post-motorcycle accident years, when his music and even look changed. For some, this was a big deal. Why the change?

"So f---ing what? They want to know what can't be known. They are searching—they are seekers," Dylan concludes. "Like in the Pete Townshend song ["The Seeker"] where he's trying to find his way to 50 million fables. For what? Why are they doing this? They don't really know. It's sad. It really is. May the Lord have mercy on them. They are lost souls. They really don't know. It's sad—it really is. It's sad for me, and it's sad for them."

Dylan's quoting of a Who song from the early 1970s in this context didn't come out of nowhere. The narrator of "The Seeker" has, among other things, inquired of Bobby Dylan, the Beatles, and Timothy Leary—and they all couldn't provide any satisfaction. This same seeker has values, but doesn't know how or why. "I won't get to get what I'm after until the day I die" is the song's bold refrain. By his own admission, the seeker acknowledges he is "a really desperate man." Although Dylan doesn't seem thrilled with the preoccupations of this type of person, he does manage an ultimate wish for their souls to be redeemed.

Since the album where Dylan spoke of his soul being redeemed was *Slow Train Coming*, would the newly written songs that didn't make *Tempest*—those "religious" ones Dylan had referred to—be like the Dylan's album of 1979? "No. No. Not at all," Dylan told Gilmore. "They're more like 'Just a Closer Walk With Thee'."

Just as Dylan had enough experience to be able to pull off *Christmas in the Heart* in 2009, it seems his experience as a believer allowed him to write some original songs in the traditional gospel vein, along the lines of his covers in the late 1990s/early 2000s.

"Has your sense of your faith changed?" Gilmore wondered. "Certainly it has, o ye of little faith," Dylan responded—in what had to be either good humor or condescending sarcasm. Dylan then asked who had the authority to say he had faith—while also claiming that he saw God's hand in everything. He acknowledged that we could have faith in anything, even faith in a calmer of the nerves like a Bloody Mary. That kind of faith, though, according to Dylan, can't move mountains like the real thing.

"You can tell whether other people have faith or no faith by the way they behave, by the s--- that comes out of their mouths. A little faith can go a long ways. It's the right thing for people to have," Dylan told Gilmore. "When we have little else, that will do. But it takes a while to acquire it. You just got to keep looking."

Gilmore then observed how people can acquire faith but then succumb to the feeling that they've lost it. Dylan wholeheartedly agreed:

"Yeah, absolutely. You get hit hard in life. People get hit with everything. We all do. We all get hit upside the head. And some of us get hit harder than others. Some of us get no chance at all. Some of us get more than one chance. No two are alike. You just have to push on. Make the best of it. Just like the Woody Guthrie song 'Hard Travelin'.'"

Dylan's theology here resembles what he referred to in his last interview with Gilmore (back in 2001) when he observed that one of God's least talked about attributes is that of being arbitrary. If one accepts the existence of God, is this what it seems like, at times, humanly speaking? Or is God truly arbitrary? Dylan told Gilmore in 2001 that he could look "arbitrary" up in the dictionary. At the beginning of his piece in 2012, Gilmore referred to *Tempest* as telling tales "of mortal ends, moral faithlessness and hard-earned (if arbitrary) grace."

"Clearly, the language of the Bible still provides imagery for your songs," Gilmore added. "Of course, what else could there be?" Dylan asks. The seventy-one-year-old goes on to assert that it's impossible to go through life without reading books and claims there's some truth in all books while citing a laundry list of titles and authors: the Egyptian Book of the Dead, the Bhagavad-Gita, the Buddhist sutras, the Koran, the Torah, the New Testament, Marcus Aurelius, Confucius, and Sun Tzu.

As for belief, Dylan says in 2012, like he did back in 1984–1985: "I believe in the Book of Revelation." This last book of the New Testament is a blueprint for Dylan's apocalyptic lyrics and imagination that have been there since 1962 but were no doubt pumped with new meaning, life, and spirit in the waning days of 1979. They remain to this day.

When it comes to Dylan's personal faith and what's behind those shades—what he believes or doesn't believe—it's ultimately between him and his God. Though he has taken off the shades, like a poet in his nakedness, and told his public through interviews that the God of history and destiny has called him. Some songs he brings to the stage express that truth, too.

On July 15, 2013, a Dylan audience in Toronto, Canada, heard Dylan debut a song entitled "Twelve Gates to the City," a gospel cover that made sense. The traditional song is perhaps most associated with the late Rev. Gary Davis who as Blind Gary first recorded "Twelve Gates to the City" in 1935. The song's lyrics owed to the Book of Revelation and the biblical idea of the "new Jerusalem" described in the twenty-first chapter. It certainly was a song Dylan knew as a young man and could've easily heard from Dave Van Ronk or Joan Baez. Another recording of the song appeared on Davis's 1961 release Blind Gary Davis: Harlem Street Singer. Davis performed the song in his set list at the inaugural Newport Folk Festival in 1959 and also aired it again at the festival in 1965, the very day Dylan "went electric."

In this one-off performance from 2013, accompanied by Wilco's Jeff Tweedy and Jim James of My Morning Jacket, Dylan may not have suspected such a robust response from the crowd as they joined in for the chorus—"Oh, what a beautiful city." At song's end, some positive nonverbal communication circulated as Dylan issued an affirmative two fists out. He then walked out from behind the keyboard and gave a pat on the back to both Tweedy and James.[33]

One of the ear and eyewitnesses that night in Toronto for Dylan's version of "Twelve Gates to the City" was Daniel Maoz, a Canadian professor of Hebrew Scriptures and Jewish scholar in residence at Wilfrid Laurier University. Having seen Dylan in concert in the 1960s, Maoz spent a good bit of his review reflecting on his mixed feelings about even attending this summer 2013 show:

"Last night was the beginning of Tisha B'Av, the commencement of the most solemn day of lament for Jews. It commemorates the destruction of Temple and Tradition in days gone by—encapsulating a history of tragedy from Moses to the Spanish Inquisition—and it is programmed to elicit sober reflection on these events until a day of restoration. The stage for Dylan's concert was framed by two columns of fire reminiscent both of the pillars of fire that guided Moses through the wilderness to a hopeful and promised future as well as of the burning embers of the ruined Temple. The bass drum in the centre of the stage also had flames seemingly burning within its skins (burning but not consuming the drum, hmmm).

On the drive to the concert, I questioned my motive for attending a Dylan concert on Tisha B'Av, an earnest day of fasting. Somewhere during the end of the evening, the flames constantly reminding me of the gravity of unforgettable history, I found my peace. Just before his predictable end-song and encore, Dylan had invited what he called 'my new friends' (Jim James of My Morning Jacket and Jeff Tweedy of Wilco) to join him in his rendition of the traditional 'Twelve Gates to the City'—whose lyrics and chorus brought to an end my ill-founded consternation and helped me realize that the answer to darkness is not struggling against it but merely turning on the light: 'And there's no more crying in the city / No more death or pain / Everything's made new, it's the gospel truth / The old things are passed away / Oh, what a beautiful city / Oh, what a beautiful city / God knows, it's a beautiful city / Twelve gates to the city, hallelu'"[34]

Jennifer Cruickshank, another concert attendee in Toronto, witnessed something she had never seen in her previous 15 Dylan concerts (her first concert was in 1997, also in Toronto):

"At the time of the show in July of 2013, I had just turned thirty-six. When Bob started singing that song ["Twelve Gates to the City"] I didn't know it, but it sounded familiar and I seemed to recognize the chorus. It was during the chorus that he sang the first part and then pointed to the audience and said, 'your turn.' The audience proceeded to sing the next couple of lines while Bob watched from behind his keyboard and then he took over. In all the concerts of his I have seen, I have never seen that.

"As far as why I think he chose 'Twelve Gates to the City,' he has always chosen classic songs to throw into his set list over the years. I personally think it's him showing his appreciation of these classics and wanting to share them. Not unlike his new covers of Frank Sinatra songs. Or this Theme Time Radio Show where he showcased many songs most people had never heard. I've always considered him a great teacher of these things, and his seemingly bottomless knowledge of musical history is well known."

Cruickshank, who considers herself an agnostic at this point, wasn't raised particularly religious but has dabbled in both Christianity and Buddhism.

"I am not too familiar with Bob's religious period. I was born in 1977. I discovered Dylan's music at around eighteen and it was a nice contrast to the stuff I was listening to at the time. I grew up with a lot of classic music thanks to my father so I already had an appreciation. But that quickly became much more. I have always thought of Bob as a real curious mind and eager student so I always thought of his religious period a result of just wanting to learn more about something that interested him at the time."[35]

Four nights after Toronto, in Bridgeport, Connecticut, Dylan performed another one-off gospel cover with Jim James and Jeff Tweedy assisting again; this time it was Blind Willie Johnson's "Let Your Light Shine on Me." The song's refrain—"Oh, let Your light from the lighthouse shine on me"—draws its inspiration from a line in the Sermon on the Mount recorded in the Gospel of Matthew, coupled with the lighthouse metaphor for Jesus's directive in the passage to "Let your light shine before men in such a way that they may see your good works, and glorify your Father who is in heaven" (Matthew 5:16, NASB).

At the beginning of the song when Dylan sang, "He healed the sick and raised the dead / Let the light from the lighthouse shine on me / Shine on / Shine on . . ." some listeners may have caught a familiar echo from the refrain of one "Precious Angel," the song that spoke of the Man who came and died a criminal's death. (Some fifty years before *Slow Train Coming*'s release, Blind Willie Johnson recorded two songs in 1929 that became companions on a vinyl record: the featured "God Don't Never Change" and its flip side, "Let Your Light Shine on Me.")

On this night in Bridgeport, similar to Toronto a few nights earlier, the crowd seemed enthusiastic, clapping along as the song began, though not knowing what was forthcoming. The persistent energy and drive from the song was evident at the Webster Bank Arena—and at song's end, Dylan came from behind his keyboard again and gave a few hand claps before briefly shaking the hands of his gospel collaborators from My Morning Jacket and Wilco as they left the stage.[36]

By fall of 2014, Dylan's set lists had settled into a somewhat predictable pattern, unusual for his tours of the last twenty-five years or so. Also unusual was the fact that compositions from the 1960s—the obvious crowd-pleasers—appeared only a few times per show while the vast majority of songs were latter day affairs from the twenty-first century—with a healthy smattering from 2012's Tempest. "All Along the Watchtower" and "Blowin' in the Wind" were two of the typical three songs from the 1960s, and they were reserved for the encore.

That is, until the final night of a three-night stand at the Dolby Theatre in Hollywood, California. Concertgoers on October 26, 2014, witnessed only one song for the encore—"Stay with Me"—and it wasn't even composed by Dylan. It immediately became a show closer staple for the rest of 2014, and a good chunk of 2015, and re-emerged in the set lists in the summer of 2016.

"I have never seen him so relaxed and apparently happy," wrote

Nancy Cobb in an online review. "Plus we had a wonderful cover of 'Stay with Me' from the film *The Cardinal* for the glorious conclusion. I was glad to see that the L.A. audience appreciated the ad-lib surprise. After all these years of receiving rudeness from his fans, he deserves it."[37]

After taking time to digest the song through listening to Dylan's versions both in the studio and onstage, writer Sean Curnyn nicely summed up this song that Dylan has closed a number of concerts with from 2014 to 2016, including his last concert as of this writing (Gilford, New Hampshire, July 17, 2016). The sentiment of "Stay with Me" communicates Dylan's ongoing sympathy for the Gospel:

"It is truly a very profound and piercing prayer, and this is something which Dylan obviously perceived better than just about anyone and then revealed so well in his own heartfelt rendition. The song captures the pain of a soul who has turned away from God in its metaphor of a lamb wandering in the darkness, growing cold, and conversely the wonder of that soul finding that wherever he may turn, God is there again.

"It's an exquisite hymn which expresses the hopelessness of life without God, despite our constant inclination to stray from Him, and the irreplaceable preciousness of those times when we can sense His presence.

"Dylan has used it as his closing number in so many of his shows now, and in a way it serves as an anchor to all of these 'popular standards' that he has lately chosen to uncover; these grand expressions of undying romantic love and/or unbearable lovelorn/loneliness are shown through the prism of 'Stay with Me' to reveal sublime angles on our relationship with God, and God's relationship with us. It is a great song, and Dylan's take on it is a helluva record."[38]

Right after debuting "Stay with Me" as an encore in Hollywood, Dylan's touring machine headed to the Bay Area for three nights in Oakland. It was during this time that Robert Love, the editor in chief of *AARP: The Magazine* (American Association of Retired People) found himself driving to a San Francisco hotel to interview Bob Dylan. The interview, months in the making—and at Dylan's request—was mainly to focus on Dylan's forthcoming album *Shadows in the Night*, a collection of American standards written between the 1920s and 1960s, and all included in the Frank Sinatra discography.

Though the interview was ultimately published in the organization's magazine (the February/March 2015 issue), the uncut version of the interview on their website (aarp.org) was where some of the gems resided. For example, although the magazine featured a sidebar with snippets of Dylan's quotes on other notable figures, including Irving Berlin, Chuck Berry, Billy Graham, Johnny Mercer, Jimmie Rodgers, and Shakespeare, we merely get this about the evangelist Graham: "This guy was rock 'n' roll personified. He filled football stadiums before Mick Jagger did." On its own, an amusing enough sentence, but its larger context in the uncut online interview reminded readers that even though Dylan's idea for an album like *Shadows in the Night* had been percolating since the late 1970s, his spiritual leanings/callings were brewing long before 1979's *Slow Train Coming*. And Billy Graham, apparently, was a big part of it.

In fact, in this poetic rant about Billy Graham, Dylan was not willing to divorce the DNA of his music from matters of salvation. Love wrote in his online introduction that his interviewee "reserves undiluted praise for Chuck Berry's poetry and Billy Graham's soul-searing hellfire." Dylan talked of the roots of the folk revival in the early 1960s and how he figured he had to go into songwriting; and though he couldn't be a hellfire rock 'n' roller, he was up to the task of writing hellfire lyrics:

"When I was growing up, Billy Graham was very popular. He was the greatest preacher and evangelist of my time—that guy could save souls and did. I went to two or three of his rallies in the '50s or '60s. This guy was like rock 'n' roll personified—volatile, explosive. He had the hair, the tone, the elocution—when he spoke, he brought the storm down. Clouds parted. Souls got saved, sometimes 30- or 40,000 of them. If you ever went to a Billy Graham rally back then, you were changed forever. There's never been a preacher like him. He could fill football stadiums before anybody. He could fill Giants Stadium more than even the Giants football team. Seems like a long time ago. Long before Mick Jagger sang his first note or Bruce [Springsteen] strapped on his first guitar—that's some of the part of rock 'n' roll that I retained. I had to. I saw Billy Graham in the flesh and heard him loud and clear."[39]

The public record shows that Dylan was at a Christian religious rally of the soul-saving variety when he met up in 1974 with the aforementioned cross-carrying evangelist Arthur Blessit. It is true that some folks have tracked Dylan's public life so closely that they are able to occasionally correct the man himself on matters of chronology; perhaps Dylan was mistaken regarding his memory of seeing Graham in the 1950s or 1960s—and yet he tells Love that he saw two or three Graham rallies. Intriguing fodder for future research and inquiry.

To add further intrigue to this evangelical scenario, in January 2016, just over a year after the AARP interview was conducted, a book by one Jess Archer was self-published entitled *Finding Home with the Beatles, Bob Dylan and Billy Graham: A Memoir of Growing Up Inside the Billy Graham Evangelistic Association*. In it, the author recounts how her father, a new employee in the Billy Graham ministry in 1981, encountered a man at a Graham rally in Baltimore, Maryland.

"I'm Bob Dylan's manager. He's here tonight. I just wanted to let someone official know," said the man. "The man walked Dad toward the seats directly above home plate and pointed six rows deep," writes Archer. "There he was, if you thought to look. Like a cardboard cutout of himself, in telltale Bob Dylan sunglasses but with a ballcap low, keeping his shoulders hunched. Unawares, people sat all around. Dad stared for a long moment, imagining a meeting between Bob Dylan and Billy Graham." Her dad, a longtime Dylan fan, struggling to maintain composure in the moment surreal, managed a "I'll see what I can do."

Archer goes on to recount how her dad proceeded up the chain of command: first, a man named Charlie Riggs said Graham didn't have the time for a meeting. Then it was on to Don Bailey, the ministry's head of public relations. Bailey said Graham was too busy. Finally, the new Graham employee boldly approached T. W. Wilson, Graham's personal assistant. "Why would Billy Graham want to meet Bob Dylan?" asked Wilson.

"If it needed explaining, Dad knew he had lost," Archer concluded. "The chasm at that time between the old men of the BGEA [Graham was sixty-two at the time.], who feared the world and hovered around Mr. Graham, and the newly converted—the artist or revolutionary thinker—was too vast. Many years later, when my father had the ear and friendship of the man himself, he told Billy about this story. Mr. Graham was shocked. 'Why did T. W. tell you that? Of course I would have met with Bob Dylan!'"[40]

And so it goes.

For the record, considering Dylan's concert schedule and the Graham rallies in Baltimore, it is highly likely Dylan took in the rally on Saturday evening, June 13, 1981, night number seven of eight for Graham at Memorial Stadium (the Orioles baseball team was on the road). Dylan would play a concert the next night on Sunday in Columbia, Maryland, about a twenty-mile drive from Baltimore—and then fly overseas for a summer European tour. The night before the Graham rally, Dylan had included in his set list Dallas Holm's "Rise Again," a song that would've fit right in with the Graham rally.

At times, Dylan's long-running affinity for certain gospel songs emerges like a wind seemingly out of nowhere. Just as Dylan concert-goers in July 2013 were privy to a couple of passionate gospel one-offs—via "Twelve Gates to the City" and "Let Your Light Shine on Me"—back in 1989 Dylan did the same for Thomas Dorsey's gospel classic "Peace in the Valley." Biographer Clinton Heylin heard the song through a tape of the show about a week later; he would never forget the performance. In 2011, while giving a talk at a Dylan conference in Vienna, Austria, he made this assertion about that 1989 performance of "Peace in the Valley" from Frejus, France:

"I believed even then that Dylan's heartfelt vocal and whole performance was giving us an insight into where he was 'at' spiritually at the time. After hearing it I wanted to say, 'So this is a guy who is no longer a Christian, but is singing this way because he likes the tune? I don't think so.' And the most important line for me (and him) is when Dylan sings

'Yes I'll be changed from the creature that I am', which he enunciates precisely, determined to get across the meaning. It is a specific reference to the Rapture, straight from Corinthians [in the New Testament]. He is telling us he still believes the same thing he believed in 1979, when he wrote the apocalyptic 'Ye Shall Be Changed'. I am prepared to state with a degree of certainty that there was no official tape made of that show by Dylan's people. So the people who were taping that show did as much of a public service as Thomas Thorpe when he published Shakespeare's sonnets." (Heylin's talk can be found in the 2015 book *Refractions of Bob Dylan*, edited by Eugen Banauch.)

For anyone who might scoff at Heylin's direction here, there was a 1990 crowd in Merrillville, Indiana, who heard Dylan cover the gospel standard "Stand by Me." Like "Peace in the Valley," Dylan had never played it before—and hasn't played it since. Yet after having been introduced by former President Jimmy Carter and honored in 2015 as Person of the Year by MusiCares (a charity outfit connected to the Grammys), Dylan delivered a half-hour speech in Los Angeles—utterly unheard of in his 50-plus year career. He brought up the song "Stand by Me." He didn't reference performing the song back in 1990, but he sure wanted to make sure no one confused it with that Ben E. King composition of the same name that hit No. 1 for weeks back in 1961 (and has since been an absolute staple of radio and time-honored in its presence on stages and in recording studios). "Not 'Stand by Me' the pop song. No," Dylan said. "The real 'Stand by Me'. The real one goes like this:

'When the storm of life is raging / Stand by me / When the storm of life is raging / Stand by me / When the world is tossing me / Like a ship upon the sea / Thou who rulest wind and water / Stand by me / In the midst of tribulation / Stand by me / In the midst of tribulation / Stand by me / When the hosts of hell assail / And my strength begins to fail / Thou who never lost a battle / Stand by me / In the midst of faults and failures / Stand by me / When I do the best I can / And my friends don't understand / Thou who knowest all about me / Stand by me.'[41]

He informed the Los Angeles crowd that he might be recording the song with the Blackwood Brothers, that it might confound expectations (but it shouldn't, he added), and that it wouldn't be anything out of the ordinary for him to do.

Though often given the "traditional" attribution, the song was copyrighted in 1905 by the Rev. Charles Albert Tindley. Its roots reached The Staple Singers, who created their rendition on their 1961 release *Swing Low*. Dylan would meet the Staple Singers not too long afterward.

Considering Dylan's immersion in American music, he may well have heard a version prior to The Staples family treatment. There's little doubt that at some point Dylan also became familiar with Sister Rosetta Tharpe's version of "Stand by Me," which happened to be released the year of Robert Zimmerman's birth.

Fast-forward to the day after Dylan's twenty-fifth birthday—an off day between his Paris concert and a tour-ending double bill at London's Royal Albert Hall—and Elvis Presley was in a studio recording "Stand by Me." The song would appear the following year on Presley's *How Great Thou Art* album. At the time of its release in early 1967, a post-motorcycle crash Dylan, may well have soaked in this second album of Presley gospel songs, considering the Bible was prominent in Dylan's Woodstock home, "Sign on the Cross" was percolating, and *John Wesley Harding* was on the eve of its creation.

In his *AARP* interview, Dylan's description of his experience of first hearing the Staple Singers' "Uncloudy Day" on the radio amounted to nothing short of a transformative moment. That moment, six decades earlier, he spoke of like it was something he had just experienced. As a young man, though obviously attracted to Mavis Staples, the overarching spiritual experience of hearing the Staple Singers present the gospel through song was a kind of foreshadowing for Dylan: In 1979 as a middle-aged man, the figure behind the gospel music genre itself, Jesus Himself, informed Dylan's experience. As he told Paul Vitello of the *Kansas City Times* in a January 1980 interview—"Let's just say I had a knee-buckling experience."

Readers of the uncut version of the AARP interview encountered this in the opening line of the opening paragraph: "I've always been drawn to spiritual songs. In 'Amazing Grace' that line—'that saved a wretch like me'—isn't that something we could all say if we were honest enough?"

Above the article there is this pullout quote from Dylan featured: "You have to believe what the words are saying and the words are as important as the melody. Unless you believe the song and have lived it, there's little sense in performing it."

By May 2016, the follow-up to *Shadows in the Night*—*Fallen Angels*—saw its release. The songs, like its predecessor, were all written by individuals or collaborators not named Bob Dylan, and mainly were drawn from the same 2014 recording sessions.

In some ways, the front cover to *Fallen Angels*—a shot of a man's hand in the foreground holding a hand of cards, which nicely conceals his face—works well with the back cover of *Shadows in the Night*: a cover revealing Dylan and a woman who's donning a Lone Ranger-like mask (and no small bust line), sharing a small table that features a plant, a candle, an ashtray, and two drinks. The well-dressed couple intently examine a vinyl record that both of them hold with one of their hands.

The songs from these two albums weave a *Chronicles*-like story of Dylan's interior life through the decades and where his heart lies during this season. He's aware of the hand he's drawn, he's choosing not to share his own songs for a season, and he's reveling in the songs of others and making them his own.

"There are moments of sadness and doubt on *Fallen Angels*—in the glum 'Melancholy Mood,' the prowling 'Maybe You'll Be There,' and the self-doubting yet openhearted 'Nevertheless,'" writes Chris Morris in *Together Through Life: A Personal Journey with the Music of Bob Dylan*. "But the profound despair with which *Shadows in the Night* was bathed never invades its putative sequel for more than a passing moment. Despite its forbidding title, with its echo of original sin, the record is about a world where love is not a catastrophe, and more than a possibility—the subject of 'Skylark'—but instead is deep, abiding, and eternal."[42]

Shadows in the Night has the opening blues of infidelity in "I'm a Fool to Want You," delivered with care and brutal honesty while the stately beginning of the album's closer, "That Lucky Old Sun," quickly unfolds into the tale of toil and longing it is—and ends in a flurry of vocal pathos that sounds like it could be the singer's last song sung.

Fallen Angels has the opening optimism of "Young at Heart" with its line of "As rich as you are / It's better by far / To be young at heart," echoing the singer from *Saved* who had lost every dime but was "richer by far with a satisfied mind." Young at heart and a satisfied mind seem to inhabit "Come Rain or Come Shine," Dylan's closing song for his 2016 release. We hear of someone who's going to love someone like no one, an act "high as a mountain, deep as a river" whether the couple is happy or unhappy together, in or out of money, and whatever the weather. Come rain or shine.

For some, Dylan albums might not be the event they used to be, but events related to the man are ever increasing. On March 14, 2016, an intermittent drizzle at twilight and threatening, dark clouds could've easily deterred people from attending a talk at the University of North Carolina-Asheville's Sherrill Center. Instead, the Mountain View Room, set up for a crowd of about a hundred, teemed with several generations of folks curious to hear about the evening's focus—Bob Dylan.

Dr. Richard Chess, a longtime English professor and director of the Center for Jewish Studies at UNC Asheville, cancelled his Monday night Spiritual Autobiographies class so his students could attend the Dylan talk. Chess introduced the featured speaker, Dr. Stephen Hazan Arnoff, by noting the two were friends and how he once, in awe, witnessed Arnoff give a clear and compelling lecture on the history of Judaism in less than an hour.

Chronologically speaking, Arnoff could be Dylan's son. He had recently taken over as CEO of the Jewish Community Center Association, the umbrella outfit that is over nearly 350 JCC locations in the United States. On this night, the public didn't know that in several days he'd be stepping down from his post.

As the crowd continued to mill into the room just above the college's basketball arena, comfortable chairs could be found and two large presentation screens could be seen, one on each side of the room. They displayed a picture of Dylan and the title of Arnoff's talk: "Bob Dylan's Begging for Salvation: Man and God and Law." As people chattered, Dylan's "Dirt Road Blues" played in the background, a song off *Time Out of Mind.*

"My mom loved Bob Dylan and I was raised listening to him and the Grateful Dead," said Michael Albinger, twenty-three, a UNC Asheville psychology major from Atlanta. Asheville native Hannah Spring, twenty, also a psychology major, had memories of Dylan's music growing up too. Another parent was the culprit: "On long road trips, Dylan was definitely on dad's play list," said Spring. Although not greatly familiar with the Dylan story, she came out on a Monday night, curious to hear about how religion had affected his career.

Though Leon Kramer, eighty-seven, had no personal history with Dylan's music (he said he was geared for other things, considering his age), he arrived at the talk with his wife, who did grow up with Bob Dylan and Joan Baez. "I don't like his voice and sometimes his personality leaves something to be desired, but his poetics are gorgeous," said Melody Kramer, seventy-six. She was interested in hearing Stephen Arnoff address Dylan's religious pursuits: "I think he went into fundamentalist Christianity, but I don't know what he is now."

Arnoff was a man on a mission, addressing the Minnesota native's journey in elliptical fashion. The packed crowd in Asheville was attentive, soaking it all in. Beginning with a story of dining in a New York City restaurant with some dear friends where the conversation eventually led to the swapping of Bob Dylan stories, he noted that with Dylan "There's just too much to talk about, like the universe." Meantime, he did manage to share the down-to-earth 2009 story of an on-tour Dylan detained by a New Jersey police officer for suspiciously roaming around—with hooded apparel in the pouring rain—near a property for sale. Reportedly near the residence that Bruce Springsteen once called home when the New Jersey native was penning the songs that became his landmark *Born to Run* album.

Speaking of running, if Dylan's faithfulness to the gypsy lifestyle these last three decades has had him running to something, perhaps it's all been part of a spiritual destiny. According to Arnoff, although Dylan has worn different masks, performed different styles of music, and hung out with a variety of collaborators and co-conspirators, religion has consistently run rampant throughout the legendary singer's work.

Arnoff's presentation was nothing if not deep, eclectic, and daring (and it mirrored his resume, which could easily be mistaken for the resumes of three or four middle-aged men of high repute). He spoke of how Dylan carried the mantle of both rock 'n' roll and the King James Bible; how excerpts from Saint Augustine's Confessions and a song clip from Paul Robeson's "I Dreamed I Saw Joe Hill Last Night" pointed up Dylan's own creative artistic process, a process where spiritual seeking was expressed and evident. How U2 singer Bono once playfully said that Dylan the lyricist "always mistakes women and God"; and how in the 1980s, when Dylan was struggling, the Grateful Dead served as translators for him, like the first-century Apostle Paul did for the Gospels.

Although Arnoff didn't delve into what happened between 1978's "Señor" and 1983's "Lord Protect My Child," i.e., Dylan's surrender to Jesus, he did go forward by tackling "Tryin' to Get to Heaven" from the 1990s. He linked the song up with nothing less than the story of a liturgical prayer uttered by an eleventh-century high priest. He then deftly leapt forward to the twenty-first century and focused on Dylan's "Ain't Talkin'" (from the 2006 album *Modern Times*) since it is here where the singer declares that he practices "a faith that's been long abandoned" and there "ain't no altars on this long and lonesome road."

So what does it all mean?

"Is Bob Dylan Jewish?" Arnoff bluntly asked, toward the end of his fast-paced and stimulating jaunt of a talk. An answer came through the photograph of Bob Dylan attending one of his son's bar mitzvahs at the Western Wall in Jerusalem in 1983: Dylan was wearing a prayer shawl, and a yarmulke and tefillin rested on his head. The answer to the Jewish question seemed obvious. Yet the next slide in the presentation remained up for a while, seemingly lingering for too long, and it featured the original album cover to *Saved*. Of all Bob Dylan album covers—and there have been dozens—this one stirred up no small amount of controversy back in the day. It is still capable of evoking derision, apathy, and praise, depending on the beholder.

The hand featured on the album cover of *Fallen Angels* in 2016 is of an unknown man holding an unknown hand of cards; maybe one day some Dylanologist will discover more details and uncover some "message." The bleeding Hand reaching down and the small hands reaching upward on the original album cover of *Saved* may be, for some, either a joyous mystery to embrace or an image to loathe, but for most its general message is evident—even if album artist Tony Wright had never revealed through an interview that he specifically captured what Dylan said he had seen in a vision.

"He never renounced the Christianity of the late 1970s, but he's been known to attend bar mitzvahs and synagogues on High Holy Days, too," offered Arnoff toward the end of his presentation. "What gives?" was a likely natural question among audience members that night in Asheville. "Syncretic" was the operative adjective Arnoff chose in describing the arc of Dylan's spiritual journey. (Here's one definition for syncretism: "the attempted reconciliation or union of different or opposing principles, practices, or parties, as in philosophy or religion."[43]

Not everyone bought into everything presented. One student who got to skip Dr. Chess's Spiritual Autobiographies class because of the talk wasn't bewildered by any supposed Dylan mystique. "I thought it [the talk] was a bit sophomoric basically because Dylan was ubiquitous when I was in my teens and twenties and was so totally understandable," the sixty-four-year-old woman said. "If you didn't live during the sixties and seventies, I suppose Dylan could be somewhat 'magical.' But, to me, he was just one of many creative minstrels of his time."

Another UNC-Asheville student, fifty-nine-year-old Robin Cape, who grew up in the military and traveled the world, was impressed by the turnout and the interest, and liked Arnoff's style. "I had no idea there were so many people who were so dedicated to exploring Dylan's music," said Cape. She thought the most interesting part of his talk was getting to understand a little more about the singer's personal angst: "I was a Joni Mitchell fanatic and can see now how Dylan gave her permission in a way to be so open and expressive of personal feelings in music."

In her early twenties, Cape attended one of Dylan's 1981 concerts that featured a good bit of Dylan's then-new gospel songs as well as his older hits. She recalls being impressed by the passion of the new songs and music. In her Spiritual Autobiographies class with Dr. Chess, what really stood out to her about Dylan was the role he played as a spiritual channel for her generation: "We were disillusioned by so much and found music as an expressive conduit for our internal explorations of meaning."

"I am not a Christian though I was raised in a Christian church," said Cape. "I believe that religion is valuable for the metaphors and for aiming our gaze and reflections toward truth that then must be revealed by our own exploration and personal experience." Though admittedly inquisitive, Cape does not think of any religion as facts about actual events or a singular truth.[44]

Whatever that might mean, no one knows just what the future holds for this septuagenarian singer, Bob Dylan—not even the sad gypsy serenading the moon. But if Dylan continues to, on occasion, appear at a Grammy event; or sing about Jesus on stages across his native land or around the world; or slip into synagogues for Rosh Hashanah or Yom Kippur—or whenever the need arises; or peck out a message on his old-school typewriter for the Internet; or release that gospel album he hinted at in a recent interview and speech; no soul should be too surprised. Dylan is exercising his gift of free will—a key gift from on high.

The songs of Bob Dylan speak in plain and subtle ways; in ambiguous and fantastic ways. His lyrics occasionally speak of the Answer in the Almighty; but they also express the humility of not knowing all of life's answers—and even being in doubt. These lyrics can also be filled with humor, wit, and sarcasm galore. These songs of Bob Dylan also communicate the sublime gospel blues that often accompany the faith journey.

Long may Zimmy run, and may he continue to faithfully paint that masterpiece.

AFTERWORD

ON THE EVE OF DYLAN'S SEVENTY-FIFTH BIRTHDAY, in May 2016, Jeffrey Salkin wrote an opinion piece for Religion News Service, reflecting on how the singer has communicated the Jewish experience in the world through his music. He let readers know he was fully aware of times in Dylan's life when "he lived as a Christian." He reminded readers that "Precious Angel" from *Slow Train Coming* is "so Christian as to be theologically anti-Semitic. What else do you make of a line like: 'You were laboring under the Law. . .'? It's as if Paul himself (and no, not McCartney—I'm talking about the 'original' Paul) had jumped across time and had joined Bob in the recording studio."

Salkin doesn't quite indict the whole album though. Another *Slow Train Coming* song curiously makes an appearance among his "Bob Dylan's Greatest Jewish Hits" list. "Man Gave Names to All the Animals" amounts to "an accurate rereading of the Genesis text, in which God gives Adam the task of naming the animals, which forever enshrines humanity as the category-creating being."

Though Salkin doesn't allude to the provocative Jesus/Judas Iscariot lyric from "With God on Our Side," he does bring up another lyric from the same song and offers it as a shining example of a rare cultural event for 1964 America: public reference to the Holocaust. He acknowledges *Anne Frank: The Diary of a Young Girl* (1952), Elie Wiesel's *Night* (1960), and a 1961 television episode of "The Twilight Zone" written by Rod Serling where the Dachau concentration camp is the context and a returning Nazi war criminal is tormented by his former victims; but his main assertion is that it really wasn't until an NBC-produced television series in 1978 that many Americans first encountered the horror of the Holocaust. (Even William L. Shirer's opus, the 1960 surprise bestseller *The Rise and Fall of the Third Reich: A History of Nazi Germany*, a book of over twelve hundred pages, only contained a few dozen pages directly related to the catastrophe. With that said, author Ron Rosenbaum, in a new introduction to the book in 2011, argued that it "made amnesia no longer an option" in America and that "Shirer reminded the world of 'what'; what happened to civilization and humanity in those years. That in itself was a major contribution to a postwar generation that came of age in the '60s, many of whom read Shirer as their parents' Book of the Month Club selection."[1])

Salkin concludes that Dylan helped American Judaism find its voice through his Holocaust allusion in "With God on Our Side."[2]

In a previous Dylan-related birthday piece (for Dylan's seventieth), Rosenbaum picks up—and then some—where Salkin left off:

"It's too often forgotten that Dylan wrote a horrifically chilling

Holocaust verse for one of his most brilliantly sarcastic songs, 'With God on Our Side,' which is in effect a sarcastic tour of official American history as intermittent slaughter, rationalized by religion, by 'American exceptionalism,' and climaxed by the aftermath of the Second World War, after which Dylan sneers about the way we forgave the Germans even though 'They murdered six million / In the ovens they fried / The Germans now too / Have God on their side.' Killer. He didn't forgive the Germans, or forgive the forgiving, and it's all there in that deliberately raw, ugly, in-your-face barbarism, 'In the ovens they fried.' No one wants that image, that metaphor made (burning) flesh conjured up before their inner eyes. We're usually content with speaking in hushed tones about 'ovens.' Dylan wasn't satisfied that we were satisfied."[3]

Those who've followed the Dylan story casually (or even closely) might not imagine that the same twenty-two-year-old kid who wrote "With God on Our Side" might've been influenced by the Catholicism that surrounded him while he grew up in the North Country. The usual suspects in the Dylan story of spiritual or religious influence are the Judaism of his childhood (and beyond) and the evangelical Christianity of his middle age (and beyond). But writer Jim Keane makes an intriguing case for the influence of Catholicism after having made a pilgrimage to Duluth and Hibbing, Minnesota.

Keane wasn't on a mission to read his own Catholicism into Dylan's journey; in fact, he decided to extend some business in Minneapolis in order to fulfill a two-decades old wish: simply to visit Dylan's old haunts. It was during his journey, in the summer of 2016, that he began to make connections and reflect on matters related to specific geographical locations.

He shared how his many travels down the Jersey shore enlightened him on sources related to the genius that is Bruce Springsteen; that he better understood the blue soul of William Butler Yeats after having driven through the Burren in Ireland; and how he learned more about Jack Kerouac from his road trip to Lowell, Massachusetts, than he had from reading any Kerouac book.

"I am a firm believer in the power of place, both as a matter of artistic influence and as a valuable source of interpretative information," declared Keane. "I became more and more intrigued with the influence of religious places (or at least a religious aesthetic) on Dylan as a young man with each new glimpse of his past."

First stop: Duluth. After noting that both of Dylan's parents are buried in a Jewish cemetery in Duluth and the former Zimmerman family home was only about two blocks from the nearest synagogue, Keane observed the fact that their former home, a duplex on Third Avenue, overlooked Lake Superior's most western tip. And in that line of sight from the home to the great lake, one cannot miss the spires of St. Josephat Polish National Catholic Church. Additionally, not too far from St. Josephat's is the Mary Star of the Sea Catholic Church.

"Religious tribalism (and anti-Semitism) being what it was and is, Dylan likely never thought to set foot in either church," Keane opined. But as a matter of fact, Keane, reports Dylan would've had to pass by St. Josephat at least twice daily on the way to school as a little boy. Keane then cites "Beyond the Horizon," Dylan's 2006 song from *Modern Times*, suggesting that St. Mary left him with one powerful auditory memory:

"Beyond the horizon, the night winds blow / The theme of a melody from many moons ago / The bells of St. Mary, how sweetly they chime"

Keane soon rolled out of Duluth and headed for Hibbing. After arriving, he discovered from the former Zimmerman home where Dylan grew up (age six to eighteen) how Hibbing High School is just out of sight from the front door. But what is very much in sight is a gigantic Catholic church named Blessed Sacrament, along with its neighboring school, Assumption School.

He makes the safe assumption that one cannot look left from Dylan's boyhood home without seeing the bell tower of Blessed Sacrament overwhelming the skyline. Just like St. Josephat in Duluth, Dylan would've passed in front of the Blessed Sacrament church and school at least twice daily. (And Dylan's younger brother David would, decades later, be at his mother-in-law's funeral in this same church.)

Keane did research along the way and discovered that this Hibbing church is substantially less attended than it was back in the 1950s. Back then, the pews were filled and the school overenrolled. "What did he think of the crowds coming and going from the school every day, or the men on the steps every Sunday morning, or the rituals and processions and religious iconography out front?" wondered Keane.

The Zimmerman family worshipped at a small synagogue on Second Avenue in Hibbing, easily accessible by foot from their home. The structure remains to this day and, according to Keane, if you gaze closely enough you'll spot the wood covering a Star of David window up top and a barely visible outline of a menorah on a wall above the window.

He reminds us that Dylan's post-bar mitzvah party in 1954 (four hundred were invited to attend) took place in a Hibbing landmark, the Androy Hotel. The hotel is not too far from where the now-defunct Zimmy's, a Dylan-themed restaurant and bar, was for a number of years.

Further down the street (on Fifth Avenue) is what used to be Abraham Zimmerman's appliance store. Dylan was known to be one of its employees from time to time and, if you were to have exited the store, right across the street was another Catholic church, Immaculate Conception. Like the Blessed Sacrament church in Hibbing, it had seen better days, attendance-wise, back in Dylan's day, so he would've likely seen the natural ebb and flow of the parish from the vantage point of his father's store.

Keane reflected on the larger context of churches beyond the Catholic affiliation in Duluth and Hibbing, and pondered what effect they might have had on Dylan:

> Hibbing is of course full of churches—Episcopalian, Lutheran, and nowadays evangelical of many stripes—so perhaps it is not so surprising that one should bump into a Catholic one now and again. But still, doesn't one wonder to what degree these sacred places influenced the aesthetics and the worldview of this balladeer of the sacred and the profane in everyday life? Most of us associate Dylan's Christian aesthetic with his controversial conversion to Christianity in the early

1980s, but his childhood feet were never far from the doors, nor his ears from the bells, of St. Mary, of St. Josephat, of Blessed Sacrament, of Immaculate Conception.[4]

Essentially resting his case, Keane then brings us to this account from Dylan's 2004 memoir *Chronicles*:

> Across the street from where I stood looking out the window was a church with a bell tower. The ringing of the bells made me feel at home, too. I'd always heard and listened to the bells. Iron, brass, silver bells—the bells sang. On Sundays, for services, on holidays. They changed when somebody important died, when people were getting married. Any special occasion would make the bells ring. You had a pleasant feeling when you heard the bells.[5]

By October of 2016, metaphoric bells were certainly ringing for some when the Swedish Academy announced that Dylan had won no less than the Nobel Prize for Literature—"for having created new poetic expressions within the great American song tradition." First nominated for the prestigious honor in 1996, very few (including most likely Dylan) would've bet on this day's arrival. After a major league ruckus ensued within fan, media, and academic circles about what the honor meant (and if he was worthy of it in the first place) and how and why the singer should or shouldn't respond, Dylan managed to continue his fall U.S. tour, record a song in honor of Tony Bennett's ninetieth birthday, quietly visit the Woody Guthrie Archives in Tulsa, Oklahoma, receive a Nobel-related e-mail of congratulations and encouragement from former U.S. president Jimmy Carter[6]—and, not so quietly, a couple of months later, miss the Nobel ceremony with his fellow honorees and the King of Sweden.

In 2017, on the eve of his latest album release, *Triplicate* (set squarely, some might say, in that "great American song tradition"), and a spring tour of Europe, Dylan granted a wide-ranging interview to the man who had last interviewed him about the affair that was the *Christmas in the Heart* album. In this Q&A in March 2017, exclusively published on Dylan's official Website (bobdylan.com), there was this nugget of an exchange: Flanagan: Which one of your songs do you think did not get the attention it deserved? Dylan: "Brownsville Girl," or maybe "In the Garden."

Although just one question among dozens from journalist, author, and novelist Bill Flanagan, the question was an interesting one, and not insignificant. And who could've guessed the response? "Brownsville Girl," co-written with playwright Sam Shepard and appearing on what many fans and critics deem one of the nadirs of Dylan's studio career—the *Knocked Out Loaded* album—is, nonetheless, an absolute gem. Its lyrics include allusions to: a Gregory Peck movie; the familiar image of a rollin' train; a Ford in need of repair; the places of San Antonio, the Alamo, Mexico, the Rocky Mountains, the panhandle of Florida, and Amarillo; tough times, bummin' rides, and avoiding the subject of money; broken hearts, and even corrupt swap meets. Images of great landscapes and deep emotions abide, along with deceptively simple dialogue. Characters are going for broke, including one soul whose real name isn't known, and the cross-country ride is for keeps—until the wheels fall off and burn. Then it's back to the Gregory Peck movie that started it all off.

Danger suddenly emerges in "Brownsville Girl" as shots ring out. The narrator instinctively runs (instead of ducking) from the imminent danger and is ultimately cornered in, of all places, a churchyard—and is identified from a photo in, of all newspapers, the *Corpus Christi Tribune*. The photo's caption? A man with no alibi. The mere length of "Brownsville Girl," basically in the ballpark of Dylan's eleven-minute epic "Desolation Row" from twenty years earlier, made it an audacious inclusion for *Dylan's Greatest Hits: Volume 3* (1994), almost like someone trespassed and went over the line of some greatest hits rule. The song's conclusion features New Orleans' French Quarter, the powerful bonds of those who suffer together, and the narrator's recollection of being told by a presumed intimate that brutally human line regarding repentance. Then, the Gregory Peck movie surfaces yet again, and the pathos-drenched refrain of the inescapable Brownsville girl.

"In the Garden," the other tune Dylan suggested to Bill Flanagan as not getting the attention it deserved, has been referenced repeatedly in this manuscript, including Dylan's onstage plea in 1986 (incidentally, the very year "Brownsville Girl" first appeared) to have the Amnesty International tour feature this song of his, a Jesus-centered song that unsuspecting crowds first encountered in the heady days of 1979–1980. For whatever reason, Dylan's suggestion in 1986 fell on deaf ears.

Of the hundreds of songs Bob Dylan has composed over five decades, it almost seems perverse for the Nobel winner to draw attention to "In the Garden," a song that also hails from what is widely perceived as another nadir of Dylan's career—the *Saved* album of 1980. Set aside any deep reflection and analysis of its lyrics—unflinchingly evangelical to the nth degree—and the music is formidable in its own right, occasionally receiving notice from some discerning ears, including old Dylan friends like the late poet Allen Ginsberg and Rabbi Manis Friedman who both have publicly acknowledged their admiration for "In the Garden" ("a great song" Ginsberg told interviewer Wes Stace in 1985; "a good song" Friedman told interviewer Martin Grossman in the late 1990s).

At some time in the not-too-distant future, Dylan might be recording "Stand by Me," another gospel song close to his heart, through its content is more about the mercy than the judgment of God. Lyrically speaking, both judgment and mercy will be on public display soon enough through the latest installment of Dylan's officially sanctioned recordings known as *The Bootleg Series*. As of this writing, *The Gospel Years* will apparently be a box set released in November of 2017, some thirty-eight years after Dylan's storied first run at San Francisco's Warfield Theatre, where he introduced his gospel songs to the masses. If an unrepentant Dylan didn't particularly regret telling people how to get their souls saved back then, as he told his old journalist friend Robert Hilburn in 1983 when discussing the gospel tours, then this latest release loudly communicates that his lack of repentance remains.

Even former punk rocker and longtime Dylan chronicler and biographer Clinton Heylin has been, in a way, welcomed into official Dylan circles: he's been called on to pen the liner notes to this official gospel release (and has already contributed the liner notes to the 1966 live box set, released in 2016). Furthermore, for good measure, the Englishman Heylin, born the year before a nineteen-year-old Dylan landed in the Big Apple, will soon be releasing his latest Dylan book—*Trouble in Mind: Bob Dylan's Gospel Years—What Really Happened.* The book will coincide with the release of Dylan's gospel offering. Apparently, Dylan's longtime right hand man Jeff Rosen has either overlooked or forgiven Heylin for the not so subtle non-dedication Heylin gave him in a 1995 book devoted to Dylan's studio recordings. Things have changed indeed, and seem to have come full circle. (As for the sheer number of books written on Dylan, no one on the planet comes close to Heylin; and those not familiar might assume him to be a one-trick pony. Far from it. His other books include biographies of Van Morrison and Sandy Denny, a history of the bootleg recording industry, song snatchers in pop music, a history or two of punk rock music, books on Orson Welles, the Beatles, Bruce Springsteen, the Sex Pistols, and British rock music, and even a tome on the sonnets of Shakespeare.)

In 2002, Dylan's then newly-composed alternate version of his *Slow Train Coming* song "Gonna Change My Way of Thinking" had the singer in a recording studio with Mavis Staples by his side, the same woman whose voice kept him up in his Hibbing bedroom late one night in the 1950s as teenager—when "Uncloudy Day" on the radio threw him for an otherworldly loop.[7] The two reunited for a summer 2016 tour. When they sang together in the studio back in 2002, one of the lyrics had the singer sitting at the welcome table. Dylan's been ready for that welcome table for decades now, and the odds are that welcome table isn't located in Minnesota, Woodstock, New York City, Malibu, or the White House.

For her part, Dylan's former wife Carolyn Dennis has processed a moment the two shared together: "I noticed a Bible in his luggage one day as he was packing. Amidst all the rumors that he was no longer Christian, I asked him if he was still a believer. His answer was short and simple, 'I believe the whole Bible.' I have always known Bob to be one that uses few words. Knowing that he was born into the Jewish faith and culture and being one of the people that he so proudly proclaimed his acceptance of Jesus Christ as Lord and Savior to, I did not push or ask anything more about it. As far as I am concerned, I didn't need to. The answer seemed complete to me and he'd answered my question. Bob has never denied being Jewish, nor has he ever denied being Christian to me."[8]

Dennis's conclusions aside, some Jesus followers have judged Dylan to not be among the true believers. This judgment sometimes originates from sources of considerable scholarly respect and evangelical influence. Randall Balmer, an Ivy League professor and for years an editor-at-large at *Christianity Today*, tackled the task of compiling *The Encyclopedia of Evangelicalism*, a large volume originally published in 2002 by the Christian publisher Westminster John Knox Press and updated in 2004 by Baylor University Press. Balmer's entry on Dylan, about a page long, climaxes with this sentence: "Dylan publicly renounced his conversion to Christianity early in 1982."[9] This bogus, unfounded rumor has faithfully persisted now for decades. What's striking about this matter-of-fact statement in Balmer's case is that the lone source he cites for his entry on Dylan is Howard Sounes' 2001 biography, which makes no such claim.

The conventional wisdom of a Dylan no longer a part of the kingdom of heaven ushered in by the radical proclamations of a first century Jew will likely dog Dylan to the grave. But Dylan, not the biggest proponent of conventional wisdom, probably couldn't care less. So who says the man can't get heavenly aid?

When Bob Dylan penned "Saving Grace" in 1979, he plainly wrote that after the death of life comes the resurrection—and wherever he is welcome is where he will be. Why bet against Dylan having a place at that heavenly welcome table? He's been hungry as a horse for a good long while. The vast majority of us aren't privy to the private moments of joy, laughter, contentment, sorrow, confusion, discouragement, doubt, and resolve that the man has experienced over the decades; yet we have witnessed the public Dylan, who has faithfully tried to get to heaven before they close the door.

NOTES

CHAPTER ONE: CHIEF COMMANDER BLUES

1. Scott Cohen, "Don't Ask Me Nothin' About Nothin,' I Might Just Tell You the Truth: Bob Dylan Revisited," *Spin* (December 1985), p. 37.
2. Christopher John Farley, "Legend of Dylan," *Time*, September 17, 2001.
3. Ronnie Keohane, "It's Alright Ma, It's Dylan's Fate and Dylan's Fate Only," Ornery Press Syndicate, October 2003.
4. Dave Engel, *Just Like Bob Zimmerman's Blues: Dylan in Minnesota*, Mesabi, Rudolph, WI: River City Memoirs, 1997, p. 37.
5. Derek Barker [Editor], *Isis: A Bob Dylan Anthology*, London: Helter Skelter Publishing, 2001, p. 21 (via Ian Woodward's transcriptions).
6. Neil Spencer, "A Diamond Voice Within," *New Musical Express*, August 15, 1981, pp. 29–31.
7. Michael Fox, "Seinfeld Writer, Bob Dylan Team Up for Offbeat New Film," *Jewish Bulletin of Northern California*, August 2003.
8. Francis Davis, "Napoleon in Rags," *Atlantic Monthly* (May 1999).
9. Davin Seay with Mary Neely, *Stairway to Heaven: The Spiritual Roots of Rock 'N' Roll*, New York: Ballantine Books, 1986, p. 333.
10. Author interview: Daniel Evearitt, December 1, 2011.
11. Lisa Randall, *Knocking on Heaven's Door: How Physics and Scientific Thinking Illuminate the Universe and the Modern World*, New York: Ecco, 2011, p. 59.
12. Ralph J. Gleason, *San Francisco Chronicle*, September 19, 1965.

CHAPTER TWO: 1961-1969: ESCAPING ON THE RUN

1. Izzy Young, The Izzy Young Notebooks, October 23, 1961 entry (originally published in *Other Scenes*, 1968, Israel G. Young).
2. Bert Cartwright, *The Bible in the Lyrics of Bob Dylan*, Romford, Essex, England: Wanted Man Study Series, 1992, p. 107.
3. Anthony Scaduto, *Bob Dylan*, London: Helter Skelter Publishing, 1996, p. 220 (originally published in 1972 by Grosset and Dunlap, New York).
4. Matthew Tempest, "Don't Look Back!," *The Bridge* #6 (Spring 2000), p. 75.
5. Colbert S. Cartwright, "The Times They Are a-Changin': The Time-Wearied Troubadour Turns 50," *Sojourners* (June 1991), p. 40.
6. Michael Corcoran, "Recommended Music," *Austin American-Statesman*, February 21, 2002.
7. Paul Williams, *Dylan—What Happened?*, South Bend, IN/Glen Ellen, CA: and books/Entwhistle Books, 1979, p. 35.
8. Clinton Heylin, *Bob Dylan: Behind the Shades Revisited*, New York: William Morrow, 2001, p. 223.
9. John Herdman, *Voice Without Restraint: Bob Dylan's Lyrics and Their Background*, New York: Delilah Books, 1982, p. 91.
10. Neil Hickey, "A Voice Still Blowin' in the Wind," *TV Guide*, 14, September 11, 1976, p. 5.
11. Stephen Davis, *Old Gods Almost Dead: The 40-Year Odyssey of the Rolling Stones*, New York: Broadway Books, 2001, p. 237.
12. Heylin, *Bob Dylan: Behind the Shades Revisited*, p. 285.
13. Howard Sounes, *Down the Highway: The Life of Bob Dylan*, New York: Grove Press, pp. 227-228.
14. John Cohen and Happy Traum, "Conversations with Bob Dylan," *Sing Out!*, October/November 1968, p. 10.
15. Nat Hentoff, *New York Times*, February 10, 1974.
16. Tim Riley, *Hard Rain: A Dylan Commentary*, New York: Alfred A. Knopf, Inc., 1992, p. 11.

CHAPTER THREE: 1970-1979: DON'T MIND THE DRIVING RAIN

1. Davin Seay with Mary Neely, *Stairway to Heaven: The Spiritual Roots of Rock 'N' Roll*, New York: Ballantine Books, 1986, pp. 193–194.
2. Ron Rosenbaum, "Bob Dylan: A Candid Conversation with the Visionary Whose Songs Changed the Times," *Playboy*, March 1978, p. 69.
3. Bex Levine, "Let the Locusts Descend," *The Daily Princetonian*, March 12, 2001.
4. Edna Gundersen, "The 'Oh Mercy' Interview: Part I," *On the Tracks* #3 (Spring 1994), p. 15 (originally published: *USA Today*, September 21, 1989).
5. *The Telegraph* #11 (April 1983), p. 1.
6. M. Enghien, *Super-Hebedo-Pop Music*, 1970.
7. Author interview: Scott Ross, March 20, 2000.
8. Robert Shelton, *No Direction Home: The Life and Music of Bob Dylan*, New York: Da Capo Press, 1997, p. 412 (originally published in 1986 by Beech Tree Books, New York).
9. Ibid, p. 414.
10. Ibid, p. 413.
11. Robert D. Campbell, "Dylan's New Morning," *Christian Century*, August 25, 1971.
12. Stephen Pickering, *Bob Dylan Approximately: A Portrait of the Jewish Poet in Search of God: A Midrash*, New York: David McKay Company, Inc., 1975, p. 22.

13. Martin Grossman (with a little help from Ronnie Schreiber and Larry Yudelson), "Tangled Up in Jews," *On the Tracks* #22 (Fall 2001), p. 46.
14. Nat Hentoff, *New York Times*, February 10, 1974.
15. Ibid
16. Author interview: Dave Kelly, April 29, 2012.
17. Howard Sounes, *Down the Highway: The Life of Bob Dylan*, New York: Grove Press, 2001, p. 274.
18. Pickering, *Bob Dylan Approximately*, p. 80, 82.
19. Ibid, p. 11.
19. Author interview: Arthur Blessit, March 18, 2003.
20. Pickering, *Bob Dylan Approximately*, p. 98.
21. Neil Hickey, "A Voice Still Blowin' in the Wind," *TV Guide*, September 11, 1976.
22. "Misc. News," *Series of Dreams* #46 (1997), p. 2 (quote appeared in the *New Yorker*).
23. Shelton, *No Direction Home*, p. 432.
24. Jim Jerome, *People*, November 10, 1975.
25. Peter Barry Chowka, "This is Allen Ginsberg?," *New Age* (April 1976).
26. Bob Spitz, *Dylan: A Biography*, New York: W.W. Norton & Company, 1991, pp. 527–528 (originally published in 1989 by McGraw-Hill, New York).
27. Author interview: T-Bone Burnett, September 20, 1999.
28. Hickey, *TV Guide*.
29. Rosenbaum, *Playboy*.
30. Jonathan Cott, "Standing Naked—the Rolling Stone Interview: Bob Dylan," *Rolling Stone*, January 26, 1978, pp. 42–43.
31. Paul Williams, *Dylan—What Happened?*, Glen Ellen, CA: Entwhistle books, 1979, p. 70.
32. Sharon Gallagher, "Faith and Hope and Rock and Roll: An Interview with T-Bone Burnett," *Radix* Vol. 21/No. 3 (Spring 1993), pp. 8–11; 28–29.
33. Steve Pond, "T-Bone Burnett: Surviving the Wild Side," *Rolling Stone*, November 24, 1983, p. 62.
34. Sharon Gallagher, "Alpha Band Interview," *Radix* (November-December 1978), p. 5.
35. Ibid.
36. Robert Christgau, Consumer Guide Reviews: "*Spark in the Dark* (1977) B+," robertchristgau.com
37. Robert Christgau, Consumer Guide Reviews: "*The Statue Makers of Hollywood* (1978) B+," robertchristgau.com
38. Larry Jaffee, "An Exclusive On the Tracks Interview: David Mansfield," *On the Tracks* #17 (Fall 1999), p. 35
39. Lloyd Sachs, *T-Bone Burnett: A Life in Pursuit*, Austin, Tx: University of Texas Press, 2016, p. 38; 219.
40. Roger Sachs and Lonnie Frisbee, *Not by Might, Nor by Power: The Great Commission* [Book Two], Santa Maria, Ca: Freedom Publications, 2016, pp. 17-20.
41. Ibid, p. 20.
42. Author interviews: Dave Whiting-Smith, January and May 2001. For the record, both "Blowin' in the Wind" and "Forever Young" were performed by Dylan at this concert in Gothenburg, Sweden, on July 11, 1978; furthermore, it's worth noting that by the following year, on December 5, 1979, in Albuquerque, New Mexico, Dylan's onstage comments between songs included the following: "I told you 'The Times They Are A-Changin' and they did. I said the answer was 'Blowin' in the Wind' and it was. I'm telling you now Jesus is coming back, and He is!--and there is no other way of salvation. I know around here you got a lot of people putting mess on you in all kinds a ways, you

don't even know which way to believe. There's only one way to believe, there's only one way--the Truth and the Life. It took me a long time to figure that out before it did come to me, and I hope it doesn't take you that long. But Jesus is coming back to set up His kingdom in Jerusalem for a thousand years. I don't know if that's news to you, but I know you don't read it in the newspapers, but it's the truth alright!" [source: Clinton Heylin (Editor), *Saved!: The Gospel Speeches of Bob Dylan, Madras*, India & New York: Hanuman Books, 1990, pp. 12-14.]

43. "Helena Springs: A Conversation with Chris Cooper," *The Telegraph* #34 (Winter 1989), pp. 72-73 (originally published in Endless Road #7).
44. Bert Cartwright, *The Bible in the Lyrics of Bob Dylan*, Romford, Essex, England: Wanted Man Study Series, 1992, p. 108.
45. *The Telegraph* #3 (February 1982), p. 2.
46. Author interview: Dave Kelly, April 29, 2012.
47. Robert Hilburn, "Dylan: 'I Learned that Jesus is Real and I Wanted That'," *Los Angeles Times*, November 23, 1980.
48. Larry Myers, "Setting the Record Straight: A Letter from Pastor Larry Myers," *On the Tracks* #4 (Fall 1994), pp. 31–32.
49. Author interview: Dave Kelly, April 29, 2012.
50. Grossman, "Tangled Up in Jews," *On the Tracks*, p. 46.
51. Larry Yudelson, "Dylan: Tangled Up in Jews," *Washington Jewish Week*, 1991.
52. Author interviews: Al Kasha, July 30, 1999; June 27, 2000.
53. Author interview: Terry Botwick, February 23, 2012.
54. Author interview: Paul Wasserman, April 2, 2001.
55. Author interview: Jerry Wexler, October 11, 2000.
56. Author interview: Dick Cooper, August 9, 2000.
57. Jerry Wexler and David Ritz, *Rhythm & the Blues: A Life in American Music*, New York: St. Martin's Press, 1993, p. 294.
58. Author interview: Barry Beckett, November 3, 2000.
59. Author interview: Micky Buckins, October 5, 2000.
60. Jon Bream, "Dylan: He Awaits a 'Slow Train' Out of His Musical Limbo," *The Minneapolis Star*, August 8, 1979, 1b, 6b.
61. Author interview: Catherine Kanner, July 20, 2000.
62. Author interview: Nick Saxton, July 20, 2000.
63. Dan Wooding, "Bob Dylan: The American Troubadour," A&E Biography, August 13, 2000.
64. Spitz, *Dylan: A Biography*, p. 528.
65. Uri Geller, "B-side Myself over Bob Dylan," *The Jewish Telegraph* [incorporating the *Jewish Gazette*], January 14, 2000 (via http://www.tcom.co.uk/hpnet/jt3.htm).
66. Michael L. Brown, *Answering Jewish Objections to Jesus: General and Historical Objections* (Volume One), Grand Rapids, MI: Baker Books, 2001, p. 3.
67. Author interview: Wasserman.
68. Author interview: Dave Kelly, April 29, 2012.
69. Ibid.
70. Ibid.
71. Ibid.
72. P. Williams, *Dylan—What Happened?*, p. 13, 84; pp. 117–118.
73. Scott Marshall, "An Exclusive On the Tracks Interview: Regina Havis," *On the Tracks* #18 (Spring 2000), pp. 15-17.

74. Ibid.
75. Author interviews: Joel Selvin, June 27; July 7, 2000.
76. Author interview: Wasserman.
77. Author interview: Tim Drummond, January 12, 2001.
78. Author interview: Spooner Oldham, July 23, 1999.
79. Wesley G. Pippert, *An Ethic of News: A Reporter's Search for the Truth*, Washington, D.C.: Georgetown University Press, 1989.
80. Author interview: Fred Tackett, August 9, 1999.
81. Author interview: Peter Barsotti, June 28, 2000.
82. "Dylan Tour Off to a Shaky Start," *Rolling Stone*, December 13, 1979.
83. Author interview: Mitch Glaser, January 24, 2001.
84. Author interview: Dave Kelly, April 29, 2012.
85. Author interviews: Tim Charles, January 22; February 16, 2001.
86. Author interview: Dave Kelly, April 29, 2012.
87. Ibid.
88. Harvey Kubernik, "Holy Bob," *Melody Maker*, November 1979.
89. Rod Macbeath, "The Bridge Interview: Bruce Gary," *The Bridge* #8, p. 22.
90. Sounes, *Down the Highway*, p. 331.
91. Heylin, "Saved!," *The Telegraph* #29, pp. 48-50.
92. Steve Berg, "Dylan and Jesus: The Scratching of Heads in Hibbing," *Minneapolis Tribune*, December 7, 1979.
93. Author interview: John Perry Barlow, August 18, 1999.
94. *Rolling Stone*, December 27, 1979-January 10, 1980, p. 240.
95. Janet Huck, Barbara Oraustark, and Ying Ying Wu, The (New) Word According to Dylan," *Newsweek*, December 17, 1979, p. 90.
96. Pickering, *Bob Dylan Approximately*, p. 203.
97. John Swenson, UPI press release, 1986.
98. Robert Hilburn, "Dylan's New Furor: Rock 'n' Religion," *Los Angeles Times*, November 18, 1979, p. 82.
99. Fred A. Bernstein, "Interviews from the *Official Jewish Mothers' Hall of Fame*"; from Bernstein's The Official Jewish Mothers' Hall of Fame, published by Doubleday, New York, 1986; reprinted here: http://www.jewhoo.com/editor/ interviews/beattyrutman/

CHAPTER FOUR: 1980-1989: RING THEM BELLS, YE HEATHEN

1. Al Aronowitz, "Bob Dylan: American Troubadour," A&E Biography Special; August 13, 2000 (incidentally, Aronowitz acknowledged participating in self-destructive binges during this time period and counted himself among the survivors).
2. Paul Williams, *Watching the River Flow: Observations on Bob Dylan's Art-in-Progress, 1966-1995*, London: Omnibus Press, p. 134.
3. Paul Vitello, "A Born-Again Dylan Believes the Times They Are a-Changin'," *Kansas City Times*, January 29, 1980.
4. Steve Turner, *Hungry for Heaven: Rock 'n' Roll & The Search for Redemption*, Downers Grove, IL: InterVarsity Press, 1995 (originally published by W.H. Allen, London, 1988).
5. John Ledbury, *Mysteriously Saved: An Astrological Investigation into Bob Dylan's Conversion to American Fundamentalism*, London: Quest Publications (self- published), 1980, p. 39.

6. Ibid, p. 29.
7. Author interview: Raymond Foye, 2001.
8. Clinton Heylin, *Bob Dylan: A Life in Stolen Moments: Day by Day: 1941-1995*, New York: Schirmer Books, 1996, p. 214.
9. Clinton Heylin, "Saved!: Bob Dylan's Conversion to Christianity" (Part Two), *The Telegraph* #29 (Spring 1988), p. 53.
10. Robert Levinson, "Larry Sloman: Rolling with the Thunder," *Isis* #104 (August-September 2002), p. 49.
11. Howard Sounes, *Down the Highway: The Life of Bob Dylan*, New York: Grove Press, 2001, p. 334.
12. Ibid, pp. 334–335.
13. Author interviews: Dave Whiting-Smith, January 8; May 21, 2001.
14. Author interviews: Peter Stone Brown, May 10-11, 2000.
15. Karen Hughes, "Dylan Follows Christ with a Passion," *The Dominion*, August 2, 1980, p. 8.
16. Author interview: Dave Kelly, April 29, 2012.
17. John Bauldie, "A Conversation with Tony Wright," *The Telegraph* #43 (Autumn 1992), p. 88, 93.
18. Ibid.
19. Author interview: Dave Kelly, April 29, 2012.
20. Sounes, *Down the Highway*, p. 336.
21. Martin Grossman (with a little help from Ronnie Schreiber and Larry Yudelson), "Tangled Up in Jews," *On the Tracks* #22 (Fall 2001), p. 47.
22. "Brief Encounter: Leonard Cohen," *The Telegraph* #28 (Winter 1987), p. 94—interview conducted on March 5, 1985 by unidentified journalist in Basel, Switzerland.
23. Author interview: Dave Kelly, April 29, 2012.
24. Robert Shelton, *No Direction Home: The Life and Music of Bob Dylan*, New York: Ballantine Books, 1986, p. 566.
25. Paul Vincent, "Backstage at the Warfield," *On the Tracks* #5 (Spring 1995), p. 14.
26. "Bob Dylan Philosophizes on Folk Songs Backstage," *The Daily Princetonian*, November 9, 1964.
27. Robert Hilburn, "Dylan: 'I Learned That Jesus is Real and I Wanted That'," *Los Angeles Times*, November 23, 1980.
28. Jerry Wexler and David Ritz, *Rhythm and the Blues: A Life in American Music*, New York: St. Martin's Press, 1994, p. 198 (originally published by Alfred A. Knopf, New York, 1993).
29. Bob Spitz, *Dylan: A Biography*, New York: W.W. Norton & Company, 1991, p. 540 (originally published by McGraw-Hill, New York, 1989).
30. Clinton Heylin, "A Vagabond Rapping in Late 1980," *The Telegraph* #24 (Summer 1986), p. 88.
31. Ernesto Bladden, KPRI-FM radio, San Diego, broadcast on November 25, 1980, four days after the interview was conducted.
32. Dolores Barclay, "Bob Dylan: Hero Folk Singer of the '60s, Turns 40," Associated Press, May 24, 1981.
33. Neil Spencer, "A Diamond Voice Within," *New Musical Express*, August 15, 1981, pp. 29-31.
34. John Bauldie, "The Wanted Man Interview: Harvey Brooks," *The Telegraph* #47 (Winter 1993), p. 82.
35. William McKeen, *Bob Dylan: A Bio-Bibliography*, Westport, CT: Greenwood Press, 1993, p. 70.
36. Imre Salusinszky, "Chimes of Freedom Flashing: Bob Dylan's Message about Freedom and Responsibility," *The Telegraph* #49 (Summer 1994), p. 23.
37. Michael Long, "What Good Came from the Sixties?," *The Weekly Standard*, January 1, 2001.
38. Sharon Churcher, "Dylan Ditching Gospel?," *New York*, March 15, 1982, p. 15.

39. Sounes, *Down the Highway*, p. 351.
40. Kurt Loder, *Rolling Stone*, April 14, 1983.
41. Derek Mankelow, "Now Hear This Robert Zimmerman—I Wrote a Song for You," *The Telegraph* #35 (Spring 1990), p. 92.
42. Michael Gray, *Mother!: The Frank Zappa Story*, New York: Proteus Books Ltd., 1985, pp. 148-149.
43. Author interview: Kasriel Kastel, October 27, 2000.
44. Author interview: Paul Wasserman, April 2, 2001.
45. "Has Born-Again Bob Dylan Returned to Judaism?," *Christianity Today*, January 13, 1984 (since this article was under a general "News" heading and had no attribution—and since no one remains on staff from that period—the interviewer in question remains a mystery for now. (I called the offices of *Christianity Today*.) However, I spoke with Rabbi Kastel and although he remembers his quotes, he doesn't remember being interviewed by *Christianity Today*: "Could I swear to it in a court of law? No. But I'd be very surprised if I would've agreed to it. I'm not denying I said it but, again, I don't remember the context. I wasn't saying it in a way that would be published because that's something that could get back to him; and that'd be a stupid thing to do because it'd be counter-productive.").
46. Author interview: Kastel, 2000.
47. Bryan Styble, "Bob Dylan's Mysteries Unveiled," *CCM Magazine*, January 1984.
48. Mark Joseph, *The Rock & Roll Rebellion: Why People of Faith Abandoned Rock Music and Why They're Coming Back*, Nashville, TN: Broadman & Holman Publishers, 1999, p. 108.
49. James W. Earl, "Beyond Desire: The Conversion of Bob Dylan," *University of Hartford Studies in Literature* 20.2 (1988), pp. 53-54.
50. Author interview: Dave Kelly, April 29, 2012.
51. Clinton Heylin, *Saved!: The Gospel Speeches of Bob Dylan*, Madras, India, & New York: Hanuman Books, 1990, p. 80.
52. Martin Keller, "Times They Are a-Changin': In Search of the Latest Bob Dylan," *Dallas Times-Herald*, November 6, 1983, H1 (this interview was originally conducted for the *Minneapolis City Pages*).
53. Gospel of John 1:29b (New International Version).
54. Heylin, "Saved!", *The Telegraph* #29, p. 41.
55. James Carroll, *Constantine's Sword: The Church and the Jews: A History*, Boston, MA: Houghton and Mifflin Company, 2001.
56. Fred Bernstein, http://www.jewhoo.com/editor/interviews/beattyrut51.man/.
57. Author interview: Zavi Cohen, January 30, 2001.
58. Ibid.
59. Sounes, *Down the Highway*, p. 356.
60. Scott Marshall, "An Exclusive On the Tracks Interview: Howard Sounes," *On the Tracks* #21 (Summer 2001), p. 47.
61. Mick Brown, "Dylan: 'Jesus, Who's Got Time to Keep Up with the Times?'," *Sunday Times*, July 1, 1984.
62. Author interview: Mitch Glaser, January 24, 2001.
63. Robert Hilburn, "Bob Dylan at 42—Rolling Down Highway 61 Again," *Los Angeles Times*, October 30, 1983.
64. Daniel Levitin, "A Conversation with Joni Mitchell," *Grammy Magazine*, March 1997.
65. Dylan and Joni Mitchell toured together again in 1998, a year when Dylan reintroduced "Gotta Serve Somebody"; it marked the first time Dylan opened concerts with this song since the gospel tours of 1979–1981.

66. Bert Cartwright, *The Bible in the Lyrics of Bob Dylan*, Romford, Essex, England: Wanted Man Study Series, 1992, p. 83.
67. Kurt Loder, "The Rolling Stone Interview: Bob Dylan," *Rolling Stone*, June 21, 1984.
68. Author interview: Ronnie Keohane, October 9, 2000.
69. Brown, *Sunday Times*.
70. Bill Flanagan, *Written in My Soul: Rock's Greatest Songwriters*, Chicago, IL: Contemporary Books, 1986.
71. Raymond Foye, "The Night Bob Came Round," *The Telegraph* #36 (Summer 1990), p. 20.
72. Wes Stace, "The Wanted Man Interview: Allen Ginsberg," *The Telegraph* #20 (Summer 1985), p. 88.
73. Cameron Crowe, liner notes to "Every Grain of Sand," *Biograph*, New York: CBS, Inc., 1985.
74. Scott Cohen, "Don't Ask Me Nothin' About Nothin', I Might Just Tell You the Truth: Bob Dylan Revisited," *Spin*, December 1985.
75. Clinton Heylin, *Bob Dylan: Behind the Shades Revisited*, New York: William Morrow, 2001, p. 590.
76. Mikal Gilmore, "Positively Dylan," *Rolling Stone*, July 17–31, 1986.
77. Bill DeYoung, "Rednecks in Space: Tom Petty & Mike Campbell on Bob Dylan, the Heartbreakers and 'Let Me Up' (1986)," billdeyoung.com, July 9, 2015.
78. Grossman, "Tangled Up in Jews," *On the Tracks* #22, p. 48.
79. Author interview: Laurence A. Schlesinger, August 1999.
80. Author interview: Glaser, 2001.
81. Robert Hilburn, "Bob Dylan's First Israel Concert a Hits Missed Affair," *Los Angeles Times*, September 7, 1987.
82. Arnold G. Fruchtenbaum, *Jesus Was a Jew*, Nashville, TN: Broadman Press, 1974.
83. Calev Ben-David, "Gotta Serve Somebody," *The Jerusalem Report*, May 30, 1991, p. 40.
84. Glenn Frankel, "Dylan's Doldrums: Israeli Concerts Fail to Ignite Audience," *The Washington Post*, September 9, 1987, D1.
85. Hilburn, *Los Angeles Times*, September 7, 1987.
86. Heylin, *Bob Dylan: Behind the Shades Revisited*, p. 619.
87. Tim Dunn, "Feats of Pride: The Award-Winning Bob Dylan," *On the Tracks* #14 (Summer 1998), p. 42.
88. Olof Bjorner; click on "Olof's Files" via the Dylan-related website, http:// www.expectingrain.com (Bjorner has done extensive research documenting Dylan's career, including comments made from the stage).
89. Ibid.
90. Ibid.
91. Stace, *The Telegraph* #20 (Summer 1985), p. 88.
92. Grossman, "Tangled Up in Jews," *On the Tracks* #22, p. 48.
93. Richard Brody, "Bob Dylan in Correspondence," *The New Yorker*, May 25, 2011.
94. Edna Gundersen, *USA Today*, September 21, 1989: reprinted in *On the Tracks* #3 (Spring 1994), "Bob Dylan: The 'Oh Mercy' Interview: Part I," p. 14.
95. Hilburn, *Los Angeles Times*, October 30, 1983.
96. Bob Dylan, "Song to Woody," Copyright 1962, 1965 by Duchess Music Corporation.
97. Sounes, *Down the Highway*, p. 390.

CHAPTER FIVE: 1990–1999: MURMURS OF PRAYERS

1. John Bauldie, "The Wanted Man Interview: David Was," *The Telegraph* #44 (Winter 1992), pp. 37–38.
2. Tom Chaffin, "As Ever, Dylan Both Iconoclast and Icon," *Atlanta Journal-Constitution*, May 27, 2001, L3.
3. Bob Dylan, "From a Man's Point of View: Adam's Rib," *Sister 2 Sister*, Vol. 2, No. 10 (July 1990), p. 1 (thanks to Mary McKenzie of *Sister 2 Sister* for the fax and permission to reprint this letter).
4. Edna Gundersen, *USA Today*, September 14, 1990.
5. Psalm 44:20–21 (New American Standard Bible).
6. Larry Yudelson, "Dylan: Tangled Up in Jews," *Washington Jewish Week*, 1991.
7. Clinton Heylin, *Bob Dylan: Behind the Shades Revisited*, New York: William Morrow, 2001, p. 663.
8. Olof Bjorner; "Olof 's Chronicles," http://www.punkhart.com/dylan/ olof (Dylan's onstage raps from Glasgow, Scotland; Boston and Amherst, Massachusetts in 1991).
9. Clinton Heylin, "Saved!: Bob Dylan's Conversion to Christianity (Part Two)," *The Telegraph* #29 (Spring 1988), p. 49.
10. Martin Keller, "Dylan Speaks," *Us*, January 2, 1984, p. 58 (interview originally conducted for the *Minneapolis City Pages* in July 1983).
11. Joe Queenan, "The Free-Fallin' Bob Dylan," *Spy*, August 1991, p. 57.
12. Matthew Zuckerman, "A Chat with Martin Carthy," *Isis: A Bob Dylan Anthology*, London: Helter Skelter Publishing, 2001, p. 60 (originally published in *Isis* #83/February 1999).
13. *The Telegraph* #38 (Spring 1991), pp. 115–116— transcription of Jack Nicholson's speech before Dylan's performance at the 1991 Grammys.
14. Reid Kopel, "The Wanted Man Interview: Kinky Friedman," *The Telegraph* #42 (Summer 1992), p. 14.
15. Queenan, *Spy*, p. 57.
16. *The Telegraph* #38 (Spring 1991), p. 117— transcription of Jack Nicholson's speech before presenting Dylan with his Lifetime Achievement Award at the 1991 Grammys.
17. Queenan, *Spy*, p. 57—transcription of Dylan's speech at the 1991 Grammys.
18. Ibid.
19. Clinton Heylin, *Bob Dylan: A Life in Stolen Moments: Day by Day: 1941–1995*, New York: Schirmer Books, 1996, p. 338.
20. Ronnie Schreiber, "Dylan's Grammy Acceptance Speech Explicated," Bob Dylan: Tangled Up in Jews (via http://www.well.com).
21. Mikal Gilmore, "The Rolling Stone Interview: Bob Dylan," *Rolling Stone*, November 22, 2001, pp. 63–64.
22. Ibid, p. 63.
23. Mike Wyvill and John Wraith, "Jotting Down Notes," *The Telegraph* #40 (Autumn 1991), p. 93.
24. John Bauldie, *The Bootleg Series: Volumes 1-3*, liner notes, 1991, p. 56.
25. Edna Gundersen, "The Times, They Haven't Changed Dylan's Genius: Best of 'The Bootleg Series'," *USA Today*, March 26, 1991, D-10.
26. Steve Morse, "Dylan Comes on Strong with a Concert of Old Favorites," *Boston Globe*, May 10, 1991, p. 32.
27. Steve Turner, "For He's a Jingle-Jangle Good Fellow!: A Spy 50th Birthday Celebration," *Spy*, August 1991, p. 57, 59, 61.
28. Alan Jacobs, "It Ain't Me, Babe" from *A Visit to Vanity Fair: Moral Essays on the Present Age*, Grand Rapids, MI: Brazos Press, 2001, p. 107.

29. Yudelson, "Dylan: Tangled Up in Jews," *Washington Jewish Week*.
30. Robert Hilburn, "Forever Dylan: On the Never-Ending Tour with Rock's Greatest Poet," *Los Angeles Times*, February 9, 1992.
31. Martin Grossman (with a little help from Ronnie Schreiber and Larry Yudelson), "Tangled Up in Jews," *On the Tracks* #22 (Fall 2001), p. 47.
32. Kurt Loder, "The Rolling Stone Interview: Bob Dylan," *Rolling Stone*, June 21, 1984, p. 17.
33. Clinton Heylin, *Bob Dylan: The Recording Sessions: 1960–1994*, New York: St. Martin's Press, 1995, p. 191.
34. Dallas Holm, lyric excerpt from "Rise Again," Copyright 1977 by Dimension Music/SESAC—all rights controlled by The Benson Company, Inc., Nashville, TN.
35. Heylin, *Bob Dylan: A Life in Stolen Moments*, p. 122.
36. Jonathan Cott, "Standing Naked—The Rolling Stone Interview: Bob Dylan," *Rolling Stone*, January 26, 1978, p. 44.
37. Sharon Gallagher, "Faith and Hope and Rock and Roll: An Interview with T-Bone Burnett," *Radix*, Vol. 21, no. 3, 1992.
38. Bert Cartwright, *The Bible in the Lyrics of Bob Dylan*, Romford, Essex, England: Wanted Man, 1992, pp. 121–122.
39. Mike Wyvill and John Wraith, "Jotting Down Notes," *The Telegraph* #46 (Summer 1993), p. 132.
40. Bob Dylan, *World Gone Wrong*, liner notes to "Lone Pilgrim," Copyright 1993, pp. 8–9.
41. Ibid, pp. 6–7.
42. Gary Hill, "Dylan Sees Some Hope," *Toronto Star*, October 16, 1993—via the newsletter *Series of Dreams* #6 (December 1993), p. 5.
43. Guy Garcia, "Rock Finds Religion...Again: New Groups Groping for Eternal Values," *New York Times*, January 2, 1994.
44. Cameron Crowe, *Biograph*, New York: CBS, Inc., 1985—liner notes to "Every Grain of Sand".
45. Richard Harland Smith, "Rock and Religion: Sustained Sour Notes," letter to the editor, *New York Times*, January 30, 1994.
46. Ellen Futterman, "Dylan Speaks," *St. Louis Post-Dispatch*, April 7, 1994— reprinted in *Series of Dreams* #10 (April 1994), p. 3.
47. Tony Norman, "Bob Dylan Springs Back to Life," *Pittsburgh Post-Gazette*— via *Series of Dreams* #15 (September 1994), p. 2.
48. Bill Parr (founder of the Slow Train Coming website) reported this after attending Dylan's concert on May 7, 1994, in Chattanooga, TN.
49. Laurence A. Schlesinger, "Trouble in Mind: A Rabbinic Perspective on Bob Dylan's 'Religious Period'," *On the Tracks* #4 (Fall 1994), p. 44.
50. Bob Dylan, *Drawn Blank*, New York: Random House, 1994.
51. Jonathan D. Lauer, "Last Songs on Bob Dylan's Studio Albums, 1974-1993," *On the Tracks* #10 (Spring 1997), p. 19.
52. John Dolen, "A Recent Interview with Bob Dylan," *On the Tracks* #7 (Spring 1996), p. 8.
53. John Dolen, "The Talk with Dylan," *On the Tracks* #7 (Spring 1996), p. 9.
54. Scott Benarde, "Rock for the Ages: Pop Stars Sing Out About Their Judaism," http://www.jewishjournal.com/home/searchview.php3?id=2953, August 27, 1999.
55. Larry Yudelson, "Dylan on Tour: Fall Tour 1995," http://www.radiohazak. com/tours.html.
56. Rick Mitchell, "Dylan Proves He's More Than a Relic," *Houston Chronicle*, November 3, 1995, p. 1.
57. Michael Sweeney, Chart Stoppers [via *Series of Dreams* #36c (Sept./Oct. 1996), p. 1].

58. Wes Stace, "The Wanted Man Interview: Allen Ginsberg," *The Telegraph* #20 (Summer 1985), p. 88.
59. Robert Eshman, "Up Front," http://www.jewishjournal.com/home/ searchview.php3?id=5738, May 30, 1997.
60. *Time*, September 8, 1997, p. 87.
61. Alan Jacobs, "It Ain't Me, Babe: Bob Dylan, Reluctant Prophet," *Books & Culture: A Christian Review*, May/June 1998, p. 18.
62. Edna Gundersen, *USA Today*, August 1997.
63. Murray Engleheart, "Maximum Bob," *Guitar World*, March 1999.
64. *Time*, September 8, 1997, p. 87.
65. "Rock of Ages: Pope John Paul II Backs Pop Laureate Bob Dylan in Concert," *People Weekly*, October 13, 1997, p. 54.
66. John Thavis, "Times They Are A-Changin': Dylan to Perform for the Pope," *Catholic Star Herald*, August 29, 1997—via *Series of Dreams* #46 (October 1997), p. 6.
67. *The Dairo* 16 (a Spanish newspaper)—via *Series of Dreams* #49 (January 1998), p. 1.
68. Christian Ter-Nedden, "A Dylan/Pope TV Broadcast Review," *On the Tracks* #12 (Winter 1997), pp. 51–52.
69. Paolo Vites, "Backstage at Bologna," *On the Tracks* #12 (Winter 1997), p. 53.
70. Clinton Heylin, "Saved!: Bob Dylan's Conversion to Christianity (Part One)," *The Telegraph* #28 (Winter 1987), pp. 82–83.
71. James Carroll, *Constantine's Sword: The Church and the Jews: A History*, Boston: Houghton and Mifflin Company, 2001, p. 314.
72. Michael L. Brown, *Answering Jewish Objections to Jesus: General and Historical Objections (Volume One)*, Grand Rapids, MI: Baker Books, 2001, p. 3 (Brown believes the figure of 150,000-200,000 is "probably a conservative estimate" and goes on to assert that these Jewish believers in Jesus include "American Jews, Russian Jews, South American Jews, and Israeli Jews. Many of them are highly educated, and some are ordained rabbis.").
73. Robert Hilburn, "Bob Dylan at 42—Rolling Down Highway 61 Again," *Los Angeles Times*, October 30, 1983.
74. *On the Tracks* #12 (Winter 1997), p. 51.
75. Grossman, "Tangled Up in Jews," *On the Tracks* #22, p. 48.
76. David Letterman, *The Late Show with David Letterman* (the monologue), CBS-TV, October 2, 1997.
77. "Shakespeare in Crocodile Slippers: Der Spiegel Interviews Bob Dylan," *Der Spiegel*, October 16, 1997.
78. Engleheart, *Guitar World*.
79. Gerri Hirshey, "Jakob's Ladder," *Rolling Stone*, June 12, 1997, p. 130.
80. Hilburn, *Los Angeles Times*, October 30, 1983.
81. Press release, December 7, 1997, "The White House: Office of the Press Secretary: Remarks by the President at Kennedy Center Honors Reception: The East Room" [on December 6, 1997] (http://clinton4.nara.gov/Wh/ new/html/19971208-2814.html).
82. R. Emmett Tyrrell, Jr., "Weekly Commentary," *The American Spectator*, December 12, 1997 (http://www.spectator.org/amspec/ retarchives/97-12-12.html).
83. Scott Marshall, "A Few Words with Shirley Caesar," *On the Tracks* #20 (Winter/Spring 2001), p. 29.
84. Howard Sounes, *Down the Highway: The Life of Bob Dylan*, New York: Grove Press, 2001, p. 326.

85. Ruth Rosen, *Jesus for Jews*, San Francisco: A Messianic Perspective, 1987, pp. 280-281.
86. Ibid, p. 285.
87. Jon Pareles, "A Wiser Voice Blowin' in the Autumn Wind," *New York Times*, September 28, 1997.
88. Sounes, *Down the Highway*, p. 414.
89. John 9:1-7 (King James Version).
90. Bill Flanagan, *Written in My Soul: Rock's Greatest Songwriters*, Chicago, IL: Contemporary Books, 1986.
91. Crowe, *Biograph*, p. 26 (the booklet).
92. Mikal Gilmore, "Positively Dylan," *Rolling Stone*, July 17-31, 1986.
93. Pareles, *New York Times*, September 28, 1997.
94. Mark Joseph, *The Rock & Roll Rebellion: Why People of Faith Abandoned Rock Music—and Why They're Coming Back*, Nashville, TN: Broadman & Holman Publishers, 1999, p. 110.
95. Ralph Stanley and Windy Smith, lyric excerpt from "Hills of Home," Trio Music Company, Inc., Fort Knox Music, 1969.
96. A.P. Carter, lyric excerpt from "Keep on the Sunny Side," Peer International, 1928.
97. David Gates, "Dylan Revisited," *Newsweek*, October 6, 1997, p. 64.
98. Robert Hilburn, "Dylan: 'I Learned That Jesus is Real and I Wanted That'," *Los Angeles Times Calendar*, November 23, 1980.
99. "Misc. News," *Series of Dreams* #46 (October 1997), p. 2.
100. Mikal Gilmore, "The Rolling Stone Interview: Bob Dylan," *Rolling Stone*, November 22, 2001, p. 61.
101. Michael Ybarra, "Tennyson, Milton and...Bob Dylan?," Special to *The Times*—via *Series of Dreams* #52 (April 1998), p. 6.
102. Alex Ross, "The Wanderer: Decades of Dylanology Have Missed the Point—the Music is the Message," *The New Yorker*, May 10, 1999 p. 58.
103. Ibid.
104. http://www.boblinks.com (February 23, 1999, Buffalo, NY; concert review posted).
105. Ibid (February 24, 1999, Amherst, MA; concert review posted).
106. Author interview: Alan Jacobs, August 6, 1999.
107. "Last Week Bob Dylan and Paul Simon Announced That They Would Tour Together," *Time*, April 19, 1999—via *Series of Dreams* #64 (April 1999), p. 4.
108. Bjorner, "Olof 's Chronicles."
109. Karen Hughes, "Dylan Follows Christ with Passion," *The Dominion*, August 2, 1980, p. 8.
110. Proverbs 17:22 (New International Version).
111. Mark Jacobson, "Tangled Up in Bob," *Rolling Stone*, April 12, 2001, p. 72.
112. Ibid.
113. Ian Woodward, "National Poetry Day and Andrew Motion," *The Wicked Messenger* #4365, via *Isis* #87 (October-November 1999), p. 14.
114. Ken F. Wilson, rec.music.dylan, September 9, 1999.
115. Davin Seay with Mary Neely, *Stairway to Heaven: The Spiritual Roots of Rock 'n' Roll*, New York: Ballantine Books, 1986, pp. 333–336.
116. Ibid.
117. Larry Yudelson, "Jewish Mothers: Mum No More," *Moment* (December 1999)—via *Series of Dreams* #71 (November/December 1999), p. 5.
118. Grossman, "Tangled Up in Jews," *On the Tracks* #22, p. 48.
119. Rob Sheffield, *Rolling Stone*, March 3, 2000.

120. Michael Gray, *Song & Dance Man III: The Art of Bob Dylan*, London: Cassell, 2000, p. xvii.
121. Author interview: Bucky Baxter, August 23, 1999.
122. Peter Garrett, "The Religion Report," June 9, 1999 (via http://www.abc. net.au).
123. http://www.pbs.org (November 2001).

CHAPTER SIX: 2000-2009: NO NEED TO CONFESS AGAIN

1. Lucy Y. Her, "Beatrice Rutman, Bob Dylan's Mother, Dies," *Minneapolis Star Tribune*, January 2000—via *On the Tracks* #18 (Winter/Spring 2000), p. 47, 52.
2. Roy Rivenburg, "How Does It Feel?: For Now, Dylan's Religion is a Complete Unknown," *Los Angeles Times*, March 6, 2000.
3. "Jewish Top-10: The Kosher Top-10 Pop and Rock Stars," June 20, 2000; http://www.jewish.co.uk/top10music.php3.
4. Bono Vox, "He's Got You, From Cradle to Grave," *Q* (October 2000), p. 2.
5. Edna Gundersen, "Forever Dylan," *USA Today*, May 18, 2001.
6. David Vest, "Whose Bob Dylan?"; http://www.mindspring.com/~dcqv/ dylan.htm
7. J.J. Goldberg, "Bob Dylan at 60: We Used to be Young Together," *Forward* (May 2001); http://www.forward.com/issues/2001/01.05.18/arts4.html.
8. "Newspapermen Eating Candy: The Rome Press Conference," *Isis* #99 (October-November 2001), pp. 47–48.
9. Edna Gundersen, "Dylan Brings It All Back Home," *USA Today*, September 10, 2001.
10. Mikal Gilmore, "The Rolling Stone Interview: Bob Dylan," *Rolling Stone*, November 22, 2001.
11. Dave Hoekstra, "Staples of Life and Liberty," *Chicago Sun-Times*, February 22, 2002 http://www.suntimes.com/output/show/cst-ftr-staples22.html.
12. John 20:29 (New International Version).
13. Marvin Olasky, "Some 20th-Century Notables Who Almost Crossed Over," *World*, March 2, 2002, p. 55.
14. Bob Dylan, "Gonna Change My Way of Thinking" (alternate version), Copyright 2001 by Special Rider Music.
15. Kinky Friedman, "My fellow Armenians": the Introduction to Larry "Ratso" Sloman's *On the Road with Bob Dylan*, New York: Three Rivers Press, 2002, p. vii.
16. Bob Dylan, "Solid Rock," Copyright 1980 by Special Rider Music.
17. David F. Dawes, "Insights into Bob Dylan's Faith Journey," *Canadian Christianity* (September 2001) http://www.canadianchristianity.com/cgi- bin/bc.cgi?bc/bccn/0901/artdylan.
18. Clinton Heylin, *Bob Dylan: Behind the Shades Revisited*, New York: William Morrow, 2001, pp. 521–522.
19. Masato Kato, "Mavis Staples Interview," *Isis* #115 (June-July 2004), p. 43.
20. Bob Dylan, "Gonna Change My Way of Thinking," *Lyrics: 1962–2001*, p. 410.
21. Michael Fox, "Seinfeld Writer, Bob Dylan Team Up for Offbeat New Film," *Jewish Bulletin of Northern California*, August 2003.
22. "Bob Dylan Made a Doctor of Music," June 24, 2004: http://calvin.st- andrews.ac.uk/external_relations/news_article.cfm?reference=662.
23. Jay Lustig, "Passion Inspires Album," *The Star-Ledger* [New Jersey], March 4, 2004.
24. David Gates, "The Book of Bob," *Newsweek*, October 4, 2004, pp. 48–51.
25. Bob Dylan, *Chronicles*, New York: Simon & Schuster, 2004.
26. Jay Michaelson, "He's Wandered the Earth an Exiled Man," *Forward*, February 4, 2005.

27. Alan Light, "Bob Dylan: Reluctant Prophet," 2004: http://www.beliefnet. com/story/156/story_15603_1.html.
28. John Tintera, "Bookshelf: Excerpts and Commentaries: Chronicles, Vol. 1," 2005: http://www.explorefaith.org/books/dylan.html.
29. Geoff Gehman, "Dylan: Forever Young," *The Morning Call*, November 13, 2004.
30. *Rolling Stone*, November 17, 2004: http://www.rollingstone.com/news/ story/6635604/qa_bob_dylan/bobdylan.
31. Nadine Epstein and Rebecca Frankel (with contributions from Andrew Muchin), "Bob Dylan: The Unauthorized Spiritual Biography," *Moment* (August 2005), pp. 44–49, pp. 79–83.
32. Larry Yudelson, "The Ballad of Zimmy the Yid: 5766 edition," October 16, 2005: http://www.shmoozenet.com/yudel/mtarchives/2005_10.html.
33. Gary Hill, "Dylan Sees Some Hope," *Toronto Star*, Oct. 16, 1993.
34. Author interview: Clarence Fountain, August 10, 1999.
35. Jonathan Lethem, "The Genius of Bob Dylan," *Rolling Stone*, Sept. 7, 2006 (posted online on Aug. 21, 2006).
36. Douglas LeBlanc, "Rolling Stone's State of the Union," Apr. 22, 2007. http://www.getreligion.org/?p=2364.
37. Interview with Jann S. Wenner, *Rolling Stone*, November 29, 1969" in Jonathan Cott's *Bob Dylan: The Essential Interviews*, New York: Wenner Books, 2006, pp. 139-160.
38. Jann S. Wenner, "Bob Dylan and Our Times: The Slow Train is Coming," Rolling Stone, September 20, 1979, pp. 94-95.
39. Author interview: Jerry Wexler, October 11, 2000.
40. Jon Pareles, "Blues from Dylan, and Heartaches from the 1920s," *New York Times*, Oct. 10, 2008.
41. Douglas Brinkley, "Bob Dylan's America," *Rolling Stone*, May 14, 2009, pp. 42–49; 76.
42. Paul Shaffer with David Ritz, *We'll Be Here for the Rest of Our Lives: A Swingin' Showbiz Saga*, New York: Flying Dolphin Press, 2009.
43. Sean Wilentz, "Dylan's Early Christmas Present," *Daily Beast* (thedailybeast.com), Oct. 13, 2009.
44. Bill Flanagan's interview with Dylan for the NASNA (North American Street Newspaper Association)—via http://www.rightwingbob.com/ weblog/archives/7221 (Tues. Nov. 24, 2009).
45. Author interview: Maria Muldaur, July 26, 1999.

CHAPTER SEVEN: 2010–2016: STAND BY ME

1. Jann Wenner, "Obama in Command: The Rolling Stone Interview," *Rolling Stone*, September 28, 2010 (http://www.rollingstone.com).
2. Wesley G. Pippert, *An Ethics of News: A Reporter's Search for the Truth*, Washington, D.C.: Georgetown University Press, 1989.
3. Jim Arnosky (Illustrator) with Bob Dylan (Lyrics), *Man Gave Names to All the Animals*, New York: Sterling, 2010.
4. Scott Menchin (Illustrator) with Bob Dylan (Lyrics), *Man Gave Names to All the Animals*, Boston, MA: Harcourt Children's Books, 1999.
5. Scott Marshall, "An Exclusive On the Tracks Interview: Regina McCrary Brown," *On the Tracks* #18 (Spring 2000), p. 18.
6. Author interviews: outide of and within Littlejohn Coliseum in Clemson, SC, on October 17, 2010.
7. Sinead O'Connor, "Gotta Serve Somebody," *Rolling Stone*, May 26, 2011, p. 69.
8. Austin Scaggs, "Marcus Mumford on Backing Dylan, Naked Songwriting and Why Arcade Fire Rule His World," *Rolling Stone*, March 4, 2011 (http:// www.rollingstone.com).

9. Hugo Daniel, "Bob Dylan's Blues: Ashen-Faced Singer's Synagogue Trip After Death of His Soulmate," *Daily Mail*, March 27, 2011 (http://www. dailymail.co.uk).
10. David Peisner, "Also a-Changin': Saving World with Songs," *New York Times*, January 13, 2012.
11. Jim Farber, "80 Stars Interpret Bob Dylan for Amnesty International Benefit CD Called 'Chimes of Freedom'," *New York Daily News*, January 24, 2012.
12. Chris Willman, "Dylan's 'Freedom' Offers Eclectic Mix of Songs," *Chicago Tribune* (via Reuters), January 24, 2012.
13. Howard Sounes, *Down the Highway: The Life of Bob Dylan*, New York: Grove Press, 2001, pp. 421–422.
14. Robert Hilburn, "Dylan's Evangelicalism Goes On," *Los Angeles Times*, November 20, 1979.
15. "Bob Dylan in Conversation with John Elderfield," bobdylan.com, Spring 2011.
16. Mikal Gilmore, "Bob Dylan on His Dark New LP," *Rolling Stone*, August 16, 2012, pp. 15–16.
17. Darren Hirst, "Bob Dylan: Religion and the Apocalypse in His New Album, *Tempest*," twilightdawning.com, November 2, 2012.
18. A.T. Bradford, "Bob Dylan: Looking at the Spiritual Undercurrents of the *Tempest* Album," crossrhythms.co.uk, November 4, 2012.
19. David Yaffe, "The Rage in Bob Dylan's *Tempest*," thedailybeast.com, September 3, 2012.
20. Neil McCormick, "Bob Dylan's *Tempest*: Rock's King Lyricist Keeps His Crown," *The Telegraph*, September 7, 2012.
21. Joe Breen, "Bob Dylan," *Irish Times*, September 7, 2012.
22. Simon Cosyns, "The Most Revealing Review of Bob Dylan's New Album Tempest Yet," *The Sun*, September 8, 2012.
23. Allan Jones, "Bob Dylan—*Tempest*," *Uncut*, September 7, 2012.
24. Hirst, twilightdawning.com
25. Bradford, crossrhythms.co.uk
26. Steve Turner, *The Gospel According to the Beatles*, Louisville, KY and London: Westminster John Knox Press, 2006, p. 191 (also, some of these quotes are taken from the website beatlesinterviews.org, which contains a transcript of David Scheff 's interview with John Lennon and Yoko Ono from September 1980, which was published in *Playboy*, January 1981).
27. Ibid.
28. beatlesinterviews.org
29. Gary Stewart, "Bob Dylan Turns Tourist as He Visits John Lennon's Liverpool Home," *Liverpool Daily Post*, May 13, 2009.
30. Mikal Gilmore, "Bob Dylan: The Rolling Stone Interview," *Rolling Stone*, September 27, 2012, pp. 42–51; 80–81.
31. Clinton Heylin, *Bob Dylan Behind the Shades: A Biography*, New York: Summit Books, 1991, p. 16.
32. Harold Lepidus, "Bob Dylan's New Interview: Critical, Provocative, or Manipulative?", examiner.com, September 12, 2012.
33. khoury2000, "Bob Dylan, Jeff Tweedy, Jim James-Twelve Gates To The City-Toronto July 15, 2013," youtube.com; published on July 17, 2013 (accessed 8/1/16).
34. Daniel Maoz, "Reviews: Toronto, Ontario, Molson Canadian Amphitheatre, July 15, 2013," boblinks.com (permission granted by writer to reprint review excerpt).
35. Author interview: Jennifer Cruickshank, April 4, 2016.
36. Frederick Matt, "BOB DYLAN, JEFF TWEEDY, JIM JAMES 'Let Your Light Shine on Me' 07-19-13 Webster Arena, Bridgeport CT," youtube.com; published on July 20, 2013 (accessed 8/1/16).
37. Nancy Cobb, "Reviews: Hollywood, California, Dolby Theatre, October 26, 2014," boblinks.com

38. Author interview: Sean Curnyn, July 31, 2016.
39. Robert Love, "Bob Dylan: The Uncut Interview," aarp.org (*AARP: The Magazine*), February/March 2015; the print magazine citation: Robert Love, "Bob Dylan Does the American Songbook His Way," *AARP: The Magazine* (February/March 2015), pp. 28–36.
40. Jess Archer, *Finding Home with the Beatles, Bob Dylan, and Billy Graham: A Memoir of Growing Up Inside the Billy Graham Evangelistic Association*, Bloomington, IN: WestBow Press, 2016, pp. 44–45.
41. "Read Bob Dylan's Complete, Riveting MusiCares Speech," rollingstone.com, Feb. 9, 2015 (Copyright 2015 Bob Dylan).
42. Chris Morris, *Together Through Life: A Personal Journey with the Music of Bob Dylan*, Los Angeles, CA: Rothco Press, 2016, p. 157.
43. *Webster's College Dictionary*, New York: Random House, 1991, p. 1355.
44. Author attended event: Moutain View Room in the Sherrill Center at UNC-Asheville on Mon. Mar. 14, 2016; interviews conducted in person as well as subsequently via e-mail. (Thanks to sister Grace for the Asheville JCC e-mail alert!)

AFTERWORD

1. Ron Rosenbaum, "Revisiting The Rise and Fall of the Third Reich," *Smithsonian* (February 2012) via smithsonianmag.com.
2. Jeffrey Salkin, "Happy 75th Birthday, Bob!," Religion News Service, religionnews.com, May 23, 2016.
3. Ron Rosenbaum, "Dylan's Birthday Present: Free Bob from the Bobolator Cult," slate.com, May 16, 2011.
4. Jim Keane, "Bob Dylan's Church(es): Travels in the North Country Fair," *America: The National Catholic Review*, http://americamagazine.org, June 24, 2016.
5. Bob Dylan, *Chronicles: Volume One*, New York: Simon & Schuster, 2004, pp. 31–32.
6. Remarks from Jimmy Carter during his Sunday School class at Maranatha Baptist Church, Plains, Ga., Sun. Oct. 23, 2016.
7. Robert Love, "Bob Dylan: The Uncut Interview," aarp.org, February/March 2015.
8. Statement for author: Carolyn Dennis, April 2017.
9. Randall Balmer, *The Encyclopedia of Evangelicalism*, Waco, Tx: Baylor University Press, 2004, pp. 221-222. This author contacted Balmer to see if he'd be willing to read over this manuscript and possibly provide a book blurb, which he generously did. It wasn't until a few months later that this author discovered the Dylan entry in his encyclopedia. (Granted, just a 10-word sentence out of a 781-page book, but those 10 words said a lot.)

INDEX

C

D

H

T

Printed in Great Britain
by Amazon

46495000R00169